IMMIGRANTS AT SCHOOL
NEW YORK CITY, 1898-1914

IMMIGRANTS AT SCHOOL
NEW YORK CITY, 1898-1914

Selma Cantor Berrol

ARNO PRESS
A New York Times Company
New York • 1978

**Publisher's Note: This book has been reproduced
from the best available copy.**

Editorial Supervision: LUCILLE MAIORCA

———◆———

First publication 1978 by Arno Press Inc.

BILINGUAL-BICULTURAL EDUCATION IN THE UNITED STATES
ISBN for complete set: 0-405-11071-5
See last pages of this volume for titles.

Manufactured in the United States of America

———◆———

Library of Congress Cataloging in Publication Data

Berrol, Selma Cantor.
    Immigrants at school, New York City, 1898-1914.

    (Bilingual-bicultural education in the United States)
    Originally presented as the author's thesis, City
University of New York, 1967.
    Bibliography: p.
    1. Minorities--Education--New York (City).
I. Title. II. Series.
LC3733.N5B47 1978   371.9'7'097471   77-90872
ISBN 0-405-11077-4

IMMIGRANTS AT SCHOOL: NEW YORK CITY, 1898-1914

by

Selma Cantor Berrol

A dissertation submitted to the
Graduate Faculty in History in partial
fulfillment of the requirements for the
degree of Doctor of Philosophy, The
City University of New York.

1967

This manuscript has been read and accepted for
the University Committee in History in satisfac-
tion of the dissertation requirement for the
degree of Doctor of Philosophy.

May 1, 1967 _____
date   Chairman of Examining Committee

May 1, 1967 _____
date   , Executive Officer

_____
Sidney I. Pomerantz
_____
Irving Howe
_____
Michael Kraus   Supervisory Committee

The City University of New York

PREFACE

As a product of the New York City public schools,
having been educated at the taxpayer's expense from kindergarten to the doctorate, I have long had considerable
interest in the educational history of our city. Similarly,
as the child of immigrant parents, my interest in the
great migration of peoples to the United States at the
turn of the century was early aroused. The difficulties
of the public schools of New York City in recent years, as
they attempt to cope with the problems raised by the newest
arrivals to the metropolis, led me to inquire into the
responses developed by the educational authorities of an
earlier day, when they were faced with a similar challenge.
Thus, the subject of this study was developed, partly from
an interest in the past, and partly from a concern for
the present.

The object of the investigation was twofold:
first, to find out what changes (if any) were made in the
educational structure of the city under the pressure of the
two largest immigrant groups, the Jews and the Italians;
and second, to determine if there were any clues to the
viability of the New York City schools of today ascertain-
able in the developments of sixty years ago. In order to

do this, it was first necessary to establish the background for change, and so the first part of the study
deals with the political, financial, and administrative
structure in which the schools operated; and with the
social and economic pattern of the "new immigration", in
relation to the schools.

The changes themselves were of such number and
variety, it required four chapters to fully discuss them:
buildings, teachers, students, programs, and problems
multiplied so fast in the fifteen year span from consolidation of the boroughs to the outbreak of World War I that
the schools of New York were "transformed" indeed. The
last part of the study is an attempt to evaluate the
changes and present their implications for today.

1898 was chosen as the starting point of the
investigation because the formation of the Greater City
of New York and the establishment of a city-wide public
school system in the Charter of 1897 meant that school
records would be unified, and changes in the educational
structure of the entire city could be more easily seen.
1914 was used as the terminal date of the study because
the outbreak of World War I in that year effectively ended the greatest influx of immigrants from Eastern and
Southern Europe.

Studies of the role played by the public schools
in changing the immigrant into an American have been
plentiful. This paper is an attempt to do the converse;
study the changes made in the schools by the impact of the
newcomers. New York City was the best place in which to
examine this question, because there was more immigration
to the Empire City than any other single area in the
United States, but changes such as occurred here also took
place in Baltimore, Philadelphia, Foston, and Cleveland,
on a smaller scale.

To a very great extent, as the following pages
will make clear, the educational innovations which appeared were part of larger reforms going on simultaneously
during the Progressive Era. The problems which manifested themselves in the great cities in the first decade of
the twentieth century were caused by the impact of urbanization and industrialization, as well as immigration,
and the responses developed by the schools were an attempt
to cope with all three. Similarly, the agents of change
were often interested in many aspects of reform, the
public schools being just one among a number of areas
which aroused their concern.

Thus, a study of immigrant impact on the public
schools of the nation's largest city can be considered
one small contribution to the knowledge of urban progressivism as a whole, and may help to demonstrate the close

connection between education and the broader aspects of American life and thought which has always existed, although it has not always been recognized.

I am indebted to Professor Lawrence A. Cremin and his most significant book, The Transformation of the Schools , for first showing me the drama of the educational changes of the Progressive Era, and to Moses Fischin for his moving and sensitive portrayal of immigrant life in New York in the years before 1914, The Promised City . Harold McCormick, historian at the Board of Education was extremely helpful in many ways, including his suggestion that I see Dr. Morris L. Siegel, who kindly answered all my many questions about the evening schools. The long afternoon's conversation with Dr. Jacob Foss was very, very valuable, since not many educators whose professional life spans the period 1904-1954, are available for interviews. Dr. Ross' referral to Milton B. Perlman, who also had a long career as student and teacher in the public schools was most important.

The advice, encouragement and professional skill of Dr. Sidney I. Pomerantz, Professor of History at the City College of New York, was of the utmost help to me, and I am grateful. I also wish to express my thanks to Professors Michael Kraus, Emeritus Professor of the City College of New York, and Irving Howe of Hunter College who

kindly consented to read this study, and offer suggestions
for its improvement. Last, but in most ways first, my
husband Edward's interest and training in sociology was of
inestimable benefit to me, and I was fortunate to be able
to make use of it.

TABLE OF CONTENTS

LIST OF TABLES

LIST OF ILLUSTRATIONS

PART I.   THE BACKGROUND FOR CHANGE

CHAPTER I

MANAGEMENT, MAYORS AND MONEY: THE CITY AND THE SCHOOLS:

1898-1914

New York City, Midnight, December 31, 1897. A cold
rain had been falling on the city for three hours, thoroughly
soaking the thousands of New Yorkers who were massed along
the streets leading from the Brooklyn Bridge to City Hall
Park. The wet but cheerful crowds had come to see the festiv-
ities arranged for the birth of Greater New York, and they
had not been disappointed. The buildings along Park Row and
the City Hall itself had been decorated with hundreds of
electric lights which dazzled the spectators, even through
the rain. At 10:15 a great parade had begun, complete with
floats and marching bands. When the parade ended a gigantic
fireworks display began and continued "until the City Hall
clock marked 12", at which time "steam whistles sounded,
the bands played more vehemently, rockets and bombs went up
faster and faster and the flag of the new city, in the
glare of the concentrated searchlights, went to the top of
the pole over the City Hall!" For the next 15 minutes there
was a "saturation of sound" as the New York Times proudly
reported, ending only when the rain changed to snow and the

celebrants, finally thinking of warmth and home, left the [1]
scene.

The next morning, for the first time, residents of Brooklyn, Richmond and Queens awoke to find that they had been "annexed to, united and consolidated with the municipal corporation known as the mayor, aldermen and commonalty of the city of New York" [2] and were now all citizens of the Greater City--the second largest in the world. Ten years of agitation, controversy and planning had resulted at last in political unity. [3]

---

[1] The New York Times, January 1, 1898, p.1.

---

[2] New York (State), Laws of 1897. Chapter 378. Charter of the City of New York, p.1. The full description of the boundaries of Greater New York is as follows: "The county of Kings, the county of Richmond, the city of Long Island City, the towns of Newtown, Flushing and Jamaica, and that part of the town of Hempstead in the county of Queens which is westerly of a straight line drawn from the southeasterly point of the town of Flushing through the middle of the channel between Rockaway Beach and Shelter Island, in the county of Queens, to the Atlantic Ocean is hereby annexed to...the city of New York."

[3] Andrew Haswell Green, prominent civic leader, had been the prime force behind the drive for consolidation. While many others supported the move, unity was impossible to achieve until Thomas C. Platt, Republican boss of New York State, gave his approval. Allan Nevins and John A. Krout (eds.), The Greater City (New York:1948), especially John Krout's Essay on the unification struggle, pp.41-56; David Ellis et al. A Short History of New York State (Ithaca:1957), pp. 376-379; Charles Garrett, The La Guardia Years (New Brunswick, N.J.:1961), P.25.

In the cities of Brooklyn and New York, prior to consolidation, differing opinions on the merits of unification had sharply divided the citizenry, the leaders and the press. All through the years of debate, Brooklyn had blown hot and cold, wishing for the benefits of joining New York, while at the same time jealous of her independence. In New York, the desire for expansion was tempered with the fear of the burdens which might result. Neither borough wished to give up the governmental institutions which it had developed and each had certain cherished ideas about municipal management which it insisted on including in the Charter. Nowhere are these divergent attitudes more apparent than in the educational provisions of that document.

The New York City position had been shaped by a series of legislative battles in 1895-1896, sometimes known as "The Great School War". As a result of that struggle, the principle of separation of business from scholastic policies in school administration had been established. This was a great victory for those elements in the city who were anti-Tammany and interested in better schools. Prior to 1895, the school system of the City of New York had been a source of great concern to many reformers. The public had been alerted to the deficiencies in the city schools by a series of articles published in The Forum in which Dr. Joseph M. Rice bitterly attacked the inefficiency, corruption and formalism which characterized public education in New York City. Even more important were the books and

articles of Jacob Riis, which laid almost every burden
borne by the "children of the poor" at the door of the
school system.

The educational structure which so disturbed the
reformers consisted of a 21 man Board of Education appointed
by the Mayor, who had little control over the schools, since
the real power was in the hands of ward trustees--semi-liter-
ate politicians appointed by the Board of Education in
response to political pressures. These trustees (five in
each of the city's 24 wards) appointed the teachers, principals and janitors, made contracts for school repairs and [4]
alterations, bought school sites and built school houses.
Favoritism and corruption were the hallmarks of this arrangement, and the schools of the city suffered as a result. In
the municipal election of 1894, the good government forces
organized a Committee of 70 and succeeded in electing
William L. Strong as Mayor, partly on a platform of school
reform. The Committee of 70 stayed in operation after the
election and one of their sub-committees drew up legislation to revise the system of ward trustees which was then
introduced into the state legislature.

---

[4]
Sol Cohen, Progressives and Urban School Reform
(New York: 1964), p. 16; A.E. Palmer, History of the New
York City Public Schools (New York: 1905), p.185.

These Pavey Bills would have transferred most of
the trustees' power to professional educators organized into
a Board of Superintendents. The bills failed to pass, due
to the opposition of Republican Boss Platt, the Tammany
Democrats and many of the city's teachers.[5] The following
year, the City Board of Education introduced its own reform
bills which would have made some improvements in the school
system, but increased the number of ward trustees and left
their powers intact. The reformers opposed these Strauss
Bills with every device they could muster and at the same
time lobbied for their own legislation. In March of 1896
they were delighted to see the Legislature pass the Stranahan-
White Bill which gave them everything they wanted. Ward
trustees were abolished and control over educational matters
was placed in the hands of a Superintendent of Schools and
his associates, especially teacher selection which also was
to be done from an eligible list established by examination.[6]

---

[5] The reason for teacher opposition to the Pavey Bills
is somewhat obscure. It might have been sheer conservatism
but more likely it represented fear on the part of the older
teachers that they would receive less favorable treatment at
the hands of a Board of Examiners than they had from the
Tammany controlled ward trustees. At least, such rumors did
circulate among the staff.

[6] Cohen, pp. 38-39; Palmer, pp. 187-188.

The passage of this bill was a great step in the direction of professionalizing the schools, and led to a number of improvements because Mayor Strong appointed an able and non-partisan Board of Education. Another result of the "school war" was the formation of the Public Education Association, originally an outgrowth of the sub-committee of the Committee of 70. The members of the Public Education Association and their allies were adamant on the need for the separation of education from politics, and exercised a strong influence on the school chapters of the Charter, so that, except for one arrangement applicable only to Brooklyn, the school system established in 1897 was rel-atively free from the problems of favoritism and corruption. [7]

While professional administration of the schools was of the utmost importance to the New Yorkers, the reten-tion of local control was equally significant to the Brooklyn delegates to the Charter Commission. They felt this could be done by establishing borough control over the schools, thus enabling Brooklyn to keep a unique feature of its educational structure--the local committee system. The origin of this device lay in the historical development of the borough. Brooklyn was originally a number of separate towns that were gradually joined together to become a city. Each of these towns had been a separate school district,

---

[7] Richard Whittemore, "Nicholas Murray Butler and Public Education" (unpublished Ph.D. dissertation, Columbia University, 1962), p.146; "The Administration of New York's Public Schools", Harper's Weekly, L (February, 1906), p. 257.

with its own organization, curriculum and standards which
were slowly brought under the partial control of the
Brooklyn Board of Education.[8]

Even when that body had established its hegemony, a
system of local control was continued through the use of
committees. Each of these groups consisted of three laymen,
appointed by the Board of Education (themselves appointed
by the Mayor) with extensive power over teachers and school
buildings. The committeemen could hire, transfer, promote
and assign teachers to the various schools in their district,
and their actions were subject only to the token approval of
the Board of Education. The individual committees could
also determine when and to what extent a school building in
their bailiwick needed repairs or additions and let the
contracts for the work, again subject to the routine approval
of the central board. A final source of their power was the
right to hire and assign janitors and maintenance personnel.[9]

This system, so similar to the ward trustees of
New York, did not lead to a war, but instead was looked upon
as a positive good, because it was claimed that the local
committees were responsive to the wishes of the people in
their districts, and that the Brooklyn school arrangement

---

[8] Palmer, pp. 226, 207.

[9] Ibid., 243-244.

was, therefore, democratic. In practice, however, since the committeemen were active in politics, the system often resulted in the appointment of poorly qualified teachers and much patronage for the political party to which the committee members belonged.

The attitudes of the Brooklyn delegates on the Charter Commission, when combined with the position of the New York representatives, resulted in an educational system which was a curious amalgam of centralization and autonomy. In an attempt to establish a city wide system, and at the same time permit the boroughs to exercise control over their own schools, the Charter created a situation likely to lead to conflict and chaos.

At the head of the Department of Education of the City of New York, stated the Charter of 1897, there was to be a 19 member Board of Education, consisting of the chairman of each of the borough school boards, ten delegates elected by the School Board of Manhattan and the Bronx and five chosen by the Brooklyn School Board, from among their members.[10]   There were 21 men serving on the Manhattan-Bronx School Board, 45 on the Brooklyn Board, and nine each in Richmond and Queens. In the latter boroughs, the school board members were newly appointed by the Mayor, but in Manhattan-Bronx and Brooklyn, the school officials were holdovers from the pre-consolidation period. As the term

---

[10] Charter of the City of New York, 1897, pp. 33-34. The affairs of the Manhattan and Bronx schools were administered by one school board, although they were separate boroughs.

of office of these "lame ducks" expired, the Mayor could replace them with men of his choosing. All school board members were unsalaried and were to serve for three years. [11]

The Charter carefully described the functions of the City and Borough School Boards. The former was to represent the entire school system before the Board of Estimate and Apportionment, requesting funds based on budgets drawn up by the borough boards. When the school requests were approved, the City Board was to apportion the money according to the number of students actually attending school in each borough plus $100 for every teacher who had worked more than 32 days in the preceding year. This power of the purse was further strengthened by the provision which permitted the City Board of Education to ask the Comptroller to withhold money from any Borough School Board not complying with the Education Law. [12]

The members of the City Board were to appoint a number of professionals to administer the schools, such as a Superintendent of Supplies, a Superintendent of Buildings, a Superintendent of Schools, a Secretary and an Auditor. The first two officials were to appoint deputies in each of the boroughs, but the purchase of supplies and the selection of janitors was left to the City Superintendent

---

11
  Ibid., pp. 380, 381.

12
  Ibid., pp. 382, 383.

in charge.[13]   A study of the topics considered by the City
Board of Education indicates that much of the work of these
men consisted of routine approvals of recommendations made
to them by the various professional administrators they had
chosen and that their work was not creative or policy-making
in any way.[14]

Control over the teaching staff was not in the hands
of the City Board, although it could set the minimum qualifications for a teaching license. Each borough school board
could add its own requirements and could, in addition, set
salaries, which did not have to be uniform throughout the
city.[15]   Except for Brooklyn, all the borough school officials

---

[13]
Ibid.,pp. 384, 385, 386.

[14]
New York (City), Department of Education, Journal
of the Board of Education, 1900 (New York: 1900), passim.
For example, the Board of Education approved advertisements
for bids for heating school buildings drawn up by the
Superintendent of Buildings, approved recommendations regarding the salaries and vacations of school clerks presented by the Superintendent of Schools, etc. They also
spent a great deal of time considering communications from
the various fiscal authorities of the city, including the
Chamberlain, who held the funds.

[15]
Charter of the City of New York, 1897, pp. 389,
394. This lack of uniformity was true only until 1899 when
the Davis Law was passed by the State Legislature, partly
to remedy this situation.

chose their staff from eligible lists established by the
Board of Examiners. The individual boards also controlled
the transfer and promotion of teachers.

In addition to staff selection, the borough school
boards chose the sites for school buildings and established
kindergartens, evening schools, high schools, teacher training schools and English-to-foreigner classes when they deem-
ed such innovations to be necessary.[16] It would appear,
therefore, that the members of the borough school boards
were much more powerful in purely educational matters than
was the City Board. This impression is reinforced by the
contrast between the duties of the borough superintendents
of schools (one for each borough, appointed by the individual
school boards) and the City Superintendent of Schools.

The former, in consultation with his associate
Superintendents, had the power to make the syllabuses, assign
teachers, choose the text-books and determine the length of
time to spend on a subject, while the latter could only
inspect the schools, prescribe the forms of reports and
prepare an Annual Report to the City Board of Education.[17]

16
   Ibid., p. 395.

17
   Ibid.; New York (City), Department of Education,
First Annual Report of the City Superintendent of Schools,
1899 (New York: 1899), p. 14.

It is clear, therefore, that the educational chapters in
the Charter of 1897 represented a victory for the Brooklyn
point of view, since that borough was left free to run its
schools much as it had been administered prior to consolidation. The local committee system continued to operate within
the framework established by the Charter. The duties of the
borough education board, which in Manhattan-Bronx, Richmond
and Queens were exercised by those bodies, in Brooklyn were
carried on by the local school committees.

About the only provision in the education section
which could be construed as a limitation on the borough
school boards was the one providing for a Board of Examiners.
The Superintendent of Schools was to nominate four men from
a list established by the City Civil Service Commission to
serve with him as examining board. Members of this board
had to be either college graduates with five years teaching
experience; hold a state certificate granted since 1875 and
have ten years experience; or hold the highest city principal
or supervisory license and have ten years of experience.
They were to be salaried and to serve a four year term.

The job of the Board of Examiners was to prepare and
hold examinations for all teaching positions in the school
system and establish eligibility lists which the City
Superintendent would then transmit to the various borough
school boards. Certain personnel were exempt from license
exams; Superintendents, Associate Superintendents, Supervisors,
Directors of Special Branches, principals and the faculties

of the teacher training schools. The staff of the evening
and vacation schools were also not required to take examinations. In addition, the teachers already in the system
had their licenses confirmed if they were graduates of recognized colleges at which they had taken one year of pedagogy,
or held a state certificate issued after 1875.[18]

The arrangements regarding the Board of Examiners
reflected the strong belief in the merit system, and the
desire to eliminate favoritism held by the New York delegates
to the Charter Commission, just as the borough school board
provisions reflected the fear of over-centralization which
dominated the Brooklyn representatives.

Regardless of the desire for independence held by the
delegations from the smaller boroughs, in one area at least,
the Charter provided for centralization. There was to be
one Mayor and he was given a role to play in the educational
affairs of the city, albeit a small one. During his four
year term he was responsible for the appointment of borough
school board members as vacancies appeared, but he could
not remove any school officials. In his role as a member
of the Board of Estimate and Apportionment, the Mayor participated in the deliberations and the votes on school budget
requests. He could also veto any budget deletions made by
the Municipal Assembly, which was the city legislature. That

---

18. Charter of the City of New York, 1897, pp. 388
389; First Annual Report of the City Superintendent of
Schools, 1899, p.43.

body needed a 5/6 vote to repass the cuts over the Mayor's
veto, and as a result, they played no important part in
19
allocating school funds.

The Charter also stated that it was the duty of the
Mayor "to keep himself informed of the doings of the several
departments" of which the Department of Education was one.
Because of this provision, the Board of Education made an
annual report to the Mayor, which unfortunately, could not
have given him much information on the "doings" of the
schools. These reports were basically statistical digests
culled from the statements of the Superintendent of Schools
and included figures on the cost of the pencils used in
each school, and the titles of all the lectures (there were
thousands) given by the Bureau in charge of that activity.
Overall, these reports had a "boondoggle" appearance, heavily
padded with long, detailed and unessential summaries which
really could not have given the Mayor a picture of school
20
problems or achievements.

19.
        Charter of the City of New York, 1897, pp. 29,30.
72,380.

20
        New York (City), Department of Education, Annual
Reports of the Board of Education, 1899-1914 (New York:
1899-1914), passim; Charter of the City of New York, 1897
p.66.

In actual practice, the Mayor's influence on the schools was limited to his appointment of school board members (whose terms never coincided with his), the extent to which he exercised power on the Board of Estimate, and his overall leadership qualities. In spite of the limited power over educational matters granted him by the Charter, the first Mayor of the consolidated city, Robert A. Van Wyck, considered the condition of the schools important enough to speak of them in detail in his inaugural address:

> The parents of children of school age and our citizens generally, have been justly indignant over the neglect (of our schools) to which is attributed the fact that thousands of applicants for instruction in the public schools have either been denied any admission whatever, or have been compelled to accept a place in half day classes . 21

The Mayor promised to remedy this condition, but did not succeed. Van Wyck had great problems with the City and the Manhattan-Bronx school boards, both of which were controlled by men who were reformers and had been appointed by William Strong after the "school war". These men disliked Van Wyck intensely because he was the representative of Tammany. At one point, the Mayor told a delegation of teachers that he was dissatisfied with the Board of Education but had no influence at all with them. [22] Mayor Van Wyck did

---

21
    Harold McCormick, "The First Fifty Years", Fiftieth Annual Report of the City Superintendent of Schools, 1948, (New York: 1948), p.5.

22
    School Journal, December 24, 1898, p.672.

not like the Superintendent of Schools, William H. Maxwell,
either, because that gentleman made little secret of his
antagonism to any protege of Boss Richard Croker, which
Van Wyck was.[23]

One of the biggest quarrels between the Mayor and
the Board of Education concerned the appointment of non-
resident teachers. Both Maxwell and the majority of the
Education Board wished to permit the licensing of qualified
teachers from anywhere in the United States, partly to
break the hold the Democratic party had on the staff, but
mostly because the graduates of the city training schools
were not always the best qualified. Van Wyck, wanting to
keep the teachers in Tammany's corner, assumed the role of
their protector. Since all the Mayor could do was quarrel
with the Board of Education, both publicly and privately,
he did not succeed in changing its policies and the
Superintendent was later able to report that teachers from
every state were employed in New York City.[24]

Similar frustration gripped Van Wyck during a hearing
on the school budget in 1900. He claimed the Board of
Education had deliberately submitted its request one month
late, so that he would not have time to look closely at it,

---

[23]
Samuel Abelow, Dr. William H. Maxwell (Brooklyn,
N.Y. 1934), p.68.

[24]
The New York Times, January 6, 1898, p.8;
January 7, 1898, p.8; Third Annual Report of the City
Superintendent of Schools, 1901, p.40.

but instead have to give his approval in a hurry, or be
labeled the villain who closed the schools.[25]   The Mayor's
anger resulted in no more than petty bickering; school
budgets were approved or cut in spite of his wishes.

Actually, the most significant factor in city-
school relationships was money or the lack of it, and
therefore the role of the Mayor in educational affairs was
secondary to that of the Board of Estimate and Apportionment, which controlled the funds. Under the 1897 Charter
that Board was made up of the Mayor, Comptroller, Corporation Counsel, President of the City Council and the
President of the Department of Taxes and Assessments.[26]
It was the duty of this group to make the city's budget
and to raise by taxes the money "necessary to provide for
the conduct of the schools". The Charter was very explicit:

> ...nothing contained in this act shall be
> construed to limit or restrict the power of
> the Board of Estimate and Apportionment...
> to fix in their discretion, and in such detail
> as they may deem expedient the amounts to be
> allowed to the board of education...   [27]

---

[25] The New York Times, October 9, 1900, p.3.

[26] Charter of the City of New York, 1897, p.72.

[27] Ibid., p.379.

Therefore, it was this Board which, to a great extent,
controlled school policy because every new program the
Department of Education wished to undertake was bound to
cost more money.

The dollars which the Board of Estimate was to
allocate to the schools were in the form of two funds, the
Special and the General.[28] The former was money which was
given in bulk to the Board of Education for the purchase
of school sites, the repair of buildings, and the buying
of school supplies. The latter was for teacher salaries
only, and was apportioned among the borough school boards
by the Board of Estimate in exact amounts.

There was also a difference in the way the money
for the two funds was raised. The Board of Estimate determined the taxes needed for the Special fund, but after 1899,
the money for the General Fund was to be raised by a state
mandated four mill tax on real estate.[29] The Superintendent

---

[28] Money for new school construction was raised throug
the sale of bonds and was not part of the annual education
budget, although approval was required from the Board of
Estimate.

[29] The New York State Education Laws did not cover
the schools of the city until 1917, although both the State
Commissioner of Education and the City Superintendent of
Schools thought they should. Instead, all the legal provisions for education in the city were in the Charter, as has
been described. The one exception to this was the imposition of the four mills tax rate. This levy was mandated
by the State in the Davis Law of 1899 which dealt mainly
with teacher salaries and established the tax levy as a
means of financing them. Rose Cohen, The Financial Control
of Education in the Consolidated City of New York (New York
1948), p. 102; McCormick, p.25; Charter of the City of New
York, 1897, p.379.

of Schools was very pleased with this mandatory tax because
it provided a fund for education which would grow with the
wealth and population of the city, and because the Department of Education could plan ahead, now that they had an assur-
ed income.[30]

The attitude of the Superintendent to the Davis Law
was not shared by the city's chief fiscal officer, the
Comptroller. In his role as head of the Department of Finance,
the Comptroller was usually the leading figure in the attacks
on school expenditures. In 1900, the man who held this
position was Bird S. Coler, a Brooklyn Democrat generally not
in sympathy with Tammany and eager to make a reputation for
himself. He attacked the education estimate for 1900-1901
on the grounds that the amount asked would comprise 1/5 of
the entire city budget and would cause a tax rate increase
of 20 points.[31]

As was to happen many times in the future, Coler
soon abandoned the purely financial aspects of his criticism
and went on to castigate the subjects taught and the methods
used in the schools. He said the children were being
taught useless things--such as drawing, sewing, and cooking,
all of which he characterized as "educational fads". In

---

[30] Second Annual Report of the City Superintendent of
Schools, 1900, pp. 66-67.

[31] The New York Times, October 9, 1900, p.3.

addition, he faulted the schools for their emphasis on higher education, saying that 95% of the children left school at 14 and therefore only the grammar schools should be improved. This last point was an attack on the expensive high school building program on which the Manhattan-Bronx school board was then embarked. He concluded that the per capita cost of education had doubled in the past few years, with no noticeable benefits to the city.[32]

Coler's attack was not successful. The budget for 1900-1901 passed with no more than the usual number of cuts, but the quarrel was significant in that it pointed up the possibilities for conflict between the city and the schools inherent in the financial arrangement.

Thus it would appear that the relationship between the city and the schools established by the 1897 Charter had unified without centralizing, had left the Mayor without real power over the schools, and had begun a pattern of financial strife which was to mark educational affairs in the city for years to come. The Charter was most successful in eliminating the influence of political patronage from school management, but in other respects, by making too many compromises between the boroughs, it had established a nearly unworkable structure, fraught with the possibilities of chaos and conflict.

---

[32] Ibid., October 16, 1900, p.11.

The dual nature of the school system could lead only to duplication and waste. Also, since the City Board was top-heavy with representatives of Manhattan and the Bronx, there were inevitable quarrels over the apportionment of funds, while at the same time, the City Superintendent of Schools felt his lack of power over teachers, textbooks and the course of study very keenly.

The Brooklyn committee system was a particularly fruitful area of conflict because the City Board and the City Superintendent attacked it constantly and the Brooklyn school board was extremely defensive about it. In his first report, Maxwell said the local committee method was:

> ...a system of appointing and promoting teachers that (had) retarded progress ever since the Brooklyn city school system was established... The young women who are licensed to teach in Brooklyn are compelled to visit the places of business and residences of members of the board to sue for appointment and to bring political and other pressure on the members to secure places.   33

The Brooklyn members of the City Board of Education were extremely angry at this comment and prevented the publication of the report until Maxwell substantiated his charges. Actually he never did, but after a suitable delay, the Brooklyn delegates permitted the report to be published,

---

33
    First Annual Report of the City Superintendent of Schools, 1899, p.117.

although they inserted a statement between the title page
and the table of contents in which they denied every one
of the Superintendent's "scandalous charges...made against
the members of the School Board of Brooklyn."

This First Annual Report of the Superintendent also
summarized the weakness of the dual system by saying it led
to superfluous administrative machinery, unnecessary clerical
work and "disharmony" among the borough Superintendents.
At the same time, the Superintendent admitted that consolidation had brought a few benefits to the school system, most
notably the inclusion of the semi-rural schools of Queens
and Richmond into a city-wide educational structure, and
better standards for teacher licensing.[34]

Maxwell also made a prediction which he obviously
hoped would come true. He said the imposition of the
mandatory four mills tax under the Davis Law would speed
revision of the education provisions of the Charter because
Manhattan would be paying the most in taxes (since it had
the greatest amount of valuable real estate) and would
therefore insist on a greater voice on how school money
was to be spent in the other boroughs. Since the dual school
system was abolished in the following year, it would appear
that his prediction was correct.[35]

---

[34]
    Ibid., pp. 86-88; 155-156; Palmer, p.298.

[35]
    William H. Maxwell, "The Schools of New York",
Municipal Affairs, IV (December, 1900), pp. 749-750.

The difficulties encountered by the schools in trying to carry out the educational provisions of the 1897
Charter were among the major reasons for Charter revision
which was finally accomplished in 1901. Under the new
educational chapters, a truly city-wide school system came
into being, to remain largely unchanged until today, although
at various times changes in the size and powers of the
Board of Education have been proposed. While minor alterations were made over the years, the policy of combining a
lay, unsalaried Board of Education and a professional
Superintendent of Schools for the entire city, was never
reversed.

The revised Charter of 1901 abolished the borough
school boards completely and placed all of their powers in
the hands of a 46 man City Board of Education and the
Superintendents this Board would choose. In order to give
some recognition to the localities, the members of the
Board of Education had to reside in the borough from which
they were appointed and the number from each was in proportion to its population. Thus, there were 22 members from
Manhattan, 14 from Brooklyn, four from the Bronx and Queens
and two from Richmond.[36] They served staggered five year
terms and worked through committees, since it was difficult
for 46 men to accomplish much when they all met together.

---

[36] New York (State), Laws of 1901. Chapter 466.
Charter of the City of New York, p.114.

The most important of these committees was the executive,
on which each borough had to be represented. Since
Manhattan had 22 representatives and the others combined
had 24, it was less likely that the largest borough could
dominate the smaller ones.

The fear of centralization runs all through the
revised Charter. For example, the city was divided into
46 districts and there was to be a seven man local school
board in each one. Five of the members of this local board
were to be appointed by the Borough President, one was to
be a member of the Board of Education and the last was to
be the District Superintendent assigned to that area. This
elaborate structure signified little, however, since the
powers of the local boards, then as now, were advisory only
and subject to the veto of the powerful Board of Superintendents.

There was some worry that the local school boards
represented retrogression and were reminiscent of the old
ward trustee system, but most observers seemed to feel that
they were a sop to the advocates of borough control and no
more than that. Since reformers such as Seth Low, Nicholas
Murray Butler and William H. Maxwell, all of whom were
staunch enemies of politics in the schools, bore the major
responsibility for the new education chapter, it seems
most likely that the local school boards were not meant to
be a force in determining policy.[37]

---

[37]
Abelow, p.96.

The Department of Education of which the Board of Education was the head, really consisted of four bureaus-- Buildings, Audit, Supplies and Superintendence, and the most important of these was the last. In addition to the relatively unimportant duties assigned to him by the 1897 Charter, the Superintenden. of Schools was now ordered to make "...plans and suggestions for the improvement of the schools and school system", enforce the compulsory education law, nominate and direct attendance officers and assign District Superintendents.[38] His most important powers were exercised in his role as chairman of the Board of Superintendents which was made up of eight Associate Superintendents, four of whom were the former borough Administrators. This board controlled curriculum, texts, methods of teaching and the appointment of teachers.[39]

Salaries were now to be fixed by the Board of Education and be uniform throughout the city. Finally, the school entry age was established at six years--for all the children. The revised Charter was greeted with enthusiasm by Superintendent Maxwell because it centralized power in the Board of Education and its executive departments and yet kept the schools close to the people through the local

---

[38] Charter of the City of New York, 1901, p.116.

[39] Palmer, P. 301.

school boards. He prepared to undertake the new policies
he felt the schools so badly needed now that he was
finally secure in his position.

Although the revised Charter made great changes in
the organization of the public schools as a whole, it left
the Mayor's relation to the system virtually untouched.
The only real change had to do with his power to appoint
the 46 man Board of Education and remove them for cause.
In other respects, his position on the Board of Estimate
was the same, as was his ability to veto the budget deletions of the Board of Aldermen. The fact that his term
of office was now two years instead of four did have an
impact on the schools because now a Mayor who really had
educational plans which he wanted to implement had a very
short time in which to do it.[40]

This factor was clearly operative during the term
of Seth Low, former Mayor of Brooklyn and well-known
reformer, who succeeded Van Wyck as Mayor of New York in

---

[40]
        Charter of the City of New York, 1901, pp. 9,16,
114,121. The bi-cameral Municipal Assembly provided for
in the 1897 Charter was eliminated in 1901, and the Board
of Aldermen, elected from 65 single member districts,became
the city legislature. The two year term for Mayor lasted
until 1904 when an amendment to the Charter reverted to a
four year term.

1901. Although handicapped by the brevity of his term in office, Low tried to fulfill his platform pledge on education which stated: "That school accomodations shall be provided for all children of school age, and that the efficiency of the schools shall be increased."[41]

The Fusionists around Low believed that his school attitudes were at least partly responsible for his election, because he carried the East Side, usually Democratic, and it was in that area that overcrowded schools were causing the greatest distress.[42]

The Superintendent of Schools, as well as reform groups generally, had great expectations when Seth Low became Mayor. In one respect, at least, these expectations were fulfilled. More money was appropriated for schools in the 18 months of the Low administration than had been allocated under the four years of Van Wyck's tenure and the "supply of schools was brought (temporarily) more abreast of demand".[43]

---

[41] *Literary Digest*, September 28, 1901, p. 365. The Fusion platform of 1901 is given in detail.

[42] Milo T. Bogard (ed.), *The Redemption of New York* (New York: 1902), p. 157.

[43] Garrett, p.40.

Although Mayor Low had no more power over the schools than Van Wyck, his interest in education led him to urge measures such as opening the school buildings in congested areas during the week-ends and the summer, and then to use his strength on the Board of Estimate to get the money for such projects.[44] Seth Low represented the exception among Mayors of this period in that he was able to influence school developments by the force of his leadership and the fact that many of the most influential groups in the city were behind him.

In spite of his efforts for the schools, Low alienated enough voters to be defeated in his 1903 bid for reelection by Democrat George B. McClellan, Jr., the son of the Union general. Mayor McClellan was aware of school problems and attempted to influence the policies of the Board of Education through his friend and relative, Egerton L. Winthrop, Jr. whose election as President of the school board he was able to arrange. In general, McClellan held a very low opinion of the members of the Board of Education. He said they were mostly uninformed and shirked their duties, a condition which he attributed to their unpaid status.[45]

---

[44] *Journal of the Board of Education of the City of New York*, June 25, 1902, p.1253.

[45] Harold Syrett (ed.), *The Gentleman and the Tiger: The Autobiography of George B. McClellan, Jr.* (New York: 1956), pp.242, 243.

Mayor McClellan was appalled by the extent of the overcrowding in the schools, as had been others before him. A solution which he favored was the erection of temporary one story school buildings on vacant city owned land, mainly property that had been set aside for small parks, but not yet developed.[46] The Board of Education, however, voted to accept this plan only as a last resort, because they felt that "the parks were the breathing spaces of the poor".[47]

Like his predecessor, Van Wyck, McClellan found that the school board was able to get the money it needed by threatening to close down popular programs, and in the midst of a great quarrel over money in 1904, the Mayor bowed to the pressure created by this threat, and used his influence to get additional funds for evening centers and recreation programs, although the Comptroller was very much opposed.[48] When he was writing his autobiography, McClellan showed a good deal of pride in the school achievements which occurred during his years in as Mayor, 1903-1909, although he was not personally responsible for these gains.[49] There

---

[46]
The New York Times, January 6, 1904, p.16.

[47]
Ibid., January 28, 1904, p.14.

[48]
Ibid., January 3, 1904, p.5; January 15, 1904, p. 14.

[49]
Syrett, pp. 259-260.

was an increase in school building in the period, but due
to the enormous growth in population, the schools were as
overcrowded as ever when the next Mayor, William J. Gaynor,
took office.

Mayor Gaynor was an independent Democrat whose
position on a number of issues agreed with the reform
elements in the city. Many changes took place in the school
system during his term of office, but Gaynor did not play a
leading role in educational affairs. This was partly
because he was overshadowed by the President of the Board
of Aldermen, John Purroy Mitchel, who initiated a controver-
sial inquiry into the schools between 1911 and 1913 which
dominated school news all through Gaynor's term.

Mitchel received a great deal of publicity as a
result of the inquiry, and this fame was at least partly
responsible for his nomination and election as Chief
Executive in 1913. As Mayor, Mitchel was enormously interested in the schools, focussing mainly on the costs and quality
of education. In a search for increased value for the
educational dollar, he forced the Board of Education to
adopt the "Gary Plan" of vocational education, over the
protests of the Superintendent of Schools and a large part
of the citizenry. The issue became so prominent it even
dominated the campaign of Mitchel's successor, John F.
Hylan. [50]

---

[50]
Sol Cohen, Progressives and Urban School Reform,
pp.80,86,88. The School Inquiry of 1911-1913 is dealt with
in more detail in chapter seven, and the Gary Plan is discussed in chapter three.

The relationship between Mitchel and the schools
would seem to indicate that it was possible for a strong
Mayor to force his plans on the Board of Education, but it
is likewise interesting to note that the "Gary Plan" was
never fully implemented and that Mitchel left office com-
plaining that delay and obstruction on the part of the
school board had prevented his plan from getting a fair
trial. This cry had been heard before and would be heard
again--it was easier for a Mayor to promise than to get the
Department of Education to implement.

The connection between the Estimate Board and the
schools was relatively unchanged in the 1901 Charter,
although the composition of the Board of Estimate was
different. The Charter stated that "(the) Mayor, Comptroller,
President of the Board of Aldermen and the presidents of the
boroughs of Manhattan, Brooklyn, the Bronx, Queens and
Richmond shall constitute a Board of Estimate and apportionment."[51]

The inclusion of the Borough Presidents led to a
good deal of "log-rolling" especially in regard to school
appropriations, because each of these gentlemen were more
interested in gaining benefits for his borough's schools
than in considering the interests of the system as a
whole. The purpose of the provision had been to reassure
the boroughs, now deprived of the protection of their own

[51]
Charter of the City of New York, 1901, p.29.

school boards, but it often had the effect of further
delaying the appropriation of school funds.

An even more serious reduction in the money available to the schools came about as a result of the action
of the State Legislature in 1903. The men in Albany cut
the mandatory tax rate established in the Davis Law to
three mills instead of four. This was done in response
to pressure from New York City property owners and the
results for the schools were disastrous. The Department
of Education was forced to ask the Board of Estimate for
deficiency appropriations every year since the three mill
tax did not raise enough money to cover the salaries of
the increased number of teachers the expanding school
system required.[52]

The conflict engendered by this situation led to a
long and noisy inquiry into the schools, called the Grout
Investigation, after the Comptroller who initiated it.
When the Department of Education asked for more money in
1904 than it had in 1903, the Board of Estimate refused
to appropriate any additional funds. The Board of
Education then cut many popular programs out of its plans,
claiming lack of money. This caused a public outcry and
the Comptroller suggested that the Board of Estimate conduct
an inquiry in order to determine whether the schools could

---

[52] Rose Cohen, Financial Control of Education, p.95.

continue these extension programs, if they were only more
efficient in spending the money allotted to them.[53]

Comptroller Grout appointed three investigators to
conduct the inquiry. They were John S. Crosby, a lawyer
who was interested in education, Robert McIntyre, newspaper-
man and Mrs. Mathilde Coffin Ford, retired assistant
Superintendent of Schools from Detroit.[54] The main conclusion of the committee was that the high cost of education
in New York stemmed from the overloading of the elementary
course of study with "frivolous subjects" such as sewing,
cooking, music, drawing, physical education and manual
training. If the schools attended to their primary business
--teaching the "three R's"-- a great deal of money could be
saved since no special teachers and fewer supervisors would
be needed.[55]

---

[53]
New York City, Board of Estimate and Apportionment, Report of an Investigation concerning the cost of
maintaining the public school system, June, 1904 (New York:
1904), pp. 6-7.

[54]
Ibid., p.8.

[55]
Ibid., p.14.

The investigators also found that the Board of
Education was carrying too much unimproved property,
which was wasteful, and was permitting too long a period
of time to elapse between the acquisition of a property
and giving out the contracts for construction.[56] The
report included a strong criticism of the methods of
purchase, storage and distribution of supplies used by the
schools and a blanket indictment of the waste and extra-
vagance practiced in certain extension activities.[57]

A special committee of the Board of Education took
on the task of answering the Comptroller. They agreed that
there was some need for tightening school administration
and reducing waste, but vehemently opposed the elimination
of any special programs or subjects. They claimed the delay
in building was due to red tape in Grout's own department
(site purchases and contracts had to be examined by the
Department of Finance) and accused the Comptroller of a

---

[56]
Ibid., pp. 138,151.

[57]
Ibid., p.223; Rose Cohen, Financial Control of
Education, p.65. Although the Grout Inquiry did investigate
the educational practices of the schools, its principal
goal (as the Coler attack before it) was to cut expenditures.
Not until the Hanus Report of 1911-1913 (discussed in
chapter seven) did the educational side of the schools get
an investigation.

desire to exploit the staffs of the schools by overloading them with tasks in order to avoid the employment of more teachers.[58]   In the end, the schools got most of their funds, after the hue and cry died down, although the Superintendent did instruct school principals to pare expenses as much as possible.[59]

Support for the Board of Education's position was forthcoming from the New York Times which said editorially, that the Comptroller was not qualified to judge the schools. Although the investigators may have been right in their judgement that the elementary schools should be improved before high schools were developed, said the Times, this was an educational decision, to be made by the educational authorities. Furthermore, the Times saw the not-so-subtle hand of Tammany in the inquiry, and said it was basically an attack on the liberal policies of Seth Low by a Comptroller who wished to curry favor with the incoming McClellan administration. The editorial thought the report would provide ammunition for the Democratic budget cutters, a prophecy which was, unfortunately, quite accurate.[60]

---

[58]
New York (City), Department of Education, Report Number two of the Special Committee of Five, February 24, 1905 (New York: 1905), pp. 3-4, 5-6.

[59]
The New York Times, February 7, 1904, p.5.

[60]
Ibid., December 26, 1903, p.6.

The basic issue in the controversies which took so much time and energy from both school and fiscal authorities was control over school finances, with the Department of Education struggling to achieve financial independence and the Finance Department attempting to limit its freedom. Also involved was the inability of city officials to adjust to the fact that greater demands on the schools simply had to cost more. In years past, a basic primary education was sufficient for the great majority, while a small minority received the classical training which enabled them to enter college. This was no longer the case. As the problems created by urbanization, immigration and industrialization increased, pressures on the schools multiplied, because many Americans looked to education for the solutions to the difficulties which vexed them.

Thus the financial struggle between the city and the schools was a substantive one, and unless the educational establishment could be adequately financed it was virtually impossible for them to cope with the tremendous demands they faced in the first decade of the 20th century. Was the relationship between the city and the schools adequate to meet the burdens placed on education at this time? In general, the structure established in the Charter of 1901 did function fairly well. Centralization was achieved, with all the benefits of a uniform curriculum and uniform salaries. Civil Service procedures were extended and political influence was largely eliminated.

Mayors were not an important influence in school affairs;
and it was only in the area of finances that the relationship became abrasive and seriously limited the power of
the schools to cope with their problems.

Thus it would seem that the crowds celebrating
in the rain at City Hall on the last day of 1897 had at
least one reason to cheer--in spite of the many, many
problems the schools had, they were better able to face
them after consolidation than before, and this boded well
for the future of the Greater City.

FIGURE 1. THE ORGANIZATION OF THE DEPARTMENT OF EDUCATION IN 1899*

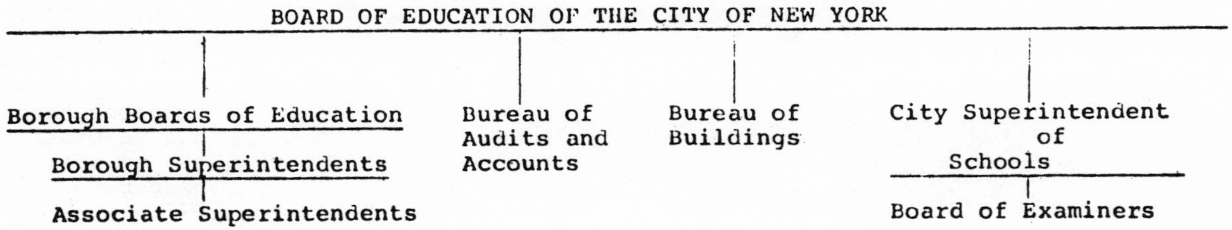

BOARD OF EDUCATION OF THE CITY OF NEW YORK

Borough Boards of Education	Bureau of Audits and Accounts	Bureau of Buildings	City Superintendent of Schools
Borough Superintendents			
Associate Superintendents			Board of Examiners

*Source: First Annual Report of the City Superintendent of Schools, 1899, p.13.

FIGURE 2. THE ORGANIZATION OF THE DEPARTMENT OF EDUCATION IN 1902.[*]

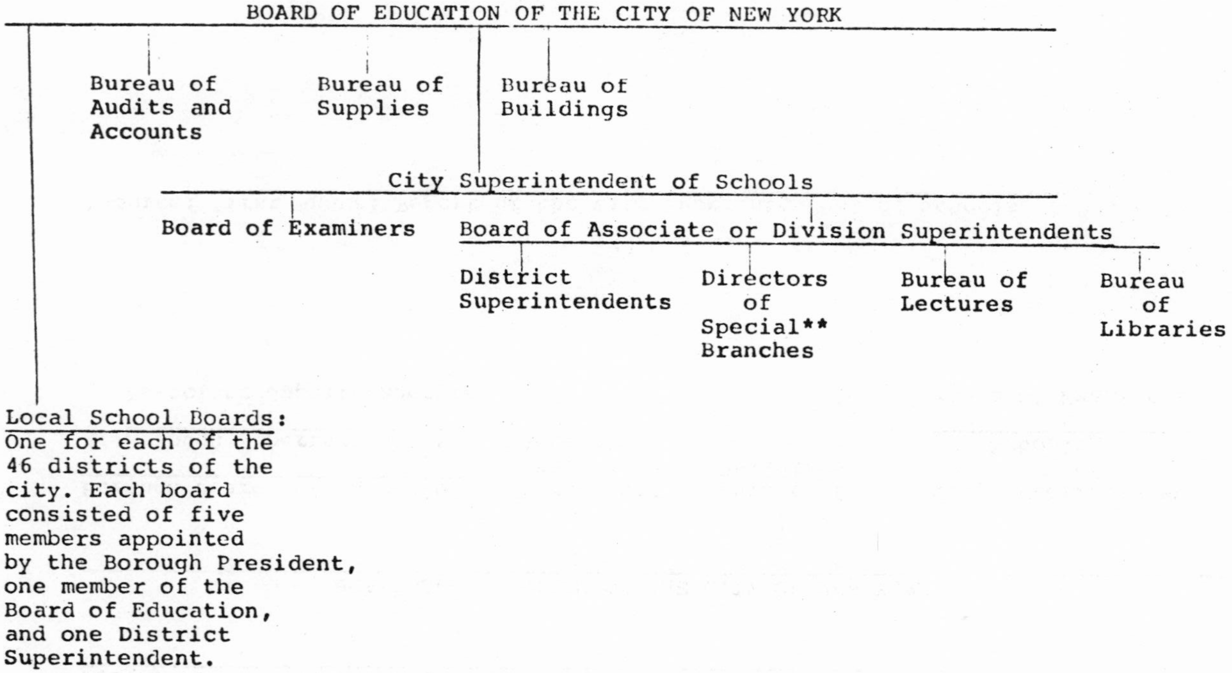

BOARD OF EDUCATION OF THE CITY OF NEW YORK

Bureau of Audits and Accounts

Bureau of Supplies

Bureau of Buildings

City Superintendent of Schools

Board of Examiners

Board of Associate or Division Superintendents

District Superintendents

Directors of Special[**] Branches

Bureau of Lectures

Bureau of Libraries

Local School Boards:
One for each of the
46 districts of the
city. Each board
consisted of five
members appointed
by the Borough President,
one member of the
Board of Education,
and one District
Superintendent.

*Source: Fourth Annual Report of the City Superintendent of Schools, 1902, pp. 12-17.

**The Directors of Special Branches included the supervisors for kindergartens, sewing, cooking, drawing and manual arts, physical education and music.

CHAPTER II.

"LAND ON SATURDAY, SETTLE ON SUNDAY, SCHOOL ON MONDAY"...[1]

To the schools of New York City, the arrival of hundreds of thousands of immigrants and the rapidity with which the children of the newcomers appeared in the class-rooms, was a fact of enormous importance, overshadowing many of the other events which occurred in the city in the years following consolidation. Actually, the Empire City was only the largest repository of the millions of new arrivals who came to America at this time, the period of heaviest immigration in United States history. Between 1898 and 1910, 9,734,972 men, women and children made the long voyage from Europe to the United States[2] and enough

[1]
Teacher proverb quoted in: Robert A. Woods, Americans in Process (Cambridge: 1902), p.292

[2]
U.S. Immigration Commission, Abstract of the Statistical Review of Immigration to the U.S., 1820-1910 (Washington: 1911), pp. 8-9. The figures for the immigration to the U.S. of the decade are:

1900	448,572
1901	487,918
1902	648,743
1903	857,046
1904	812,870
1905	1,026,499
1906	1,100,735
1907	1,285,348
1908	782,870
1909	751,786
1910	1,041,570

As can be seen, 1907 was the single year of heaviest immigration although in 1905, 1906 and 1910 almost as many persons came.

of these millions remained in New York to give that city

the largest foreign born population in the nation. By

1914, 40.8% of New York's population of five million had

been born abroad, and formed a large percentage of the

inhabitants in each of the five boroughs.[3]

In 1920, the percentage of foreign born in New

York City had dropped to 36.1% but the census of that

year showed that 33.3% of the native whites in the city

were the children of foreign born parents. These two

groups of first and second generation New Yorkers togeth-

er comprised 69.4% of the total population of the city,

and an even larger percentage of the inhabitants in

Manhattan and the Bronx.[4] This situation was not new

---

[3] "Foreign Born of United States" National Geographic,
XXVI (September, 1914) p.271. The % of foreign born population
in the boroughs was:

Manhattan	47.9%
Brooklyn	35.2%
Bronx	34.7%
Queens	27.9%
Richmond	28.4%

[4] U.S. Bureau of the Census. Abstract of the 14th Census
(Washington: 1923), p.50. The exact percentages for the various
boroughs are as follows:

Manhattan	73.1%
Brooklyn	67.9%
Bronx	73.3%
Queens	55.3%
Richmond	55.9%

because even in 1890, 80% of the people of the city were
either foreign born or of foreign parentage.[5] What was
new was the national origin of the newcomers.

In 1900, the largest single group of foreign born
in New York City had been from Germany, and the second
largest from Ireland. Partly because of heavy earlier
migrations, economic conditions improved in Germany after
the 1880's and the government attempted to limit emigration.
The passage of social legislation also made the fatherland
more attractive, and thus, fewer Germans came to the United
States in the last decades of the 19th century. These
factors were operative in regard to the previously heavy
Irish and Scandinavian immigration as well. In addition,
England directed her emigrants to the Commonwealth nations
after 1880, and therefore, fewer natives of the British
Isles came to America.[6]

Thus, the source of major immigration changed to
Southern and Eastern Europe, where neither improved economic
conditions nor stringent government restrictions prevented
anyone from leaving. As a result, 71.9% of the immigrants

5.
   Sol Cohen, Progressives and Urban School Reform
(New York: 1964), p.5.

6.
   Maldwyn A. Jones, American Immigration (Chicago:
1960), p.196.

O

who arrived in the United States between 1901 and 1910
were from Southeastern Europe, and by 1914, the German
and Irish foreign born in New York City had been greatly
outnumbered by the Russians and Italians.[7] Most of the
Russians were Jews, and combined with their co-religionists
from Germany, Poland, Austria-Hungary, Rumania and Lithuania,
they numbered 1,643,000 or about 27% of the population of
New York by 1920.[8] The emigrants from Italy, who numbered
390,832 in 1920[9] were largely from the southern part of
that country and from Sicily. The two most populous
boroughs, Manhattan and Brooklyn, also had the greatest
number of Russian Jews and South Italians. In the Bronx,
Queens and Richmond, the Germans were still the largest
group.[10] It is clear, therefore, that the ethnic strains
in New York City were greatly changed by the "new" immigration.

---

[7]
U.S., Bureau of the Census. Abstract of the 12th
Census. (Washington: 1904), p.104; Abstract of the 14th
Census, p.176;

[8]
Morris C. Horowitz and Lawrence Kaplan, Jewish
Population of the New York Area, 1900- 1975. (New York, 1959),
p.15.

[9]
Abstract of the 14th Census, p.312.

[10]
National Geographic - XXVI, p. 271.

Why did so many people leave their homes in
Southern and Eastern Europe and make the arduous trip to
America at this time? A young Russian Jew who left his
ancestral village in 1902 for the long voyage to New York
told of his hopes.

> I was going to America and building castles in
> the air about making lots of money and getting an
> education. I would come home dressed and thinking
> like a nobleman. I would bring nice presents to
> all the family and gold and diamonds for my
> mother...11

Implicit in this statement is the tremendous desire
for self-improvement which motivated the individuals who
undertook the great migration to the United States.
Hundreds and thousands of men and women used considerable
ingenuity in order to escape to America where they sought
the opportunity to advance themselves politically, economic-
ally, socially, and culturally, in order to achieve a better
life than was open to them in the Old World.

To get an education and make "lots of money" were
the most important reasons which motivated so many Russian
Jews to leave their towns and villages and come to America.
The possibility of doing both was the "pull" which the
new world exerted. Nowhere was there more opportunity to
achieve these goals than in New York City where free public

11
Hyman Cantor, unpublished autobiography, 1935.

education from kindergarten to college was available for the diligent, although this was probably not appreciated by the bulk of the newcomers until after they arrived here.

The Russian Jews had long been familiar with the hostility of the government but the restrictions on them were greatly increased after the assassination of Czar Alexander II in 1881. It had never been easy for a Jewish child to get a secular education in Russia, but after the May Orders of 1882, which followed terrible pogroms, quotas drastically reduced Jewish attendance at Russian gymnasiums and universities. Even worse, economic opportunity was further decreased, and the always precarious position of the Jew in Russia became increasingly hopeless.[12]

Under such circumstances, the rejective "push" of Europe and the attractive "pull" of America combined to bring a million and a half Jews to the United States between 1899 and 1910, and to keep them here. So vast and permanent was the Jewish immigration, it was really a migration. As a group, the Jews showed the lowest rate of returnees, and the family nature of their emigration showed a high amount of commitment to a new life in the United States.[13]

---

[12] John R. Commons, Races and Immigrants in America, (New York; 1930), p.91.

[13] Samuel Joseph, "Jewish Immigration to the United States" in Philip Davis (ed.), Immigration and Americanization (Boston: 1920) p.136.

More than half of the Jews entering the United
States in an average year such as 1912 were women and
children[14] and this pattern, repeated all through the
decade 1900-1910 guaranteed a new and larger school population for the city. Indeed, many of the immigrants
remained in New York City, congested as it was, precisely
because of the educational opportunities no other city in
America could match. It was this group which was to exercise so large an influence on the schools of New York in
the years to come.

As early as 1901, the United States Industrial
Commission recognized that "of the newer people coming in,
the Italians and Hebrews are the most important as affecting city conditions, both on account of their absolute
numbers and their tendency to remain in cities".[15] What
of the Italian immigrant and his goals? The poverty,
drought, antiquated land holding system and overcrowding
of Southern Italy were the dominant "push" factors in
the case of the nearly two million South Italians who came
to America between 1899 and 1910.[16] The "pull" was the

---

[14] American Jewish Yearbook, 1913 (Philadelphia: 1913),
p.45.

[15] U.S., Industrial Commission, Reports on Immigration
(Washington: 1901), Vol. XV, p.xlvi.

[16] Statistical Review of Immigration, p.9.

chance at a job, albeit a laborer's job, and the possibility of returning home with some money.

Although the first immigrants of any group tended
to be male and transient, the Italian "bird of passage"
(migratory laborer who came to the United States in good
times and returned to Italy during depressions) continued
to dominate the immigration statistics until 1903. After
that year, family immigration became as pronounced among
the Italians as it had always been among the Jews.[17]

A desire for education did not appear to be a
dominant motive for the coming of the Italians. A maladmin-
istered, totally inadequate, compulsory education system
did exist in Italy, although very few peasant families took
advantage of it. The few village boys who did complete a
primary education found it difficult to go on to secondary
schools and impossible to get a professional position if
they did.[18] Because of this, education was not viewed as
the route to success, and nothing in the South Italian
peasant's experience led him to expect rewards from schooling. Therefore, when the nature of Italian immigration
changed, and became more permanent and family oriented,
the schools of New York City were confronted with a different

---

[17]
U.S. Industrial Commission, Report, Vol. XV, p.473.

[18]
Leonard Covello, "The Social Background of the
Italo-American School Child"; (Unpublished doctoral disserta-
tion, New York University, 1944), Vol. II, p.384.

experience--the need to educate an unwilling group of
scholars--and this was as much an influence on them as
was the urgent pressure of the Jewish children.

Whether from Minsk or Palermo, or more likely,
tiny villages near these cities, the newcomers to New York
lived primarily among their own countrymen, attempting to
reproduce the security of the families they had left
behind. The Italians grouped themselves according to the
provinces from which they came, and often an entire tenement in "Little Italy" would be inhabited by people from
the same village. Different areas of the Lower East
Side were occupied by Jews from different parts of
Eastern Europe, although the Russian Jews were always
the largest group.[19]

The immigrant communities were often temporary
and fluid; as their income increased or diminished, or as
they became aware of better housing opportunities, the
immigrant families moved.[20] These changes of address
were a great problem to the school officials, both

---

[19]
U.S. Industrial Commission, Report, Vol. XV,
.474; Moses Rischin, The Promised City,(New York:
1964)p.76.

[20]
E.A. Goldenweiser, "Immigrants in Cities"
The Survey, XXV, (January 7, 1911), p.602.

because of the shifting registers which resulted, and
because of the difficulties of tracing absentees, truant
or legitimate. The major outlines of the ghetto--Jewish
or Italian--stayed the same, although people did move out;
Jews to Williamsburg or Brownsville in Brooklyn and Italians
to East Harlem. New immigrants took the place of those able
to move elsewhere, just as the latter had displaced the
original Irish and German residents.[21]

The two wards with the highest population density
were the 10th, whose boundaries were Division, Rivington,
Norfolk streets and the Bowery and which had such a large
Jewish population it was called "New Israel", and the
14th, whose limits were Canal and Houston Streets, the
Bowery and Broadway and which was called "Little Italy".
These central areas of foreign settlement were surrounded
by other sections in which the same ethnic groups lived
in slightly fewer numbers, such as the Italian 6th ward
which included the infamous Five Points and the Mulberry
Bend, and the Jewish 7th, 11th and 13th wards which together took in almost the entire area from the East River to
the Bowery.[22]

---

[21]
    U.S., Immigration Commission. Immigrants in Cities
(Washington: 1911) Vol. LXVI, p.58 (map).

[22]
    Roy Lubove, The Proresssives and the Slums:Tenement
House Reform in New York City, 1890-1917 (Pittsburgh: 1962)
p.264.

Within this relatively small portion of Manhattan,
n which the bulk of the "new" immigrants lived, the key-
ote was crowding--in the streets, the tenement apartments
nd the classrooms. There were a great many schools in
ivision I, which is how the Board of Education designated
he area, but never enough.[23]

Besides being filled to capacity, a condition not
nique to the Lower East Side, the schools of the ghetto
ere set apart from the rest of the city by the religious
omogeneity of the children who attended them.

In a study conducted in 1905, it was found that of
he total number of pupils (64,605) in a school district on
he Lower East Side below Houston Street, 61,103 or 94.5%
ere Jews, and 10 of the 38 schools in the district had
nrollments which were 99% Jewish, while the remaining
8 had registrations which were over 90% Jewish.[24] A
etired principal who attended P.S. 75 on Norfolk street
etween 1892 and 1900 recalls a totally Jewish student body.[25]

---

[23]
In 1910, there were 64 elementary schools in the
ix wards making up the Lower East Side. Mary Fabian Matthews,
"The Role of the Public School in the Assimilation of the
talian Immigrant Child in New York City, 1900-1914."
Unpublished Ph.D. dissertation, Fordham University, 1966),
.323-324.

[24]
Charles Bernheimer (ed.), The Russian Jew in the
nited States (Philadelphia: 1905) p.185.

[25]
Conversation with Dr. Jacob Ross, October 17, 1966.

None of this is surprising since the neighborhood school was the accepted urban pattern and the neighborhoods were homogeneous in the extreme.

The fact that his child was likely to attend school mainly with co-religionists did not appear to be a cause of concern to the immigrant parent. Community groups formed by the newcomers did correspond with the Board of Superintendents regarding overcrowding, released time for religious training and the teaching of foreign languages, but no objections were made to the homogeneity of the pupil population in any given school, nor was this condition viewed as harmful.[26]

On the contrary, the newer arrivals were informed about the school, and taken there by fellow-countrymen who were only a little less "green". In the same way, those children who spoke a little English translated for the totally Yiddish or Italian speaking youngsters, and all this was looked upon as healthy and desirable.

The school personnel considered it easier to teach English to a class in which all the youngsters spoke the same foreign language. Superintendent Maxwell, in an address to the Educational Alliance in 1902, indicated that he hoped for great success in Americanizing the Jewish immigrant, precisely because almost all the Yiddish speaking children were

---

[26] New York (City) Department of Education, Minutes of the Board of Superintendents, 1902-1914, passim.

in the same schools.[27] The children naturally found it
easier to attend classes with their neighbors and friends
and the segregated groups provided security for the otherwise anxious immigrant youngsters.

Only the social workers, especially those active
in the settlement house movement, raised some questions
about the ethnic homogeneity of the schools. The assimilation of the immigrant would be retarded, it was feared, and
the learning of English would be impeded when the children
used their native tongue everywhere but in the classroom.
Certainly, it was true that at recess, going to and from
school, in playground activities, and in ordinary conversation, the Italian children spoke to each other in their
first language, and the Jewish children did the same.

But even the settlement workers concentrated their
fire less on the homogeneity of the schools and more on the
methods of Americanization they saw practiced there, and
on the over-crowding, rigid curriculum and lack of social
services. Articulate social workers commented angrily on
the gulf the teachers were creating between the foreign
born parents and their native born children. By derogating
old world culture and language and extolling only what
was American, the teachers diminished the status of the
parents in the children's eyes, the result being family
breakup and juvenile delinquency. Grace Abbott, Jane
Addams and Sophinisba Breckenridge exhorted the schools to

---

[27] Educational Alliance, Annual Reports, 10th Report,
1902 (New York:1902) p.42.

recognize the importance of the foreign cultures and to emphasize the value of the contribution each of the immigrant groups could make to the American mosaic. Folk dancing and the celebration of national holidays were urged as the means by which the immigrant child could continue to be proud of his heritage, even while learning the ways of the New World.[28]

Whether the new ways, or the respect for the old could best be accomplished in segregated schools rather than in ethnically diversified ones, was simply not the major question among those concerned with the schools. Indeed, it was really those groups most hostile to the immigrants who castigated the in-bred ghettos and blamed the newcomers for choosing to live among their own.

In general, therefore, other aspects of the relationship between the immigrants and the schools took precedence over "de facto segregation". The center of interest, was the immigrant child himself. The speed with which the newly arrived youngsters were enrolled in the public school was a

---

[28]
Grace Abbott, The Immigrant and the Community (New York: 1917) p.226; Grace Abbott, "The Education of Foreigners in American Citizenship" Proceedings of the Buffalo Conference for Good City Government, 1910, p.376; Jane Addams, "The Public School and the Immigrant Child", National Education Association Proceedings, 1908, p.99; Sophinsba Breckenridge New Homes for Old, (New York: 1921) p.231.

matter of comment. A former student at P.S. 110, located on Cannon Street near Delancey, noted that in 1905, "Sometimes as many as 125 children are admitted to the school in a single day, usually the day following the arrival of the steamer, Jewish or Italian...[29]"

The school personnel who came in contact with the newly arrived children formed opinions about them and these ideas were widely repeated. Like all stereotypes, the descriptions were probably accurate for many of the youngsters, but ignored the exceptions, who were numerous. The importance of these opinions lies in the fact that they were so widely held, and therefore influenced the attitude of the schools to the children. Also, the way in which the educational authorities saw the immigrant youngsters helped shape the proposals they advanced to meet the challenge posed by the newcomers, often with mixed results.

A frequent comment was that the young Italians were less school-minded than their Jewish contemporaries. A teacher in a predominantly Italian school said:

> ...Italian children were usually more crude in manner, speech and dress than non-Italian children ...It was common for Italian boys and girls to leave school to help out the family income...These children, especially the boys, were a source of constant irritation for the teachers...they created difficulties for the schools. [30]

[29] Kellog Durland and Louis Sessa, "The Italian Invasion of the Ghetto", University Settlement Studies, I, (January, 1906), p.112.

[30] Covello, Social Background of the Italo-American Child, Vol I, p.448.

Kate Claghorn, professor at the New York School of Social Work, investigated the immigrant child at school in New York and found that "...Italian children are...more or less difficult to discipline and are irresponsible...They are fair students, better than the Irish, but not as good as the Hebrews and Germans at book work. They show great talent for manual work, drawing, etc. One defect they have is lack of application."[31]

This observation was part of the larger report of the United States Industrial Commission which was less harsh. "Coming under the influence of the public schools, they (Italian children) are generally satisfactory pupils, mainly in the line of manual work and the industrial arts, however, rather than in bookwork"[32] A popular magazine article about the foreign born children at P.S. 1 on Henry Street repeated this idea. "...the Italians are unquestionably the most artistic in the manual training shops..."[33]

A retired principal who began his long career in 1904 at P.S. 189 near Catharine Slip with a fifth grade class which was largely Italian recalled that his first pupils were of low caliber, from deprived backgrounds and

---

[31]
U.S. Industrial Commission Report, Vol. XV, p.475.

[32]
Ibid., Vol. XV, p.xlvi.

[33]
A. R. Dugmore, "New Citizens for the Republic", World's Work, V. (Jan. 1903), p.3325.

difficult to discipline. They could best be reached through
athletics and outings, not classroom work.[34]   One observer
who was cognizant of the learning difficulties of these
Italian youngsters felt that "The public schools were wasting the children's artistic and manual ability in the academically confining school program" of the day.[35]

This opinion was shared by a student of those
Italian children who attended the Children's Aid Society
Industrial School and found that they did indeed excel in
artistic and handicraft ability. She noted that the regular
elementary schools failed to value this gift and that therefore the Italian children did not gain in self respect and
confidence when they attended public school.[36]

An Italian-American professional objected to the
non-academic stereotype of the Italian school child and
accumulated evidence from school principals to controvert
the image. The principal of Washington Irving High School
described most Italian school children as average in ability,
although emotional and excitable. He found that the girls

34
   Conversation with Dr. Jacob Ross, October 17,1966.

35
   John Mariano, The Italian Contribution to American
Democracy (Boston: 1921), p. 294.

36
   Lillian Brandt, "A Transplanted Birthright",
Charities,XII (Jan. 1904), p.499.

were shy and inarticulate which he attributed to the strict
paternal discipline in their homes. One of the first Italian-
American elementary school principals to be appointed in
New York, Anthony Pugliese, said the Italian children "...
showed particular ability along the lines of music and the
other arts and in manual work..." but were not inferior in
intellectual subjects--.except in learning English.[37]

Two studies done by social scientists during this
period shed some light on the ability of the Italian children.
In 1920, Miss Katharine Murdoch, teacher at the New York
School of Social Work, gave the Pressy Intelligence test to
1700 5th grade boys in two schools and found that those of
Italian descent placed lowest, even though she used only
English speaking youngsters.[38]   Leonard Ayres study of
school retardation in New York City, done for the Russell
Sage Institute, in 1909 found that the largest number of
overage children were of Italian origin. Both studies
indicated that the Jewish pupils were doing much better in
the schools of the day. Miss Murdoch's investigation concluded that the Jewish and native born children rated
equally high on her intelligence tests, and Ayres reported

---

[37]
    Antonio Stella, Some Aspects of Italian Immigration
to the United States, (New York: 1924) pp. 50,51.

[38]
    Katharine Murdoch, "A Study of Race Differences in
New York City" School and Society XI (January 1920), pp. 147-
150.

that the Russian Jewish children were only a little more
average than the German and native born youngsters and
much less retarded than the English, Irish or Italian
students he tested.[39]

It is likely that there was a correlation between
the greater literacy of the Jewish male immigrant and the
better school adjustment made by the children of this
group. An investigation of the literacy of a number of
immigrant families living on 14 selected blocks of Lower
Manhattan by the Immigration Commission found that 57.4%
of the Italian families and 85.8% of the Jewish families
were partly literate.[40]   Statistics gathered a little
earlier, between 1899 and 1900 indicated that only 26%
of the Jews entering the United States were illiterate
while 65.4% of the Italians were in that condition.[41]

---

[39]
Leonard P. Ayres, Laggards in our Schools
(New York: 1909) p.107. The term overage referred to the
number of grades a child was retarded in relation to his
age; a nine year old in grade I for example, would be
considered three years overage.

[40]
U.S. Immigration Commission, Immigrants in Cities,
Vol. LXVI, p.238.

[41]
U.S. Statistical Review of Immigration, p.51.

Abraham Cahan, editor of the largest Yiddish newspaper in
America, said that the Russian Jewish male was rarely
illiterate and for this reason found it easier to learn
English.[42]   The women in the Jewish immigrant family often
could not read or write since they rarely received any
but the most rudimentary religious training. It was their
spiritual study that prepared the Jewish boys for the secular
education available in America. Kate Claghorn indicated
that "One of the most striking social phenomena in New York
City today (1901) is the way in which the Jews have taken
possession of the public schools, in the highest as well as
the lowest grades". Furthermore, "In the lower schools,
Jewish children are the delight of their teachers for their
cleverness...obedience and general good conduct, and the
vacation schools, night schools, social settlements, libraries, bathing places, parks and playgrounds of the East Side
are fairly besieged with Jewish children eager to take advantage" of every opportunity.[43]

A year later, Superintendent Maxwell spoke of the
"national genius for education" of the Jews,[44]   and still
another social investigation noted that the Jewish boys
would only join a club if it could contribute to their

---

[42]
    Bernheimer (ed.) p.32.

[43]
    U.S. Industrial Commission Reports, Vol. XV, P.478.

[44]
    Educational Alliance Reports, 10th Report, 1902,
p. 42.

"power of achievement" and never for frivolity![45] The dili-
gence of the Jewish school children was further attested to
by a very low absentee rate in Lower East Side Schools, caused
almost entirely by illness.[46]

A magazine article describing the student body at
P.S. 1 on Henry Street found that "The Russian and Polish
Jews had a school standing far out of proportion to their
numbers,"[47] while the testimony of the teachers working on
the lower East Side indicated that the Jewish children at
these schools were among the brightest then attending the
public schools. They described these youngsters as docile,
bright, attentive and studious, very patriotic and responsive
to imaginative stimuli. Rarely shy, the Jewish students were
encouraged to show off by their proud instructors,[48] which
practice did not delight everyone.

A non-Jewish teacher said "We have to recognize
their ability. They are mentally alert, colorful, intelligent...mentally, the Jewish children are the backbone of
my class but they can be an insufferable nuisance because
of their constant desire to distinguish themselves."[49]

---

[45] Joseph Lee, Constructive and Preventive Philanthropy (New York, 1902) p.199.

[46] Rischin, p.200.

[47] Dugmore, World's Work, V, P3325.

[48] Bernheimer (ed.) pp. 186-187, 189.

An immigrant Jewish girl recalled vividly how much she
liked to distinguish herself, and attributed her school
success to "her...aptitude for language, and her ambition,
which made her bend her mind earnestly to her task." 50
The hunger for approval demonstrated by children like this
one might have been a reaction to the widespread disapproval
which was the lot of the Jews in Europe. It may also have
stemmed from a desire to demonstrate to the Gentile teachers
the superiority of intellect with which many were endowed.
Or, considering the sacrifices being made by many families
to keep their children in school, it might have been necessary for the child to seek proof of his worthiness through
the applause of his instructors.

Even the library personnel reinforced the image
of the bookish Jewish child. The librarians at the Seward
Park Branch of the New York Public Library, located in
the heart of the East Side, often found themselves overwhelmed by the number of children who came to use their facilities. 51

49
Pauline Young, "The Reorganization of Jewish
Family Life in America", Social Forces, VII, (December, 1928),
p. 243.
50
Mary Antin, The Promised Land, (Boston: 1912)
p. 206.
51
John F. Carr, (ed.) Bridging the Gulf in Library
Work with the Foreign Born (New York: 1917) p.28.

A survey by the New York Evening Post into the kinds of books read in some of the poor districts of New York found that "Hebrews form the best and largest class of readers among the foreign element...the children (are) attracted to the library first, then draw in (the) adults."[52]

Actually, the best proof of the happy marriage between the Jewish boys and girls and the public schools was the large Jewish attendance at the College of the City of New York and the Normal College (Hunter) as well as at the Teacher Training Schools early in the century.[53]

Teaching as a profession was appealing to the Jewish students because it gave security and status and the training cost little. It was also true that other lines of endeavor, which had much appeal, were not open to college trained Jews at this time. Private employment, other than in retailing was difficult to obtain, but a job in the public sector, gained through competitive examination, was a possible route to upward mobility, and thus teaching, along with other civil service positions, became the career choice of many a graduate. Although the greatest number of Jewish staff members were not to appear in the public schools until the late 1920's, even by 1914, enough were present

---

[52] Literary Digest, January 13, 1900, p.43.

[53] Bernheimer, (ed.) p.191; S. Willis Rudy, The College of the City of N.Y. (New York: 1949) p.292.

among the faculty to challenge the previous Irish prepon-
54
derence.

Even though higher education at C.C.N.Y. or the
Normal College was free, most of the students had to find
some means of support while they were at school, unless
their family could help them. As a result, many a boy
made a "college match"---married a factory girl who had
accumulated some savings and who was willing to work until
he could support them both. Others used less drastic means,
such as tutoring their fellow immigrants, or teaching in the
55
evening schools in order to complete their college course.

From the evidence at hand, the success of the
majority of Jewish school children cannot be denied but it
is nonetheless important to recognize that there were slow
learners and mavericks in the group, and that the favorable
picture presented above did not apply to all. District
Superintendent Julia Richman, for example, found that
many of the Jewish children in her care were in serious
difficulty at school. Upon investigation, she discovered
that poverty, illness, malnutrition, part-time work and
even rape by the boarders who shared their homes figured

54
        I am indebted to Prof. Sidney Pomerantz for the
sense of much of this paragraph.

55
        Bernheimer (ed.) p.33, Abraham Cahan, The Rise
of David Levinsky, (New York 1913), p.76.

56

in the lives of the pupils and prevented them from learning.

Whether or not the cause was poor home conditions, in 1904, 260 Jewish boys and girls were in the Randall's Island House of Refuge for juvenile delinquents, and 262 Jewish children under 16 were at the Juvenile Asylum for committing misdemeanors.[57] "In 1909, some 3,000 Jewish youngsters came before the Juvenile Court" for various offenses.[58] In addition to evidence of crime, there is other proof that the rosiness of the Jewish school adjustment may have been somewhat exaggerated.

By 1910, most of the schools on the Lower East Side had classes for the overage child and for those about-to-drop-out. If most of the pupils in a school that was 99% Jewish were doing so well, why were remedial classes needed? If most of the Jewish youngsters were bent on higher education, why were cram classes for the almost 14 year olds formed? While the evidence of contemporaries overwhelmingly indicates that the Jewish school child was highly valued, it may be that the success of some was spread over all, when in fact,

---

56
  Julia Pichman, "A Social Need of the Public Schools", Forum, XLIII (February, 1910), p.164-167.

57
  Bernheimer, p.73.

58
  Rischin, p.90.

the slow learners and the non-academic were present in all
immigrant groups.

An investigator for the U.S. Immigration Commission,
Ronald P. Faulkner, studied the relationship between the
immigrants and the schools and came to the conclusion that
when the child of foreign background did not do well
academically it was due to "various conditions of his home
life which are unfavorable to the best progress of the
children in the school", but that no blanket indictment
or praise could be given to any immigrant group.[59] This
conclusion was borne out by a series of non-verbal intelligence tests administered to immigrant children at Ellis
Island by psychologist Bertha Boody who determined that the
differences between the youngsters were individual and not
common to any one race or nationality.[60]

Although the fact that individual Italian children
often did as well as Jewish children must be kept in mind,
evidence that the adult elements in the two groups did have
different attitudes toward formal education does exist.
There is abundant proof that contemporaries were aware of
the Jewish enthusiasm for education. They were called the
"People of the Book" and the respect with which they treated

---

[59]
        Ronald P. Faulkner, "Immigrants & Education"
Paul Monroe, (ed.) Cyclopedia of Education, (New York: 1918)
p.395,
[60]
        Bertha M. Boody, A Psychological Study of Immigrant
Children at Ellis Island (Baltimore: 1926) p.151.

a learned man was often noted. Lillian Wald commented on:
"The passion of the Russian Jews for intellectual attainment
and their willingness to forego every comfort...(and submit)
to bad housing, excessive hours and poor working conditions"
so that their children might use the educational opportunities
offered in New York City.[61]   A widowed Jewish mother wrote
to the editor of the Jewish Daily Forward saying that she
needed the help of her fifteen year old son to make a living
for her other four children, but that the boy had "inclina-
tions to study and (went) to school dancing!" She concluded
by saying she would keep him in school somehow because she
"lay great hopes on her child".[62]

This favoring parental attitude to schooling is
only one of a number of explanations for the academic success
of many of the Jewish children. For example, to those boys
who had begun their education in the chedarim of Eastern
Europe, the three "R's", American style, seemed very easy.[63]
Also, school was presented in positive terms to the children.
A friendly observer of the ghetto, Hutchins Hapgood, told

---

[61] Lillian Wald, The House on Henry Street (New York: 1915), p.99.

[62] Robert Park and Herbert Miller, Old World Traits Transplanted (New York: 1921), p.7.

[63] Samuel Joseph, History of the Baron de Hirsch Fund (Philadelphia; 1935) p.256. The cheder (chedarim) was the religious school open only to boys at which Hebrew and ritual were taught directly from the ancient books.

how a five year old was introduced to the <u>cheder</u>. "Before beginning to learn the first letter of the alphabet, he is given a taste of honey, and when he declares it to be sweet, he is told that study...is (even) sweeter than honey. Shortly afterward, a coin falls from the ceiling, and the boy is told that an angel dropped it from heaven as a reward for learning his first lesson."[64] This combination of intellectualism and practicality, combined with self discipline, was very likely the key to the Jewish school posture. It would almost appear that the school attitude of the Jews was akin to the Protestant ethic--a willingness to postpone pleasure and income in order to eventually increase the possibility of both.

Jacob Riis saw an area in which both the Italian and Jewish parents were in agreement. Both groups felt that "education pays off as an investment, and therefore the child is sent to school. The moment his immediate value as a worker overbalances the gain in prospect by keeping him at his books, he goes to the shop."[65] An attitude like this was based on the old world concept that a child was important only as a member of the family and must therefore contribute his share. Furthermore, many immigrant parents did not understand that the complexity of urban life required more education, nor that the American society really offered

---

[64]
Hutchins Hapgood, The Spirit of the Ghetto (New York: 1902), p.22.

[65]
Jacob A. Riis, The Children of the Poor (New York: 1892), p.38.

opportunities for the educated unlike the situation in
Europe.

This negative view of education was most common
to the Italian born parent, for reasons which stemmed from
their European experience, where compulsory education bore
no relation whatever to material success. The general
attitude of the Italian peasant was that group wisdom was
transmitted through channels other than formal education
and that a man's happiness lay with his land and his family.
Education might actually be harmful, because in the case
of the girls, literacy might break down accepted social
patterns and would permit daughters to communicate with
young men without parental supervision. For all children,
education would weaken family ties and respect for parents,
a prophecy which unfortunately came true for some in
America.

With such opinions about schools, it is not surprising that the Italian immigrants often found themselves in
conflict with the compulsory character of American education,
and used expressions such as "America took our children" or
"the school took our children" to show how they felt. There
was not too much objection to school for children up to age
ten, because it at least served a baby-sitting function,
but there was strong antagonism to supporting a child over
that age, partly because the parent did not believe the
child would repay him for his sacrifices and partly because

a twelve year old was not considered a child. [66] This view
of Italian hostility to education has not stood unchallenged.
A non-Italian student of South Italian folkways noted that
the immigrant from Italy saw eduction "as a magic wand that
fits everyone for some pleasant and well-paying position"
and that therefore," the poorest families sacrifice to get
their first child or two through grammar school and then
make these children, as soon as they can, get working papers
and help carry the education of their younger brothers and
sisters at least as far, preferably further." [67] And
another observer stated that Italian parents "are quick to
see how essential it (education) is to progress and they are
determined that their children shall not be hampered for the
lack of it like themselves". [68] Still another saw "that it was
only the compulsion of extreme poverty that led (Italian]

---

[66]
    Covello, Social Background of the Italo-American
School Child, Vol. II, pp. 405,412,455,457,467,473,488,511.
I am indebted to Dr. Covello's massive three volume dissertation for this discussion of Italian school attitudes, but
must add that in his autobiography, The Heart is the Teacher
(New York: 1958) he points out that his own father, a
South Italian immigrant, encouraged him to go to school as
a way out of a hard economic life (p.41) and that his first
wife was an Italian immigrant girl who was a graduate of
the Normal College. (p.55) Therefore, not all Italian parents
shared the hostility to education which he describes in his
dissertation.

[67]
    Phyllis Williams, South Italian Folkways in Europe
and America (New Haven: 1938), pp. 129,130,134.

[68]
    Elliot Lord, The Italians in America, (New York:
1906), p.240.

parents to take their children from school."[69]

Sister Mary Fabian Matthews, in a recent dissertation on the assimilation of the Italian school child in this period asserts that the reputed indifference of Italian parents to education was probably exaggerated. She maintains that such poor adjustment between the adults of Italian background and the schools as did exist, was probably due to the gulf created by the school. If the educational authorities had done more to value the Italian culture, the parents would have responded. The fact that teachers, for example, were forbidden to write notes to the parents in Italian, even when they had knowledge of the language, made the mothers and fathers more dependent on their children and widened the gap between the generations, possibly increasing the latent hostility to formal education already existing among individuals in this group. But at bottom, Sister Mary feels that the lack of the Protestant ethic among the parents from Southern Italy was the most important factor in the situation:

---

[69] Robert Foerster, Italian Emigration of our Times, (Cambridge, 1924) p.377.

>Amidst such poverty as the early immigrants
>experienced, deferred gratification would have
>had little appeal; the immediate opportunity
>for employment would be far more desirable than
>the possibility of a more gainful occupation at
>the expense of a prolonged education. 70

Although reluctant scholars, short-sighted parents
and brilliant, ambitious students existed among the Jews
and Italians, in numbers at least, the children of the
former group did make a more successful school adjustment.
While many different reasons for this have been presented,
one more may be of considerable significance. The Jews
were a town people, living in an urbanized manner even
while residing in rural villages. Partly because of this
way of life, they developed skills and attitudes which
were suitable to the educational methods then in use in
the schools. The emphasis on arithmetic, drill on voca-
bulary, and recitation in unison, which was the pedagogy
of the day, suited the Jewish children far better than it
did the Italian youngsters, who, coming from a rural folk
who had lived close to the soil, had never developed the
abilities and values which led to school success. When
the schools recognized individual differences and adopted
flexible methods, a greater number of the Italian children
became better scholars.

It is clear, therefore, that because of differing
attitudes, skills and values, all the immigrant children

70
  Matthews, p.282.

presented the schools with both daily and long range
problems which had to be solved in the context of overcrowding and lack of funds. On the one hand, programs
for handling the non-academic had to be devised and on
the other, high schools and accelerated courses had to be
built for the eager and ambitious. All immigrant youngsters needed lessons in health, nutrition and urban living.
Italian or Jewish, the immigrant youngsters were poor and
required help with many problems which had never before
considered the concern of the schools. Without a long
range plan, but rather in response to daily pressures, the
schools attempted to meet the needs of the newcomers.
The changes which came about as a result of these efforts
led to an educational pattern which was quite different
in 1914 from that in 1898.

PART II. THE CHANGES

CHAPTER III

THE "UPWARD PROGRESS" OF THE SCHOOLS.

Carnegie Hall was the scene of an anniversary cele-
oration on the evening of October 24, 1912. William Henry
Maxwell, Superintendent of Schools of the City of New York,
was being honored for twenty-five years of service to
education in New York. Present on the platform were such
luminaries as Seth Low and Nicholas Murray Butler, while
in the audience were many distinguished men and women who
had been invited to join in the tribute, on elaborate engrav-
ed invitations.[1]

When Maxwell was finally called upon to address the
group, he spoke on his favorite topic-- the achievements of
the public schools of the city, during the past decade.
Although he was never a man for apologetics, on this occas-
ion he did make a point of stating that the progress of the
schools had been an uphill struggle, because of the conditions that confronted them. "...the rapid increase and
constant migration of our home population...the influx of
vast hordes of people from abroad, alien in language, alien
in modes of thought, and alien in tradition..." had combined

---

[1] Invitation and program found in vertical file 902
in Room 722 at Board of Education headquarters, 110 Livingston
St.,Brooklyn, N.Y.

to present the schools with the most serious obstacles yet
discovered to the upward progress of public education."[2]

No one in New York knew better how real these
obstacles were. Maxwell, a Scotch-Irish immigrant himself,
had come to the United States in 1874, at the age of 22,
anxious to get a position as a teacher, the profession, for
which he had been trained at Queens College, Galway, Ireland.
He was not able to achieve this ambition because, as a newcomer, he lacked the "patronage of a ward boss", necessary
for appointment to the schools at that time. With regret,
he turned instead to newspaper work and was first a reporter and later managing editor of the Brooklyn Times but the
inability to get a teaching job on his merits undoubtedly
contributed to his lifelong attitude toward civil service.[3]

While working at the newspaper and teaching in the
evening schools, Maxwell wrote a "series of powerful
articles on the needs and future development of public

---

[2] William Henry Maxwell, A Quarter Century of Public
School Development (New York: 1912), pp. 372, 380.

[3] John S. Brubacher, "William Henry Maxwell" in the
Dictionary of American Biography, Dumas Malone (ed.), Volume
XII, (New York: 1933), p.445; "City Superintendent Maxwell
of New York", Educational Review, XXVII (January, 1904), p.5.

school systems". This, and the fact that he got to know many influential Brooklynites during his newspaper tenure, won him appointment as Associate Superintendent in 1882. He remained in this position for four years and in 1887, became the Superintendent of Schools for the City of Brooklyn, in which capacity he served for over a decade.[4]

Maxwell was entirely aware of how bad the schools of Brooklyn were and also of how little he could do to make them better, due to the cherished local committee system. None the less, he did bring about certain changes during his term as Superintendent which foreshadowed the improvements he was later to oversee in New York City as a whole. First, by means of a double pronged attack, consisting of higher salaries based on experience and training and the passage of a State law requiring any city teacher to be at least a High School or Training School graduate, Maxwell was able to upgrade the staff of the Brooklyn schools.

He then turned his attention to the problem of overcrowding which up to this point, had been handled by simply turning away children when a given school was too full. Regretfully, but feeling that some education was better than none, the Superintendent instituted double time classes, an innovation hailed by the financial authorities, if not the educational.

---

[4] "Maxwell" in the Dictionary of American Biography. p.445. The Mayor of Brooklyn at the time of Maxwell's appointment as Associate Superintendent was Seth Low with whom Maxwell maintained a close association for many years.

Maxwell's own academic preparation had been in
English literature, and his special training enabled him
to change the content and methodology of this subject.
Previously, the children never saw a complete book but
instead used readers--collections of excerpts from famous
classics, which the Superintendent thought was appalling.
Now they were to read the literature in the original which
would certainly give them a more complete picture. The
changes in the teaching of English were among the few
Maxwell was able to make, although he wrote extensively
on the need for manual training, commercial education,
physical training and vacation schools. A little was done
in some of these areas, most notably the establishment of
a Manual Training High School but resistance by the local
committees, old time teachers and politicians worried about
taxes, prevented much progress.[5]

Therefore, when the Board of Education of the newly
unified City of New York invited him to be the Superintendent
of Schools for the entire city, he was very pleased, although
under no illusions about how much could be done under the

---

[5]
Maxwell, Quarter Century, pp. 10-15; Educational
Review, XXVII, p.7; Harold C. Syrett, The City of Brooklyn
(New York: 1944), p.117.

confusing Charter of 1897. [6] Maxwell's election as Superintendent was greeted with joy by the good government elements
in the city, mostly because of his well known opinions on
civil service, and the need to remove politics from the
schools.

The New York Times called him "intelligent and
mature" and rejoiced when they heard that he was disliked
by the Manhattan-Bronx Superintendent, John Jasper, because
that gentleman was an old line Tammany appointee and represented an element in the educational system that the Times
thought needed to be reformed.[7]

The man chosen to be the head of the Department of
Education was now 46 years old, six feet tall and with a
girth appropriate to his height. He wore a large walrus
mustache and only a dropped eyelid marred an otherwise imposing appearance.[8] In personality, he was direct, honest

---

[6] New York (City) Dept. of Education Journal of the
Board of Education, March 15, 1898, p.57. Maxwell was not
their first choice. Andrew Draper, the New York State
Commissioner of Education had been asked, (Journal, March 7,
1898, p.40) but had declined and recommended Maxwell
(Journal, March 15, 1898, p. 56) who was elected by 11 out
of 19 votes, with almost all his support coming from the
Brooklyn representatives on the Board of Education.

[7] The New York Times, May 4, 1897, p.6, March 15, 1898,
P. 6.

[8] Picture of William Henry Maxwell in Board of Education
vertical file 902.

and outspoken and could be considered harsh or truthful,
depending on one's point of view. His clarity, forceful-
ness and willingness to fight for what he considered right
were outstanding. By his own estimate, he never carried
out a policy of which he did not approve, and he never
avoided an issue which he considered important. Altogether,
he was the right man for the job, which was nothing less
than to construct a school system for a complicated, cosmopolitan city.

What were the educational matters which he considered important? Better trained teachers, including more men,
to be paid professional salaries and licensed by examinations
and who were to place the interests of the schools above
their own, even when the salary increases to which they
were legally entitled were not forthcoming.[9] Financial
independence for education because the schools had to have
a sure and certain income in order to expand and develop
the new programs demanded by the problems of immigration
and urbanization.[10] His plans included all the new ideas

9
New York Times, November 14, 1899, p.5, William Henry
Maxwell, "The Schools of New York", Municipal Affairs, IV
December, 1900) p.748.

10
"Maxwell" in the Dictionary of American Biography, p.446;
Maxwell, Municipal Affairs IV, p.747.

then being discussed in educational circles, ranging from
physical education, manual training, domestic science,
music, health services, and lunch programs to the extension
of the schools into summer and evening work.

Cognizant of the new educational theories promulga-
ted by John Dewey and other "progressive" educators, he
wanted movable furniture in the classrooms and urged a
diversified course of study, suited to the individual child,
because he said children would not learn if the lessons
were not geared to their life situations.[11]   One of his
major concerns was the extent of non-learning, as evidenced
in the figures regarding retardation and non-promotion that
came to his desk, and he held a weekly "clinic" on Thursday
afternoons to examine "interesting" cases of non-achievers.[12]

Almost as numerous as his plans for school improvements, were the educational ideas he opposed. In an
address entitled "On a Certain Arrogance in Educational
Theorists", Maxwell attacked the proponents of vocational
education, saying that the idea originated with manufacturers
who wished to shift the burden of training workers to the

---

[11]
    Harold McCormick, "The First Fifty Years", in the
Fiftieth Annual Report of the New York City Superintendent
of Schools, 1948, p.6; William Henry Maxwell, "The City
and the Child", Publications of the National Recreation
Association of America, XXVI, no date, pp. 7,9; Maxwell,
Quarter Century, pp. 58-62.

[12]
    McCormick, p.32.

public schools, when it was really their own obligation.
"I am in favor of whatever reasonable education will fit
young people for their life work...", he said, but he was
against narrow vocational education which would sacrifice
general education, "every child's birthright". Also, a
public school was not the best place to train a skilled
workman; the machinery would need constant replacement
and the cost to the taxpayers would be overwhelming.[13]

For somewhat similar reasons, the Superintendent
opposed permitting children to chose their course of
study at the end of 6th grade, because he felt that no
child of that age could make an intelligent decision about
his life's work and might place himself in a trade school
when he had the potential to go to college.

In his major ideals, Maxwell was the very incarna-
tion of the American conception of education--that the public
school was to be a ladder upward and, he thought that for it
to fill the role, the curriculum would have to be diversified
and flexible, the process of learning be "made a delight"
and all the children be kept in school as long as possible.[14]

---

[13] William Henry Maxwell, "On a Certain Arrogance in
Educational Theorists", Educational Review, XLVII (February,
1914), pp. 175-177.

[14] William Henry Maxwell, "My Ideals as Superintendent"
Educational Review, (November 1911) XLII, pp. 453-456.

There could be no better set of aims for a schoolman
who had to cope with the problems of the immigrant child.
In every area in which the children from the congested districts
came in contact with the schools, the Superintendent was
ready to take action. Was child labor keeping youngsters
from their books? Maxwell served on the Child Labor Committee of New York and was responsible for the stronger law of
1903 and the Newsboy Law. Was slum housing at the root of
the trouble? Maxwell served as adviser to the Tenement
House Commission which drew up the Law of 1901. Was poor
health the real cause of retardation? The Superintendent
agitated for medical inspection, school nurses and nutritious lunches. Would a flexible curriculum be the answer?
He served on the two major National Education Association
Commissions (Committee of 10 and Committee of 15) of his
era, both designed to modernize the content of the schools,
was the President of the National Education Association from
1904-1905, and even found the time to be co-editor with Nicholas
Murray Butler of the Educational Review, potent publication

in the school world.[15]

Small wonder then, that so much praise came to him, when, after two operations, he had to retire as Superintendent in 1918. A special amendment to the Education Chapter of the Charter of 1901 was passed in order to permit him to retire as Superintendent Emeritus, at full pay.[16] The evaluations made of his career at that time said he was the ablest executive yet seen in American education and that he was responsible for a "revolution" in the New York City public school system![17]

---

[15] This is not to say that Maxwell did not have both critics and enemies. He was in frequent conflict with the teachers, over their resistance to new programs and certain administrative matters such as his opposition to licensing married women. Unquestionably autocratic, he demanded dedication from his staff and fought the idea that teachers should share in policy making. Even his ethics were questioned during the Grout investigation when it was determined that many of the books used in the teaching of English literature were edited by Maxwell, and that the change in the booklist came about when he was made Superintendent. New York (City), Board of Estimate and Apportionment, Reports of an Investigation concerning the cost of maintaining the public school system. 1904 (New York: 1904), pp. 31-41.

[16] New York (City) Dept. of Education, Election of William H. Maxwell as City Superintendent of Schools Emeritus. New York: 1918, passim.

[17] School Journal, March, 1913, p.166. By 1913, the Journal had become a monthly periodical, claiming to be the voice of progressive education, but actually speaking mostly for the professional educator, and against the interference of lay people in school affairs, Prior to 1913, it had been a weekly newspaper, designed to give ideas to the classroom teacher.; "City Superintendent Maxwell:, Educational Review XXVII (January, 1904), p.18.

The school problem which most required revolutionary
handling was the oldest---overcrowding. Although some
critics jeered at Maxwell's preoccupation with the shortage
of seats, saying that he "confused sitting with learning",
the statistics of the period make clear why he had to devote
so much attention to the problem. Between 1899 and 1914,
school enrollment in New York increased by 60%, from 493,849
to 792,595 and the schools were obliged to provide seats
for 20,000 children a year, just to keep up with the entering students.[18]   When the fact that a shortage of space had
existed in Manhattan and Brooklyn since 1894, at least, is
considered, the dimensions of the problem and the reasons
for the Superintendent's concern become clear.

In 1894, Charles C. Wehrum, a member of the Board of
Education, but a strong supporter of reform candidate
William L. Strong, undertook a survey of the schools of the
City of New York in order to show how Tammany had neglected
education and found much evidence of overcrowding, as well
as other abuses. At P.S. #2 on Henry Street, at P.S. #4
on Rivington Street, and at P.S. #20 on Chrystie Street,
he noted that almost 1,000 children had been turned away
for lack of room, while at P.S. #7 at Hester and Chrystie,
a brand new building was so crowded--an annex had to be
organized immediately.[19]   Lillian Wald described the schools

---

[18]
William Henry Maxwell, "School Achievements in New
York", Educational Review, (October, 1912) p.308., XLIV.

[19]
Charles C. Wehrum, Description of Grammar and
Primary Schools in the City of New York and their Requirements
(New York; 1894)pp.10,11,12.

of the East Side in 1895 and said "The classes were over-crowded, there were frequently as many as 60 pupils in a single room and often three children on a seat."[20]   In the same year, John Jasper, Superintendent of the Manhattan-Bronx schools reported that 24,000 children could not be admitted to school because of lack of room and the situation became worse in 1896, when 28,825 youngsters were denied entrance.[21]   The greatest impact of the overcrowding was felt on the Lower East Side. The annual report of the New York City Board of Education for 1895 said:"Schools which five years ago were fully adequate to the wants of the neighborhood have been filled to their utmost capacity..."[22]

The problem not unique in Manhattan; in 1896 there were classes of 100-150 each in Brooklyn, although 70 was more the norm. Even with such enormous class sizes, 5,305 children could not enter school in that borough.[23]

---

[20] Lillian Wald, The House on Henry Street (New York: 1915) p.47.

[21] A. E. Palmer, History of the New York Public Schools (New York: 1905) p.193. The children who were turned away entered school a year or two later, thus complicating their educational careers considerably.

[22] New York (City) Department of Education, Annual Report, 1896, p.127.

[23] Palmer, pp. 247,248.

In the following year, the president of the Manhattan-Bronx school board described a dreadful annex of P.S. 4 on Pitt St. which he said had to be used for first and second graders because the main building was so crowded, even though rats had been seen there.[24]   Each September, the newspapers would report many instances of overcrowding but in 1897, the New York Times described a particular incident at P.S. 75 on Norfolk St. in which 500 children who could not be admitted stood outside the building for hours and a near riot ensued. The principal had already taken 2,000 children into his school, which was built to hold 1,500 but another 500 was just too much.[25]

An elderly gentleman who was an entering pupil at P.S. #2 on Henry Street in 1898 vividly recalled the extent of the overcrowding at that school. Because of the shortage of seats, the first grade boys were sent to temporary quarters in the parish house of a nearby Catholic church, which horrified his orthodox Jewish parents.[26]

---

[24]
New York (City) Department of Education, The Organization of the School Board for the Boroughs of Manhattan and the Bronx, February 13, 1901, p.177.

[25]
New York Times, September 15, 1897, p.12.

[26]
Conversation with Milton B. Perlman, October 19,1966.

Right after the city was consolidated, the situation got worse, if that was possible. The School Journal reported that 25,000 children were denied admittance to the schools on opening day, 1896.[27] As in many other respects, there was great variation in the amount of overcrowding. The schools of Richmond and Queens, largely rural and in many cases ungraded, one room school-houses, were plagued with transportation problems and teacher shortages but were not overcrowded at all. Brooklyn, though, was in very bad shape and needed at least 46 new schools or replacements for old ones, by Superintendent Maxwell's estimate.[28]

Even in 1903, a survey of the schools of New York by Adele Marie Shaw for World's Work, reported no improvement. She reported seeing classes of 65 in Brooklyn where there were only seats for 25, so the youngsters sat three in a seat, which led to bad posture and worse handwriting.[29]

---

[27] School Journal, September 17, 1898, p.240.

[28] New York (City) Department of Education, First Annual Report of the City Superintendent of Schools, 1899, (New York: 1899), p.29.

[29] Adele Marie Shaw " The True Character of the New York Public Schools" The World's Work, VII (November, 1903), pp. 4209, 4206.

At the same time, the always concerned New York Times
bemoaned the fact that 60,000 to 75,000 children had been
turned away from the public schools and said they would
have to go to parochial schools or be on the street, which
was dreadful.[30]   Between 1905 and 1910, conditions on
the East Side remained so crowded, an army hospital ship
was converted into a school and 10,000 children received
instruction on it, at its mooring at the foot of Corlear's
Hook.[31]

The Superintendent's Report for 1905 indicated
that the most overcrowded districts were in lower Manhattan
and the Brownsville and Williamsburg districts of Brooklyn,
areas in which the greatest numbers of immigrants were
living.[32]   In the following year, Maxwell saw a little
relief for the Lower East Side, "...unless the increase
in population by immigration becomes greater than now seems
probable", because the opening of P.S. #62 and 63 in 1906
had helped a great deal.[33]

---

[30]
New York Times, September 6, 1903, p.6.

[31]
Moses Rischin, The Promised City (New York: 1964)
p. 100.

[32]
Seventh Annual Report of the City Superintendent
of Schools, 1905, p.57.

[33]
Eighth Annual Report of the City Superintendent
of Schools, 1906, p.135.

Brooklyn, however, now became the major area of concern. The opening of the Williamsburg Bridge led to a great shift in population, with the result that the schools in Williamsburg showed a 55% increase in registers in five years, while those of Brownsville grew 22% in an even shorter time.[34]

One year later, in 1907, Superintendent Maxwell stated in an article he wrote for the Nation, that while the city-wide average of pupils to teachers was 43--this figure was misleading, because although classes on the upper West Side and in the outlying sections were small-- in the schools of "the lower East Side of Manhattan, and (in) the Brownsville district of Brooklyn, classes are very large" and ranged from 55 to 65 children per unit. He estimated that it would cost $1,500,000 a year to bring all classes down to the 40 per teacher he thought was bearable (although not ideal) not counting the cost of new buildings. This was manifestly a terrible price for the city to pay, he went on, but essential nonetheless, when the large number of foreign born and non-English speaking children were con- sidered, as well as the fact that the great majority of the youngsters went to work at 14. Because of these special problems, elementary education in New York City had to be

---

[34]
Ibid., pp. 163,409.

of the very best quality, a condition not possible to
achieve in large classes.[35]

Maxwell's report for this year (1907) listed the
districts in which classroom congestion was the worst.
These included a few on the East Side, two in East Harlem,
which had become another "Little Italy", one in the South-
east Bronx, caused by the construction of the IRT subway,
and three in Long Island City to which people were moving
in anticipation of the soon to be opened Blackwell's Island
Bridge. The schools of Brooklyn were now in worse condition than any other area of the city. Eleven districts
(comprising Williamsburg, Greenpoint and Brownsville) were
terribly congested with children whose parents had moved
to the "suburbs" in order to get away from the crush of
the Lower East Side.[36]

By 1908, the pattern had shifted a bit so that the
schools of Brooklyn, while still the worst congested, were
in slightly better shape than they had been earlier and
the Lower East Side reported almost enough seats, but the
Bronx now had four districts which were badly overcrowded.[37]

---

[35]
William Henry Maxwell, "The Present Needs of the
Public Schools", The Nation, LXXXIV (April 25,1907), p.380.

[36]
Ninth Annual Report of the City Superintendent of
Schools, 1907, p.46.

[37]
Tenth Annual Report of the City Superintendent of
Schools, 1908, p.51.

The rapid and uneven growth of the city led a group of
civic minded citizens to organize a Committee on the
Congestion of Population in New York which began an investigation of the problem in 1908.

The Chairman of the Committee was Professor Frank
J. Goodnow of Columbia University, and the executive board
of eighteen included a number of active urban progressives.
Frederick C. Howe of the Peoples Institute, Florence Kelley
of the National Consumers' League, Paul A. Kellogg of the
University Settlement, Henry Moskowitz of Madison House,
and Mary Simkhovitch of Greenwich House were all members
of the Committee. Their report, entitled, "The True Story
of the Worst Congestion in any Civilized City" appeared in
1911 and contained information on tenements, land values,
industrial uses of land, park policies, the social and
economic costs of congestion, and the measures essential
to prevent further congestion in New York City.

A large portion of the summary concerned the public
schools, and how they reflected the congestion of the
neighborhoods they served. The investigators found that out
of 469 schools in Greater New York, only 120 or 1/5 averaged
an adequate number of rooms, and that only when badly lighted
and ventilated rooms were included. About 1/3 or 162 of
the schools averaged over 46 pupils to a room. Below 14th
street the situation was especially bad. Less than 1/5 of
the schools in Division I had enough rooms, particularly in

the kindergarten and primary grades. The Committee estimated that 33 new buildings would be needed in Manhattan and
seven in the Bronx in order to bring class size down to 35.[38]

In his next annual report, for 1910, Maxwell went
into more detail, explaining that two Brownsville districts,
#39 and #40, were the most congested in the city, with
children up to 4th grade able to go to school for only half
a day. In a school in one of these districts, he knew of
three classes with registers of 82! Although the schools of
the Lower East Side were no longer in such fearful shape,
even there a class with 106 youngsters was in existence.

The problems caused by overcrowding prevented the
schools from undertaking new programs; for example,
Associate Superintendent Meleny, in charge of the Division
in which Brownsville was located, complained that he could
not institute classes for the newly arrived children who
needed English remedial work because such classes could
only have thirty children in them. Since the rooms had

---

[38]
    New York City Committee on the Congestion of
Population, The True Story of the Worst Congestion in Any
Civilized City, 1911, pp. 6-10, The Committee published
its report of 282 pages and submitted it to the Mayor
and the Board of Aldermen on February 28, 1911. They also
summarized the results in a small pamphlet which sold for
fifteen cents.

seats for 45, this would mean wasting 15 seats and in view
of the congestion, he could not do it.[39]   This particular
problem was partially solved in 1911, by keeping 50-60
children in a room, but using two teachers so that some
individual help could be given to the non-English speaking
pupils.[40]

By 1912, the shift, but not the disappearance, of
overcrowding was clearly discernible from the Superintendent's
report. Only one Lower East Side district was still crowded,
but two in Harlem, three in the South Bronx and six in
Brooklyn (all in Brownsville) were in very bad shape. In
terms of actual numbers, the Bronx districts were now the
most crowded.[41]

In 1914, the Superintendent indicated the most
congested districts in this order: East Harlem, East Bronx,
Williamsburg and Brownsville and said the children in these
areas most urgently needed new schools.[42]

---

[39]
  Twelfth Annual Report of the City Superintendent
of Schools, 1910, pp. 69, 94, 267.

[40]
  Thirteenth Annual Report of the City Superintendent
of Schools, 1911, p.257.

[41]
  Fourteenth Annual Report of the City Superintendent
of Schools, 1912, pp. 50,57.

[42]
  Sixteenth Annual Report of the City Superintendent
of Schools, 1914, pp. 83-84.

The pattern of overcrowding, so clearly connected to the movement of immigrant population within the city, and the extension of transit facilities, presented the schools with the first, and in terms of day to day management, the greatest of their problems. Congestion in the schools was an old story, but never was the impact felt so strongly as when immigration reached the huge proportions it did in the first decade of the 20th century. Shifting neighborhood populations was similarly familiar to New York, but never did the movement of people present so many difficulties to the schools as it did when the people of the Lower East Side migrated into different areas of the city seeking a better life.

Could the problems have been lessened and could the movement of peoples have been accommodated if the educational authorities had planned better, or had more money at their disposal? The question is difficult to answer, because the causes of overcrowding in the schools were multiple and varied, although the impact of immigration appeared to be foremost.

Because so many of the Italian and Jewish immigrants came as families, "...every tenement on the lower East Side fairly swarmed with children" and the greatest number of pupils were found in that part of the city..."[43]   The educational

---

[43] School Journal, September 17, 1898, p.240.

authorities were very much aware of the impact of immigration on the registers of the schools. One of the largest increases was noted in 1902, "due to a great increase in immigration".[44] The results of the school census of 1906 furnished additional evidence of the number of aliens in school. 17% of the entire enrollment of the public schools was foreign born, according to the figures gathered by this survey.[45] Although the expansion of the school population caused him great problems, Superintendent Maxwell tried to be positive about it in his 8th report. "This wonderfully rapid growth (in school population) is doubtless to be accounted for by the vast numbers of immigrants who land and settle in this city".[46] The Superintendent was quite right, because the census figures for 1910 indicated that, as a result of a decade of extra-ordinarily heavy immigration, almost three quarters of the school children of the city were from immigrant homes.

---

[44]
Seventh Annual Report of the City Superintendent of Schools, 1905, p.36.

[45]
Ninth Annual Report of the City Superintendent of Schools, 1907, p.335.

[46]
Eighth Annual Report of the City Superintendent of Schools, 1906, p.30.

The largest number of youngsters of foreign background were present in Brooklyn and Manhattan. In the former borough,. out of 282,610 children of school age (6-14), 181,073 were either foreign born or the children of immigrants. Similarly in Manhattan, 253,251 children out of a total school age population of 343,780 had an immigrant background.[47] In 1908, the United States Immigration Commission found that the Russian Jewish children were the single largest group among those from immigrant families in New York City and that the Italians were outnumbered only by the "Hebrews" and the Germans. Percentagewise, Jewish children comprised 33.6% of the school population and Italians 10.5% and thus, over 44% of the school children of the city were of the "new" immigration. The greatest number of children of these two ethnic groups were in grades two to four of elementary school. The number dwindled as the grades went higher, since fewer of the youngsters with immigrant backgrounds remained to complete the entire eight year course of study.[48]

---

[47]
U.S. Bureau of the Census, Abstract of the 13th Census (Washington: 1910). p.623. The figures for the entire city were as follows: There were 770,037 white persons aged 6-14 in the city of whom 16% were foreign born and 57% native born of foreign parents. 91% of the latter group attended school as did 88.9% of the former.

[48]
U.S., Immigration Commission, Abstract of the Report on the Children of Immigrants in Schools (Washington: 1911) pp.16-17, 22-23. A total of 191,448 Jewish children were in school, of whom 109,039 were Russian Jews, and a total of 59,645 Italian youngsters were in school.

The statistics regarding the numbers of school
children from immigrant homes and the clear evidence of
overcrowding in the districts in which they predominated
leaves little doubt that immigration and school congestion
were intimately related. There were, however, other causes.
Adele Shaw noted that a decrease in child mortality had an
effect on school population as did the lowering of the
school entry age from seven to six years in the Charter
of 1901.[49] The Secretary of the Board of Education also
noted the change in the age of starting school, saying
that it completely wiped out any increase in sittings
gained as a result of the great building program conducted
under Mayor Low.[50]

The Brooklyn schools were overcrowded not only
because of the great influx of people from the Lower East
Side, but because of what Maxwell called "...marvelously
bad judgment" of the school board which had built no
schools for two years before consolidation, in the hope
of sharing the cost of any such schools with all the
boroughs, after unification.[51] Queens on the other hand,

49
 Shaw, World's Work, VII, (1903), p.4205.

50
 Palmer, p.305.

51
 First Annual Report of the City Superintendent
of Schools, 1899, pp. 35-36, Fourth Annual Report of the
City Superintendent of Schools, 1902, p.28. Also, the
City of Brooklyn had exceeded its debt limit just prior
to consolidation and was in technical bankruptcy.

had planned differently. The school district of Woodhaven had built three new schools just prior to 1898, which were totally unnecessary and stood empty two years after they were completed. The bonds which the school district had issued to pay for the construction of these buildings were "now part of the debt of the city of New York", and so were the new schoolhouses, but the children to fill them lived elsewhere.[52]

Actually, the situation in Woodhaven illustrated the major difficulty the schools faced in trying to cope with overcrowding. There were empty seats in many parts of the city and even half filled classrooms in grades four through eight in many otherwise jammed schools. The need for seats was most urgent in grades one to three and only in certain areas of the city--districts marked by high immigrant density. The reason for the congestion in the primary grades was threefold. First, up to 1903, all non-English speaking children, regardless of age, were placed in Grade I. Thus, big boys and girls were occupying seats meant for the six year olds. Secondly, many children were not promoted and so the repeaters were crowded into first or second grade classes with those youngsters just starting school. After third grade, the crush decreased because many of the children who had entered school

---

[52] First Annual Report of the City Superintendent of Schools, 1899, p.38.

late, due to their arrival in America at age 10 or older, reached 14 and obtained working papers.

Aware as they were of both the great number of immigrant children and the greater difficulties of educating them, the school authorities were particularly disturbed by the fact that the greatest shortage of seats occurred in the most foreign sections of the city. The Associate Superintendent in charge of Division I which encompassed the area below 14th street said in 1907:

> The people of this part of the city are perhaps more thoroughly foreign, either by birth or parentage, than those of any other part of equal extent. The educational problems presented are therefore of peculiar interest, and when complicated as they have been for years by part time classes, they are problems of peculiar difficulty. 53

The year before, Superintendent Maxwell had argued against part time schooling in immigrant neighborhoods for much the same reasons.

> The burden laid upon the public school of teaching these children English as a foreign language, and of training them into American citizenship, is, under the best of conditions, exceedingly heavy. To accomplish these tasks when the children are with their teachers only three and one half hours out of the 24 is almost an impossibility...

And yet that was exactly the situation for many of the children of the "congested neighborhoods" whose parents, if not they themselves, were foreign born. [54]

53
Ninth Annual Report of the City Superintendent of Schools, 1907, p.159.

54
Eighth Annual Report of the City Superintendent of Schools, 1906, p.44.

Overcrowding was perennial and so were attempts
to apportion blame. The public and the newspapers usually
found the school authorities to be at fault but Maxwell
always shifted the blame to the Board of Estimate for
their "meagre" appropriations, their short sighted policies,
and their refusal to recognize the tremendous problems of
the schools. The enrollment and building figures supported
the Superintendent's position. There were only 38 more
schools in the city in 1914 than there had been in 1899,
while almost 300,000 more children were enrolled. Even
when allowances are made for the school buildings that
were enlarged or remodeled to seat more youngsters, there
still appears to be no reason for surprise at the extent
of overcrowding in the areas of high population density---
there simply were not enough new schools built.[55]

Because of the shortage, many buildings which were
in deplorable physical condition were still in use. As
with everything else in New York, there were great contrasts.
An observer noted that the city had "antiquated, foul (and)
unsanitary school houses...as well as many progressive features
such as fine school buildings..."[56] The child unfortunate
enough to attend school in any of the buildings described
in Charles Wehrum's 1894 report, (most of which were still
in use ten years later) was probably in daily physical discomfort and possibly even danger. Most of the schools the

---

[55]
First through Sixteenth Annual Reports, of the
City Superintendent of Schools, 1899-1914, and see Tables
I and II on enrollments and school buildings.

[56]
Charles Zueblin, A Decade of Civic Development
(Chicago:1905) p.115.

Commissioner described were dark, due to the lack of yard
space between them and the surrounding tenements. They
burned gas all day and were poorly ventilated, causing the
"air to be foul". The water closets were inadequate and
unsanitary, and the coat closets (one to a floor and unventilated) gave off a dreadful odor, especially in wet
weather. Many rooms had insufficient furniture and in
some schools, Wehrum saw children doing their lessons on
their knees. One building in particular lacked a rear
fire-escape and in many the fire exits were impossible to
locate.

Several of the schools had noise problems, from
the adjoining stores or the "El" rumbling less than ten
feet away. Some schoolhouses were worse than others---
P.S. #34 on Broome Street had falling ceilings and
"offensive water closets". School #38 on Clarke Street
had no cellar, no rear stairway and shared rodents and
vermin with a pie bakery next door. Wehrum found that
20 of the 37 schools he inspected required extensive
alterations or replacement. All but three of the 20 were
below 14th Street and consequently got the largest number
of immigrant children.[57]

In the following year, a survey of school buildings
by one of the leading reform groups in the city, Good
Government Club E, found similar conditions: unsanitary
toilets, inadequate exits and lack of light and air.[58]

---

[57] Wehrum, pp. 10-14, 21-26

[58] Good Government Club E, Public School Buildings
in New York City, p.5

Overcrowding at a main building sometimes made the use of an annex essential, whatever the condition. This was the case in 1901 when P.S. #4 used a very old building on Pitt Street for its overflow until the large number of rats present in the school forced them to make other arrangements.[59]

When Adele Shaw inspected the schools for her 1903 expose she found many of the same conditions that Wehrum had uncovered. There were dirty toilets located right outside of classrooms, inadequate lighting, lack of play space and "unventilated wardrobes where wet wraps were packed to ferment in seclusion".[60]

The very worst school on the Lower East Side, made famous by Jacob Riis and preserved in photographs, was the old Essex Street Market school. Here the children sat on long benches and had no desks at all. Because of its location in the heart of the East Side shopping area, it was assailed with smells and noise. This was one of the first schools slated for replacement and was abandoned by 1902.

---

[59] Organization of the School Board of Manhattan-Bronx, p.177.

[60] Shaw, World's Work, VII, p.4210

It is clear that there was no lack of knowledge
about the physical defects of the old schools in the
area below 14th Street and the school building program
concentrated its efforts in this section of the city. Of
the nine new buildings completed between 1898 and 1900, six
were on the Lower East Side.[61] So great was the need for
seats, buildings which held 2,000 pupils each were often
placed just a few blocks apart.[62] Two years later, most
of the new buildings were still going to Lower Manhattan.[63]
Mayor Low surveyed the extent of East Side building in 1902
and reported that 14,430 seats had been added between 1898
and 1902, and that the Department of Education had plans
for 25,000 more in 1903-1904. Low explained that it took
two years between the approval of a bond issue for school
construction and the completion of a building, and urged
the school administrators to estimate pupil increases in

---

[61]
    First Annual Report of the City Superintendent of
Schools, 1899, p.25.

[62]
    Department of Education. Fifth Annual Report, 1902,
p.204.

[63]
    Third Annual Report of the City Superintendent of
of Schools, 1901, p.13. Of the 15 new buildings erected
between 1900 and 1901, eight were in Manhattan, three in
Brooklyn, and four in Richmond which was replacing its
"little red schoolhouses".

advance.[64] A different kind of planning was done by the
Board of Education in 1906 when P.S. 62 was opened as a
school for 7th and 8th graders only in the hope that this
would free more classrooms for the younger children in
the nearby schools.[65]

Since the lower end of Manhattan Island was so
built up, it was often difficult to find the land on which
to build a school, no matter how much it was needed. Such
was the situation on Pitt Street in 1902, and the solution
was ingenious. The Department of Education accepted the
offer of the Commissioner of Bridges and took a small plot
under the Williamsburg Bridge on which it built a one story
school, "architecturally adapted to the needs of the plot
and the noises around it."[66]

The school official responsible for this innovation
and for all of the extensive building of the period was the
architect and Superintendent of Buildings for the Department
of Education, C. B. Snyder.[67] He was a busy man and

---

[64]
Seth Low, "The New York Schools", Educational
Review, XXIV (November, 1902), p.429

[65]
Eighth Annual Report of the City Superintendent of
Schools, 1906, p.135.

[66]
Department of Education. Seventh Annual Report,
1904, p.274

[67]
A total of 102 buildings were erected between
1899 and 1904, including high schools as well as elementary
ones. Most of these were not newly organized schools, of
course, but rather replacements for inadequate existing ones.
cont'd

plagued by many difficulties. Even when the funds at his
disposal were relatively ample (as they were when Seth
Low was Mayor) labor troubles, delay in letting contracts
due to municipal red tape and lack of competent draftsmen
made his job very hard.[68] The President of the Board of
Education in 1902 noted that Superintendent Snyder was
greatly overworked and requested that he be released from
his responsibilities for the school janitors, at least.[69]

Snyder was very well thought of by many people
interested in the schools. He had been the architect for
the New York City Schools since 1895, first hired during
the reform wave that followed the election of Mayor Strong.
He was responsible for a revolutionary concept in school
architecture; namely that the buildings be planned for
multi-purpose/and use be constructed in ways that would make
them more useful to the community as a whole.[70]

---

67 cont'd
The building program did increase the number of
seats. By 1905, the Superintendent estimated that 297,625
new sittings had been added. Palmer, p.286,304; Fourth Annual
Report of the City Superintendent of Schools, 1902, pp.24-25;
Fifth Annual Report, 1903, p.28; Seventh Annual Report, 1905
p.27. By 1909 the bulk of the new building was going to
Brooklyn, especially Brownsville, although even in 1902,
45% of the new sittings had been going to that Borough.
Fourth Annual Report of the City Superintendent of Schools,
1902, p.28; Eleventh Annual Report, 1909, p.23.

68
Department of Education, Sixth Annual Report,1903,
162-163.

69
Department of Education, Journal of the Board of
Education, February 3, 1902, vol. I p.223.

70
New York Times, February 23, 1898, p.6.

For example, he opposed the use of classrooms with sliding doors which could be moved to create a makeshift auditorium, favoring instead the construction of a large formal room which would be suitable for the evening lecture programs the schools held. [71] When planning P.S. 62 on Hester St., Snyder insisted that the principal's office be placed on the first floor instead of upstairs as was customary, so as to make that official more accessible to the parents of the pupils. [72]

The first of the "revolutionary" new schools planned by Snyder, was P.S. 108 in the notorious Mulberry Bend area of Little Italy. According to the New York Times, the new school was designed to be handsome and commodious in order to set an example of beauty to the people of Mulberry Bend and also to be used for free lectures, entertainment and as a community center for the neighborhood. The auditorium was to seat 1200 people and there were to be two playgrounds on the roof and at ground level, the better to provide recreation for the children of this crowded district. There were to be gym and shower bath facilities as well. [73] All in all,

---

[71] Department of Education, Fifth Annual Report, 1902, p. 197.

[72] Department of Education, Seventh Annual Report, 1904, p.277.

[73] New York Times, December 14, 1902, p.27.

this school illustrates Snyder's main idea; that the school was not just a collection of rooms in which to house pupils and teachers, but that it could serve a wider educative purpose as well.

Jacob Riis was one of the Superintendent's admirers. In his opinion, Snyder's greatest contribution was the H style of building, which was designed to get the maximum light and air possible on the small plots available in Lower Manhattan. [74] Another advantage of this style of building was the fact that it was possible to build one solid blank wall, thus blocking out the ugly sights and sounds of the adjoining tenements but still enabling the building to get light and air from the open court. [75]

Snyder believed that building tall schoolhouses was the only way to get enough schools into congested areas like the Lower East Side. Most of the buildings he planned were five stories high with the gym and manual training shops on the top floor, but at one time he did propose an eight story elevator school for Essex Street, which the horrified Board of Education vetoed! [76]

---

[74]
Jacob Riis, The Battle With the Slum, (New York: 1902) p.353; Seventh Annual Report of the Superintendent of Schools, 1905, p.287.

[75]
Gilbert Morrison, "School Architecture and Hygeiene" in Nicholas Murray Butler, (ed.) Education in the United States, (New York, 1910) p.443.

[76]
Department of Education, Seventh Annual Report, 1904, p.301

There were some who thought the Superintendent wrong and
suggested that the children from the slums should be trans-
ported to schools on the outskirts of the city, [77] but Snyder
insisted on neighborhood schools built high and adapted to
the needs of the community, and his ideas were stamped on
all of the 38 schools erected while he was in charge of
building.

Even the inventive and energetic Snyder and his
corps of engineers were not able to build sufficient schools
fast enough for the thousands of new arrivals, if the large
amounts of money needed had been available and therefore, the
educational authorities had to devise other means to cope
with the problem of overcrowding. The most used of these
was part time scheduling. This device had originated in
Brooklyn as early as 1891 and was being used in a large
number of schools in that borough by 1896 when over 12,000
children were receiving only a half-day education.

Because part time plans were always criticized,
Brooklyn began to use split or end to end sessions in 1897
which at least gave each child four hours of schooling instead
of two and under the usual part time system. [78] The use of
the half-day device to cope with overcrowding had spread
to the New York City Schools by 1898 when Superintendent

---

[77] Fletcher Dressler, "American Schoolhouses" in
U.S. Bureau of Education Bulletin #5, p.8.

[78] Palmer, pp. 246-248.

Jasper ordered a school to go on split session whenever
class registers exceeded 70.[79]

Although the system was in widespread use in both
boroughs by 1899, Brooklyn had 20,275 children on part
time in that year, while Manhattan-Bronx had only 4,679.[80]
This proporation was continued into the next year as
Superintendent Maxwell pointed out when he indicated that
68,929 of the school children of the city were on part-
time, with 42,619 of these in Brooklyn and over 20,000 in
Manhattan-Bronx.[81]

The spread of half time schooling was one of the
few educational matters on which parents voiced an
opinion. The inconvenience and manifest retardation of
learning were very real to them. In an attempt to answer
their complaints the School Journal suggested that part
time classes be alternated so that one group went on
Monday, Wednesday and Friday in the morning and on
Tuesday and Thursday in the afternoon, and that the groups
reverse positions during the following week! Perhaps
to save everyone's sanity, this plan was not adopted.[82]

---

[79]
School Journal, September 24, 1898, p.264.

[80]
First Annual Report of the City Superintendent of
Schools, 1899, p.35.

[81]
Maxwell, Municipal Affairs IV, p.743.

[82]
School Journal, September 20, 1902, p.269

The more usual answer to the criticisms was given by the
Department of Education in its 3rd Annual Report which
stated that three hours of schooling was better than none.[83]

Although disliked and bemoaned, the use of part
time devices continued to grow with the school population.
It was, after all, the simplest and least expensive way to
get some learning for everyone. By 1904, Adele Shaw noted
that 89,316 children in New York City were on a half-day
basis, an increase of 20,000 over 1900.[84]   There was more
disagreement regarding the grades most injured by part time
education. Many observers thought the upper grades, where
children were preparing for high school or jobs, needed
full time schooling and that first grade was the level at
which three hours would be enough.

Superintendent Maxwell strongly disagreed, saying
that it might be enough in a "homogeneous American community" where a six year old could get "suitable opportunities
for recreation and guidance during the rest of the day",
but three hours was not enough in New York City because
"of the great mass of foreign, non-English speaking children
who enter our lower classes, the fact that our tenement
house children have no place to play but the street, and
the difficulties of housekeeping in the tenement house

---

[83]
        Department of Education, Third Annual Report,1900,
p.22.
[84]
        Shaw, World's Work, VII, p.4205.

apartments in which the majority of our population reside."[85]

Therefore, the Superintendent rejected calling half time for the first grade full time because the immigrant youngsters needed more, not less from the schools. Always the realist, Maxwell refused to see any virtue in part time education and would only admit that it was better than having classes of 100 or turning children away entirely.

An analysis of the schools on part time in 1905 indicated that 63% were in Division I and in the Brownsville section of Brooklyn, while of the 118 schools of the city with predominantly native born students, only 16% were on a split schedule.[86] Because of this, any attempt to reduce class registers or set up small special classes in these overcrowded areas resulted in the need for even more part time scheduling. Therefore, the educational authorities had to constantly weigh the balance to see which was the lesser evil, or the greater good. This kind of soul searching led Maxwell to discover moral as well as practical reasons against half time education. "It is a very serious defect in school administration to habituate children to play first and work afterward" he said, thinking of the youngsters who attended school only in the

---

[85]
Fifteenth Annual Report of the City Superintendent of Schools, 1913, pp. 66-67.

[86]
Seventh Annual Report of the City Superintendent of Schools, 1905, p.57.

afternoon. Every child needed five hours education daily,
but especially "the extraordinary number of children in our
chools to whom English is a foreign language. 87

His concern extended to the immigrant mother as
ell and he noted how preparing lunch several times a day
hen the children were on different schedules added to the
nervous strain" of tenement life, whereas five hours of
ull time schooling could be a blessing to the overworked,
                        88
arried woman.

By 1914, the differences had been largely resolved.
irst graders went to school for four hours and end-to-end
essions were in use in some 7th and 8th grade classes.
n between, most children attended school the normal five
ours, except those in especially congested districts.
art-time schedules, educationally unsound and socially
armful though they were, remained the traditional escape
oute for the overcrowded schools, at least for interim
eriods until the supply of buildings could catch up with
he demand. Because of the many defects of this arrange-
ent, there were numerous attempts made to find other
olutions to overcrowding.

87
    Fifteenth Annual Report of the City Superintendent
f Schools, 1913, p.55

88
    Ibid., 1913, p.56

As early as 1901, the Board of Education was urging Maxwell to select school sites _before_ the population moved in order to avoid a jam-up such as occurred in Brownsville.[89] The Superintendent was in full agreement, but rarely had the funds available in the school budget to do this kind of advance planning.[90] Fully aware of the financial as well as educational advantages of early site selection, he specifically discussed his plans to acquire land and build four schools in Long Island City before the completion of the Blackwell's Island Bridge, but the ponderous municipal and educational bureaucracy could not move fast enough.[91]

Because congestion was not uniform throughout the city, at various times different members of the Board of Education suggested that contracts be made with "stage companies" and the city railroad companies to move older children from congested to under-utilized schools, but there is no evidence that this was ever done, although the Teachers Association of Manhattan-Bronx, among others, favored such a scheme. Since a great many native and middle class New Yorkers had moved uptown in order to avoid

---

[89] Department of Education, _Third Annual Report_, 1900, p.23

[90] Department of Education, _Fourth Annual Report_, 1901, p.18

[91] Seventh Annual Report of the City Superintendent of Schools, 1905, p.50; _Eighth Annual Report_, 1906, p.46

the congested schools and the cosmopolitan population below 14th Street, it is quite unlikely that they would have accepted such "bussing".[92]   Adele Shaw saw no possibility that the schools could ever cope with the great numbers of immigrant children, unless they received gigantic sums of money. Since this was not likely to happen, she thought immigration restriction was the only other answer.[93]

By 1914, however, a new plan imported from Gary, Indiana seemed to offer hope of combining quality educa-tion with part time schedules and as a result, was seized upon eagerly by groups as disparate as the Public Educa-tion Association and the Board of Estimate. William Wirt, Superintendent of Schools in the steel city of Gary, had developed a "platoon" plan where children traveled in groups and spent from 9:00 to 5:00 P.M. in school. The arrangement called for much shop and gym equipment, because over half of the long day was spent in such activi-ies. While some "platoons" were using the classrooms for academic work, others were in the kitchen, assisting the cooks to prepare meals for the school, or in the mainten-nce shops making repairs, or in the gym.

---

[92]
Journal of the Board of Education, February 3, 902, p.222.

[93]
Shaw, World's Work, VII, p.4221.

Since the eight hour day left the children with little free time, music and drawing lessons as well as released time for religious education were included in the school day. Auditoriums were also used much more, for assembly programs featuring movies and stereoptican slides for some youngsters, while the rest were otherwise engaged. The Gary Plan required precision planning and much equipment, which most New York City elementary schools did not have. It was estimated that seven million dollars would be needed to minimally equip 50 schools for the plan.[94]

It would have taken 42 millions to eliminate part time schooling under regular scheduling and therefore the Gary Plan was unquestionably less expensive. That is why it was so appealing, although Wirt and the Public Education Association also gave many educational reasons in its favor. Education under the platoon system, they said, would enrich the children, be closer to real life, provide realistic vocational training and enable the teachers to get closer to the lives of their pupils, because they

---

[94] William Wirt, A Report on a Plan of Organization for Cooperative and Continuation Courses, Submitted to the Department of Education, City of New York, July 30, 1914, pp.3-4; Public Education Association Official Wirt Reports to the Board of Education, (New York: 1916) p.22,28.

would do the work of attendance officers, school nurses, and social workers during the eight hour school day. It was especially suited, they felt, to a cosmopolitan city like New York.[95]

The Board of Estimate, under Mayor Mitchel's pressure appropriated five million dollars to begin the new arrangement, over the intense opposition of the school authorities, who took the five million but refused to implement the plan. Since the money represented funds that had been taken away from other items requested by the Board of Education, the situation resulted in an impasse. After much dispute, marked by accusations of self interest and inertia directed against the Department of Education, the plan was finally placed in operation, half-heartedly and in just a few schools. Superintendent Maxwell summed the matter up in his 16th Report when he said the only difference between the Gary Plan and any other part time device was superior equipment. If the city fiscal authorities were ready to supply the schools with all the devices called for by the Wirt plan, great educational advances could be made within the normal school day. Without vast expenditures, no plan would work, including this one.[96]

---

[95] Wirt, Report to the Department of Education, pp.2,4, 11; Public Education Association, Official Wirt Reports, p.16.

[96] Sixteenth Annual Report of the City Superintendent of Schools, 1914, p.57.

Parents, especially immigrant parents, did not like the proposed changes, Jewish parents objected to the released time provisions and the emphasis on vocational education. Italian parents objected to the longer day, which made the holding of part time jobs impossible. As with many other educational proposals, a combination of disillusionment, inertia, lack of enough money and staff opposition caused the Gary Plan to peter out, and when Mayor Mitchel was defeated for re-election in 1917, partly over this plan which he had made such an issue, the whole matter was dropped.[97]

Obviously, the key to relief from overcrowding was more schools and more teachers, unless immigration was to decrease a great deal. But more schools were expensive and enough money was never forthcoming. Therefore, the Department of Education improvised and in some areas of the city did better than in others. Overall, overcrowding remained the single most serious concern of the schools, complicating all the others and taxing the resources of the staff to the utmost because after all, it was the teachers of the city who daily faced all the problems which the heavy immigration had brought to the schools. The difficulties of communicating with the alien children, especially amidst the less than ideal physical conditions, made the job of teacher in New York at this time a challenging assignment indeed. In spite of this, the number of men and women who

---

[97] Sol Cohen, Progressives and Urban School Reform (New York: 1964) 92-93,96.

took on the job more than doubled in this period, since the size of the staff grew with the number of pupils and schools, going from 9,305 in 1899 to 20,448 in 1914.[98]

Midway in the period, the Immigration Commission determined that while the great majority of the teachers of the city were native born, almost half were the children of foreign born parents. Only a small number (about 1,000) had been born abroad themselves, the bulk of this group being Russian Jews. The largest single ethnic group among all the teachers were the Irish, who made up almost 20% of the total. Those of German background comprised 8% of the staff while 6% of the teachers were Jewish. Very few Italians were part of the faculty at this time, and there were only a few Scotch or Scotch-Irish, teachers.[99]

It is apparent, therefore, that a wide cultural gap separated the teachers from their students. Even those not too many generations removed from a foreign background would have little knowledge of the new ethnic groups whose children were in their classes. Probably even the teachers who made up the Jewish 6% of the staff were German Jews whose families had come to New York many years before.

While it certainly was not necessary for the Russian Jewish and Italian children to be taught by people of their

---

[98]
First to Sixteenth Annual Reports of the City Superintendent of Schools, 1899-1914, passim.

[99]
Abstract of the Report on the Children of Immigrants in the Schools, pp. 54-55.

own background, the educational authorities did attempt to
match the ethnic groups, where possible. The personnel of
P.S. 120 on Rivington St. in the very heart of the Jewish
ghetto, for example, was headed by a Jewish principal and
assistant principal and had 25 Jewish teachers out of a
staff of 68 while P.S. 2 on Henry St. had 17 Jewish
teachers out of a total of 57. On the other hand, P.S. 20
on Mott St. in Little Italy had an Italian principal, four
Italian teachers and only four Jewish ones on their staff
of 56. The schools of the upper West Side had faculties
which were almost completely English, Irish, German or
Scotch.[100]

Considering the small number of Jewish and Italian
teachers in the system as a whole, it does appear that there
was an attempt at matching backgrounds. The reasons for
this are not clear. It could have been merely convenience;
perhaps the teachers were assigned to schools near their
homes, although the Directory of the Board of Education
indicated that many had addresses in distant parts of the
city. It may have been part of a plan for better communication between the students and their teachers, or it may
have been simply a matter of the newest staff members being
assigned to the most difficult schools, while those in the
system longer were sent to more desirable middle class
neighborhoods. There is no doubt that teaching in the

---

[100]
New York (City), Department of Education, **Directory
of the Board of Education**, 1914, pp. 58-59, 82-83, 84-85.

schools below 14th St. was more difficult, and the number

of teachers who requested transfers was high. The princi-

pals objected strenuously to the shifting of their personnel
[101]
because it made their task even more difficult.

Regardless of ethnic background, a typical teacher

of the period was likely to be an unmarried woman, since

a Board of Education by-law did not permit a married woman

to teach unless she was widowed or had an incapacitated
[102]
husband.   The Jewish and Italian children must have found

women teachers a new experience since both the instructors

in the chedarim of Eastern Europe and those in the village

schools of Italy were always male. Within the immigrant

family as well, the inferior status of the women members

was one of the facts of life, and the children were accus-

tomed to strong paternal rather than maternal discipline,

especially in important matters. Since women, in the ex-

perience of these children, were likely to be both ignorant

and dependent, to what extent could they respect either the

female teacher or what she taught?

The necessity to take orders from a woman, previously

considered of low status, must have presented difficult

adjustment problems for the youngsters and may have accounted

---

[101]
Sixteenth Annual Report ∧1914, pp. 60-61.
of the City Superintendent of Schools
[102]
McCormick, p. 48. This was true until 1920 in
spite of a number of suits brought by women teachers.

for some of the disciplinary problems faced by the staff of the schools. The methods used to enforce order in the classroom, however, soon convinced the children that the teacher, although a woman, was the boss.. Corporal punishment was used, although technically forbidden, and washing out offending mouths with soap was a favorite punishment, much to the dismay of the Jewish youngsters because the soap used was not kosher!

The educational authorities were aware that more male teachers would have been desirable, but as in many other areas, financial considerations overruled pedagogical ones. Until 1912, women were paid much less than men, even when the grade they taught and their qualifications were identical. As a result, it was easier on the school budget to hire women, and the additional amounts required to pay men were reserved mostly for positions above the elementary level. Since the bulk of the children did not go past sixth grade, most of them never saw a male teacher, and this may have had some detrimental educational results, especially for the child of foreign background.[103]

---

[103] Palmer, p.405, Shaw, World's Work, VII p.4219; Fourteenth Annual Report of the City Superintendent of Schools, 1912, p. 271. After many years of agitation, the State Legislature passed the "Equal Pay Law" in 1911 which equalized salaries by lowering men's pay 20% and raising women's pay 25%. Maxwell opposed this law because he felt it would drive the minority of male teachers out of the system. On the other hand, he did not favor raising pay rates for all teachers, either, because he thought other needs of the schools must come first.

Male or female, on the whole the teachers of New
York City were not well qualified in many subjects especially
in view of the special challenges presented to them by the
immigrant youngsters, Adele Shaw found teachers who used
incorrect English grammar and had poor speech; great deficiencies in any instructor but especially serious in one
[104]
teaching children to whom English was a foreign language.
The Board of Examiners found, to their distress, that many
of the applicants for License #1 (grades 1-6) who came
before them, were not well prepared in English, arithmetic,
U.S. history or science, although their training in methodology was adequate.[105]   The communication of knowledge, even
under ideal circumstances, was never easy but when students
had language and cultural deficiencies, and teachers were
inadequately trained, as was the case of most of this period,
the fact that any learning took place seems almost miraculous.

Of course, there were differences of opinion regarding teacher training and so eminent an educator as Dr.
Thomas Hunter, President of the Normal College, which was
the chief supplier of instructors for the New York City
schools, did not feel that his graduates were inadequately
prepared. Superintendent Maxwell, however, did, and
criticized the College for not teaching the pedagogy of

---

[104]
    Shaw, World's Work, VII, p.4206.

[105]
    Twelfth Annual Report of the City Superintendent
of Schools, 1910, p.287.

music, drawing, sewing or physical education, "activities
which now (post 1902) formed a very essential part of the
elementary school curriculum."[106]   The results of the inadequate preparation of the teachers in the "new subjects" were
distressing.

        Many schools did not teach physical education, for
example, even though the cramped classrooms and inadequate
play space of the tenement district cried out for such
activities; or, if taught at all, the exercises consisted
of marching around the school yard under the watchful eye
of the teacher or doing calisthenics in class. This half-
hearted instruction was often equally true of music, drawing
and sewing. Happily, not all teachers were unable to conduct
the new subjects; graduates of the Teacher Training Schools,
although less well prepared academically, were better instructed in the new pedagogy because Maxwell was able to
exert his influence on the staff of the Training Schools
in a way that he never could on the colleges.

---

[106]
        Fourth Annual Report of the City Superintendent
of Schools, 1902, p.98. This Hunter-Maxwell quarrel had
its roots in their disagreement over the preparatory school
the Normal College, as well as C.C.N.Y. operated. Maxwell
felt these college-attached literary High Schools were not
necessary, now that the Board of Education had organized
academic high schools like Morris and De Witt Clinton, but
the colleges clung to their preparatory schools and many
students were attracted to them because it was possible to
complete a combined high school-college course in seven
years and emerge a teacher at 20 years of age or younger.

In view of the demands and difficulties faced by the teachers of the period, it is almost surprising that the Board of Examiners was able to license the 11,143 people it did between 1899 and 1914. The security guaranteed by the merit system with its permanent tenure after a probationary period, and the higher salaries offered by the Davis Law of 1900, probably compensated somewhat for the hardships of the job.[107] Whatever the reason, there was no shortage of applicants for teaching jobs, and if funds had been available, Maxwell could have staffed the schools twice over, even in the "congested districts". In general, the new teachers constantly coming in to the classrooms were better qualified than the older "political" appointees and thus strengthened the system.

Whether by accident or design, thousands of middle class young women found themselves teaching the children of the newcomers and facing the enormous gulf that separated them from their charges. Many teachers, rigid and prejudiced, did not try to bridge the gap, but simply relied on discipline and drill to get them through the day or year. Many others, aware and sympathetic, tried to establish rapport, but found the barriers too high. Even the pronunciation of the unfamiliar foreign names was hard, both for the teacher

---

[107] Second Annual Report of the City Superintendent of Schools, 1900, pp.66-67. The Davis Law provided uniform and higher salary schedules throughout the city as well as the money to pay for them.

and her "suffering, redfaced little charges".[108]   Reading
poetry and conducting the nature study required by the
syllabus were exercises in futility, because the beauties
of nature were meaningless to the children of the Lower
East Side and the poetry was incomprehensible.

Because the middle class teachers were unaware of
the realities in the daily life of the children, they were
unable to relate their teaching to that life and as a
result, education was separated from all that made up the
child's world outside the classroom.[109]   The white gloved,
respectable lady teachers were unable to understand many
of the immigrant attitudes and fears, just as the foreigners could not see the importance of some of the teacher's
ideas.

An incident/which occurred on the Lower East Side in 1908
illustrated this lack of communication. According to the
best medical opinion of the day, enlarged adenoids caused
mental sluggishness. Therefore, it became the mission of
many teachers to arrange for the removal of the adenoids of

108
        Catherine Brody, "A New York Childhood", The
American Mercury, XIV (May, 1928), p.62

109
        Wald, p.106; Jane Addams, "The Public School
and the Immigrant Child" in National Education Association,
Proceedings, 1908, p.101; Robert Hunter, Poverty, (New York:
1904) p.212.

a large number of their pupils. A clinic was available,
but the immigrant mothers were unwilling or unable to make
use of it. The teachers therefore arranged to have a team
of doctors from Gouverneur Hospital perform a mass
adenoidectomy <u>at</u> the school. Somehow the news got out and
80 screaming mothers descended on the schoolhouse and
dragged their children, adenoids intact, to the safety of
home! While the physical health of the children was of
the utmost importance to the teachers, the parents tended
to view small appetites and lack of energy more philosophic-
ally because of the poverty and congestion in their daily
lives.[110]

Similarly, the cleanliness campaign conducted by
the teachers created great difficulties for the immigrant
youngsters. It sometimes seemed to these children that the
chief object of school, beyond all marks and studies, was
to be clean and have a clean head. "Daily lectures were
delivered on nail brushes, hair ribbons, shoe polish, pins,
buttons and other means to grace."[111] The results of these

---

[110] William Maxwell, "Stories from the Lives of Real
Teachers."<u>World's Work</u>,XVIII (August, 1909), p.11878;
Myra Kelly, <u>Wards of Liberty</u>, (New York: 1907) p.116.

[111] Brody, <u>American Mercury</u>, XIV, p.63; Myra Kelly,
<u>Little Citizens</u> (New York: 1904) p.126.

efforts were apparent in the starched aprons and ribbons
of many of the little girls, but the costs were high.

In many of the tenements, water had to be fetched
from six floors below, since the apartments had no taps.
Mothers were harried and found the amount of bathing, washing and ironing demanded by the teacher's standards almost
impossible to accomplish. The concentration on cleanliness was probably a permissible sublimation of the basic
hostility felt by many of the teachers to the "little
aliens" in their care. While evidence of actual cruelty
was rare, and the use of bigoted epithets unusual, the
energy and time expended on cleaning the children was out
of proportion to the realities. It may also have been a
substitute for teaching, especially for teaching the new
subjects introduced into the elementary school after 1902,
to which many of the school personnel were opposed.

Even in the absence of hostility to the children
themselves, most teachers were determined to eradicate all
evidence of foreign background and substitute American
ideas and ideals in their charges instead. Partly because
they knew nothing about Italy, matters Italian were never
discussed, other than Columbus' fortunate voyage. Knowing
even less about the Jewish heritage, the teachers ignored
it and concentrated instead on wiping out any vestiges of

the dialect that remained in their pupil's speech. [112]

Teachers as a group were rarely in advance of their
times and therefore a good part of the school staff tended
to view the poverty and problems of the immigrant children
with a pragmatic eye. Those youngsters strong enough or
bright enough would survive and prosper and the rest were
not the concern of the teacher, especially after school
hours. [113] Attitudes such as these were not encouraged by
the Superintendent who believed both teachers and principals
had to enter into the life of the community and concern
themselves directly with the problems of their charges.
He urged them to make home visits and praised their efforts
to improve the physical health of their pupils. [114]

While many teachers ignored the Superintendent's
aims, many others were aware of the changing conditions in
the schools and the need to change with them. Just as the
immigrant influx forced the erection of more and better
schoolhouses and the employment of more teachers, the
problem of the foreign children forced at least a part of
the school staff to become cognizant of the need to teach
the "whole child". The doctrines of progressive education,

---

[112]
Leonard Covello, The Heart is the Teacher (New
York: 1958) p.43; Michael Gold, Jews Without Money (New
York: 1946) p.37.

[113]
John Spargo, The Bitter Cry of the Children
(New York: 1909) p.77.

[114]
Maxwell, World's Work, XVIII, p.11878.

although known only to the highest echelon of the teaching
profession, were now applicable to the daily routine of
the classroom, When the teachers concerned themselves with
the health and cleanliness of the foreign youngsters, they
were really practicing what progressive educators preached,
although they took the action for practical, not theoretical
reasons. No larger plan, no educational philosophy lay
behind the attempt to relate school and life; it was simply
the most direct response·to the pressures of the alien
children, but in its eventual result, it led to better teaching and thus, better education.

Similarly, the enlargement of the school system at
either end--high school and kindergarten--was another development accelerated by the demands of the newcomers. Both
types of schools had been established in other parts of the
United States for many years, but in New York City, their
development had been retarded by the corruption and inertia
which marked the schools prior to consolidation. Therefore,
when the period began there were functioning high schools
only in Brooklyn and just a scattering of kindergartens
in all the boroughs.

The first public kindergarten had been organized
in New York City in 1893 but spread rapidly so that by
1899, 6,524 children were attending these "children's
gardens".[115]

115
      Palmer, p.193; First Annual Report of the City
Superintendent of Schools,   1899, p.41

The number of youngsters in kindergartens continued
to increase all through the period, making an enormous
jump in 1903, when the revised Charter prohibited children
under six from entering first grade. Youngsters aged
five to six now entered kindergarten instead. By 1914,
over 22,000 children were enrolled in public kindergartens
and almost no elementary school in the city was without at
least two such classes.[116]

Only a shortage of classroom space, lack of teachers
and the perennial absence of funds prevented the kindergartens from expanding even faster, for they were very popular
with everyone; parents, educators, social workers and
children. Attendance was never compulsory and yet there
were always more applicants than room. The settlement
houses that had pioneered in the formation of such classes
frequently offered space to the Board of Education, providing that the licensed teachers and the supplies needed were
paid for out of Department of Education funds. Usually
these offers were accepted, and public kindergartens were
established at the Greenwich House, Welcome House, Hebrew
Technical Institute, Madison House and the Educational
Alliance, as well as at the regular public schools.[117]

116
Figures are derived from percentages of increase
in kindergarten population given in the First through
Sixteenth Annual Reports of the City Superintendent of
Schools, 1899-1914; Eleventh Report, 1909, p.481.
117
New York (City), Department of Education, Minutes
of the Board of Superintendents, June 14, 1906, p.814; March 8,
1907, p. 367; Educational Alliance, Reports, Fifth Report, 1897,
p.18; Journal of the Board of Education, October 26,1898,p.593.

An alumnus of the Educational Alliance kindergarten remembered vividly what a fine time he had experienced there. Graham crackers and milk were served, the teachers were very kind, and he was much "smarter" than the other children when he entered first grade.[118]

Although popular all over the city, (even the Coler and Grout reports never criticized them) kindergartens met the special needs of the immigrant poor in many different ways, and as a result, there were more of them below 14th St. than anywhere else in the city. Most important, they provided good, free care for young children, thus enabling mothers to hold part time jobs or do homework to augment the family income. The extent of women labor among the immigrants was considerable. As charwomen in both homes and offices, and as workers in the garment industry, either at home or in factories, a woman might earn a greatly needed five to six dollars a month which would considerably benefit her family.[119] Those housewives whose earnings were essential had always worked, leaving their young children in the care of the older ones who were therefore kept from attending school. The function of the kindergarten as a baby sitter was one of its most attractive features, valued equally by working mothers and school

---

[118] Conversation with Milton Perlman, October 19, 1966.

[119] Robert Foerster, Italian Emigration of Our Times (Cambridge: 1924) 380.

120
authorities.

Prior to 1902, the school administration considered kindergartens essential to relieve overcrowding in the first grade, always the level with the heaviest enrollment. Until the Charter was revised and prevented it, mothers who worked would send their five year olds to first grade if no kindergartens were available and they would be admitted on a first come, first served basis, thus occupying a seat that could have gone to an older child more able to profit from instruction. When a kindergarten was established at a school, however, the number of applicants to first grade

121

decreased and there was more room for the older students.

Kindergartens were valuable for reasons other than convenience. Miss Fanniebelle Curtis, Supervisor of Kindergartens during this decade, was proud of the way they taught patriotism early in the life of the immigrant toddlers. By singing "America" and playing games like "Soldier Boy" the "patriotic impulses of our many foreign children" were

122

aroused. Even more important, the interest of the immigrant mother was engaged. Most kindergarten teachers established mother's clubs where the foreign born house-wives learned something about their adopted land and had a

120
Jacob Riis, The Children of the Poor (New York: 1892) p.181; Ninth Annual Report of the City Superintendent of Schools, 1907, p.337; Lawrence A. Cremin, The Transformation of the School (New York; 1961) p.61.
121
First Annual Report of the City Superintendent of Schools, 1899, p.121.
122
Twelfth Annual Report of the City Superintendent of Schools, 1910, pp 29-30.

rare opportunity to improve their English. As Superintendent Maxwell put it, "It is one of the tragedies of the
great immigration movement...that while foreign born men...
try to learn English because they find it necessary in their
daily vocations, the mothers who remain at home...get
separated in feeling and aims in life from their children...
who desire to speak English..."[123]   At the mother's clubs
an immigrant woman could practice her English and learn
more about the ways of her adopted land, thus shortening
the distance between herself and her Americanized children.

There were also educational reasons of
importance for kindergartens. They improved the social
adjustment of the immigrant children, bringing them in
contact with American customs and ideas at an early, im-
pressionable age through the use of the tool they already
knew--play--and thus the rest of their educational road
was made a little smoother. Because kindergartens could
experiment, many child centered methods were developed
there, which were later to be of use to teachers in the
higher grades.[124]

---

[123]
Sixteenth Annual Report / 1914, p.74.
                        of the City Superintendent of Schools
[124]
Merle Curti, The Social Ideas of American Educators,
(Paterson, N.J.: 1959), p.342; Robert A. Woods, City Wilderness
(Cambridge: 1898) p.237; Mariana Van Rensalaer, "Our Public
Schools: A Reply", North American Review, CLXIX, (July 1899),
p.83. It is interesting to note the parallel with the
popularity today of the "Head Start" program which serves
a similar group of children.

Clearly then, the impetus towards the development of kindergartens was greatly increased by the needs of the immigrant poor who saw much practical value in them, and thus the growth in numbers and influence of these classes can be attributed, at least in part, to the demands of this group. Similarly, the enormous increase in high schools was an attempt to meet different needs of other of the newcomers.

There were some public secondary schools in the United States all through the 19th century but they were exclusively for college preparation and used by only a tiny segment of the school population. Since only middle class children attended them, the course of study was formal and classical and emphasized the skills that would be needed in a liberal arts college. As late as 1893, the Report of the Committee on Secondary School Studies of the National Education Association saw the high school as a "downward extension of the college",[125] but even at that date, many educators, especially those in large cities, knew better. Demands that the high school be adapted to the realities of industrialization and teach skills which could be used in the business world were heard all through the 1890's and heeded by some.

---

[125] Lawrence A. Cremin, "Revolution in Secondary Education" in The Teachers College Record, LVI (Nov. 1954) pp.296-297.

The City of Brooklyn had pioneered in the development of high schools in the New York metropolitan area.
As early as 1866, post 8th grade classes had been organized
and in 1878 such classes were consolidated into one central
building on Livingston Street called the Central Grammar
School. Eight years later, a new structure was erected
at .Nostrand Ave. and Halsey St. and became a full-fledged
high school for girls. Boys remained at Livingston Street
until 1892 when they received a building of their own.
From their inception, the Brooklyn high schools offered
diversified courses: English (college preparatory),
language, commercial, and scientific. In 1894, a further
step toward specialization was taken with the establishment of the Manual Training High School which offered a
three year course in regular academic subjects plus
mechanical drawing, joining, forging, pattern making,
126
sewing and iron-work.

Brooklyn was far in advance of her sister boroughs
in this area. Queens and Richmond had only a few high
school departments, housed in elementary schools, which
offered just a year of post elementary school work, while
Manhattan and the Bronx had no high schools of any kind
until 1897, except for the college preparatory course given
at the Normal College and the College of the City of New
York. Three high schools were organized in New York City

126
Palmer, 239-240.

in 1897, after years of agitation. Boy's High School, later to become De Witt Clinton, was established at Tenth Ave. and 58th St., Girl's High School, later to be Wadleigh, on Eighth Ave. and 114th St. and the Gouverneur Morris High School at 165th St. and Boston Road in the Bronx.[127] From this point on, there was a constant increase in the numbers, size and offerings of the high schools, so that by 1914, the city had 23 such schools, with enrollments of thousands.[128]

All this was accomplished in the face of considerable opposition. The high school building program was very expensive, partly because Superintendent Snyder planned elegant and elaborate buildings with great auditoriums, complete with organs and historical murals. Morris and De Witt Clinton were particular showplaces and their Romanesque style battlements were truly impressive, although possibly inappropriate.[129] The cost disturbed many, because the needs of the schools as a whole were overwhelming and because the bulk (over 90%) of all the children never attended high school. Superintendent Maxwell, however, strongly favored the erection of more high schools, saying:

> It is only through a high school education that the son of a poor man obtains an approach to equality with the son of a rich man in opportunity for success in life.

127
   Palmer, 189.

128
   First Through Sixteenth Annual Reports of the City Superintendent of Schools, 1899-1914, passim.

129
   Department of Education, Ninth Annual Report, 1906, p. 343-349.

Carrying this idea further, he urged the establishment of a manual training high school and a commercial one,
relating this directly to the needs of business and industry in New York City,[130] and even more to needs of the increasing number of non-academic adolescents, who, if left untrained could get only dead-end jobs when they left school
at 14.[131] He thought the training a technical high school
could give would even improve the public morality because
if the "...young girls who are obliged to earn their living
at an early age" could earn more as a result of a high school
education they would not be tempted into immorality to "obtain
fine rainment and gentle living"![132]

At first, the Superintendent's ideas bore little
fruit, and only academic high schools were organized. When
the educational authorities became aware of the great
number of high school graduates who never got past the
first year, their attention turned to remedial measures.
The reasons for the large number of high school drop-outs
were mostly economic, that is, the need for an income
producing job, but it was also true that many youngsters

---

[130] Maxwell, _Municipal Affairs_, IV, December, 1900
p.744.

[131] First Annual Report of the City Superintendent of
Schools, 1899, pp. 108, 109.

[132] Fourth Annual Report of the City Superintendent
of Schools, 1902, pp. 74-75.

entered high school who were unable to do the difficult
classical studies demanded of them. Since there was
little guidance or remedial work available, they soon
fell by the wayside and dropped out.

The great new high schools were simply too expensive to be utilized by only a tiny segment of the population, and therefore the course of study had to be made
more attractive in order to retain more of the students.
Thus, a choice of courses was developed, similar to those
available in Brooklyn years earlier. Unfortunately however,
a commercial or industrial course in an academic high
school was likely to become a dumping ground for the duller
students and the manual training work was inadequate
because of equipment deficiencies. Although aware of the
fact that the academic high schools were not meeting the
needs of their new students; working class boys and girls
who would not go on to college, the school authorities
were unable to make any great changes and for years the
pattern of high enrollments followed by large numbers of
dropouts continued.

A partial answer to the problem, which gradually
evolved, was the establishment of technical high schools,
the best example of which was Washington Irving High School,
located just north of 14th St. but drawing its 6,000 girl
students largely from the tenements of the Lower East Side.
While a small proportion of the girls (1,000) were preparing
to go to college, the great majority were being trained to

enter the business and industrial life of the city, and
therefore the school was equipped with a salesroom, a bank,
an employment office, and an entire floor of cooking and
sewing rooms. The trades taught were directly related to
the economic life of the city and consisted of millinery,
dressmaking and costume design. The teachers of commercial
subjects at the school made efforts to find out what skills
prospective employers might want and trained their students
to master them.

Since many of the girls would marry young, Washington
Irving also contained a housekeeping flat and devoted itself to studies that "directly bear upon the practical concerns
of life", offering courses in marriage, baby care, personal
hygiene, household sanitation and first aid. There were
lessons in table manners, and even a set of model stairs, so
that the girls could lean the lady like way to climb them.
The teachers at Washington Irving were said to believe that
"under present social conditions...it is for them to take
over many of the duties performed by parents," and even
cultural equipment such as a theatre and a conservatory were
part of the school. All in all, this kind of high school was
a direct attempt to meet the most obvious needs of the
immigrant adolescent girls; to equip them for jobs, marriage
and urban living, while raising their standards and aspira-
tions.[133]   It was very successful and only the financial

---

[133] Burton Hendrick, "Six Thousand Girls at School",
McClure's XLI (May, 1913), pp. 51-56.

inability to support a daughter through high school prevented more parents from sending their girls to Washington Irving.

A similar institution for boys, called Stuyvesant
High School also offering a technical education, was
established with equal success, but the basic problem was
not met by these schools. The bulk of the working class
youngsters, for scholastic or economic reasons, would not
go to school for four years after 8th grade and thus delay
their entrance into the labor market until they were 18, no
matter how much the school tailored the curriculum to
their needs. Therefore, by 1912, the schools had to turn,
albeit reluctantly, to the two year vocational school,
where the boy or girl who needed to work could acquire the
necessary skills in a short time, leaving the high schools
to those youngsters able to postpone working a little
longer. [134]

Although the high school did not become an upward
route for the majority of the poor youngsters at this
time, the school system had been enriched by their addition
and in years to come, as the age of school leaving rose
to 16, they were more fully utilized.

By 1914, in spite of the "serious obstacles" to
which Superintendent Maxwell had referred to in his

---

[134]
Fourteenth Annual Report of the City Superintendent
of Schools, 1912, pp. 144-145.

anniversary address, it was apparent that the schools of
New York City had made "upward progress", at least in such
basic areas as buildings and staff. The achievements had
been accomplished in the fact of many difficulties and
often were less than ideal solutions, but none the less,
did represent a real attempt to meet the deluge of problems
that public education had to deal with in the first decade
of the 20th century.

TABLE 1. SCHOOLS IN HIGH IMMIGRANT AREAS   1905   GRADES ONE THROUGH EIGHT

A. MANHATTAN

NUMBER	ADDRESS	REGISTER	NUMBER ON PART TIME
1.	Henry and Oliver Streets	2,769	631
2.	116 Henry Street	3,148	485
4.	203 Rivington Street	2,063	574
7.	Chrystie and Hester Streets	2,508	0
12.	371 Madison Street	1,833	1,060
13.	239 East Houston Street	2,786	998
20.	Rivington and Forsythe Streets	3,587	884
21.	222 Mott Street	1,854	0
22.	Stanton and Sheriff Streets	2,896	0
23.	Mulberry and Bayard Streets	1,882	380
21.	200 Monroe Street	3,071	1,459
34.	108 Broome Street	2,216	0
35.	160 Chrystie Street	1,497	290
42.	Hester Street near Ludlow Street	2,398	213
57.	176 East 115th Street	2,922	207
62.	Hester, Essex, and Norfolk Streets	3,337	3,337
72.	Lexington and 106th Streets	2,255	0
75.	25 Norfolk Street	2,144	0
83.	216 East 110th Street	2,343	843
88.	300 Rivington Street	2,392	1,038
92.	154 Broome Street	2,197	106
97.	Pitt and Delancey Streets	776	0
98.	38 Sheriff Street	822	0
103.	119th Street and Madison Avenue	2,825	378
108.	62 Mott Street	782	180
109.	99th Street and Second Avenue	2,859	235
120.	187 Broome Street	80	0
121.	227 East 102nd Street	1,583	0
137.	Grand and Essex Street	1,571	954
140.	116 Norfolk Street	1,162	0
144.	30 Allen Street	1,557	0
147.	East Broadway and Scammel Street	2,637	623
160.	Rivington and Suffolk Streets	2,962	1,119
161.	105 Ludlow Street	1,838	435
168.	104th Street and 2nd Avenue	3,449	824
170.	111th Street, East of Lenox Avenue	3,100	0
171.	103rd and 104th Streets, near Madison	3,183	458
172.	108th and 109th Streets, and 2nd ave.	1,933	456
174.	Attorney and Rivington Streets	1,470	0
184.	116th and 117th Streets, East of Lenox	3,001	0
188.	Manhattan, East Houston & Lewis Sts.	4,537	866

NUMBER	ADDRESS	REGISTER	NUMBER ON PART TIME

B. BROOKLYN'

NUMBER	ADDRESS	REGISTER	NUMBER ON PART TIME
19.	South 2nd and Keap Streets	1,670	0
21.	McKibben Street and Graham Avenue	1,353	997
37.	South 4th Street and Berry Street	1,561	212
50.	South 4th Street and Havemeyer Street	779	190
64.	Belmont Avenue and Berriman Street	1,727	485
66.	Osborn Street and Sutter Avenue	837	837
84.	Glenmore Street and Stone Avenue	4,646	2,377
109.	Dumont and Powell Streets	2,477	2,398
125.	Blake Avenue and Thatford Street	2,779	2,236

SOURCE: Seventh Annual Report of the City Superintendent of Schools, pp. 506-545; pp 520-526.

TABLE 2. NUMBER OF STUDENTS ENROLLED IN DAY SCHOOLS.   1899-1914

1899	493,849
1900	518,073
1901	553,198
1902	588,614
1903	495,045
1904	530,658
1905	622,201
1906	645,882
1907	653,153
1908	673,466
1909	685,655
1910	711,630
1911	733,548
1912	748,218
1913	765,950
1914	792,595

TABLE 3. NUMBER OF ELEMENTARY SCHOOLS.*   1899-1914

1899	466
1900	483
1901	496
1902	489
1903	481
1904	492
1905	482
1906	485
1907	486
1908	490
1909	502
1910	498
1911	497
1912	496
1913	499
1914	504

The apparent lack of growth in certain years is accounted for by the
fact that the Superintendent was attempting to consolidate the organization; elementary, primary, and grammar schools, when located under one
roof, were now to be one school, with one principal. Also, when an old
building was replaced, it was always with a larger school, thus increasing the number of seats, although in the roster of the schools, this
did not show.

Source for Tables II-IX are the First through Sixteenth Annual Reports of
the City Superintendent of Schools, 1899-1914.

TABLE 4. NUMBER OF TEACHERS IN THE DAY SCHOOLS   1899-1914

1899	9,305
1900	11,362
1901	12,212
1902	12,069
1903	12,696
1904	13,327
1905	13,777
1906	15,878
1907	16,000
1908	16,489
1909	17,073
1910	17,724
1911	18,718
1912	18,892
1913	20,128
1914	20,448

TABLE 5. NUMBER OF KINDERGARTEN CLASSES   1899-1914

1899	101
1900	85
1901	135
1902	243
1903	420
1904	449
1905	491
1906	549
1907	601
1908	678
1909	765
1910	811
1911	847
1912	847
1913	868
1914	913

TABLE 6. NUMBER OF CHILDREN IN HIGH SCHOOLS   1899-1914

1899	13,731
1900	17,018
1901	19,013
1902	21,461
1903	23,701
1904	27,794
1905	30,340
1906	31,949
1907	33,387
1908	37,477
1909	43,903
1910	50,902
1911	54,286
1912	56,788
1913	61,262
1914	67,923

FIG. 5. SCHOOL DISTRICTS OF THE LOWER EAST SIDE, 1910.

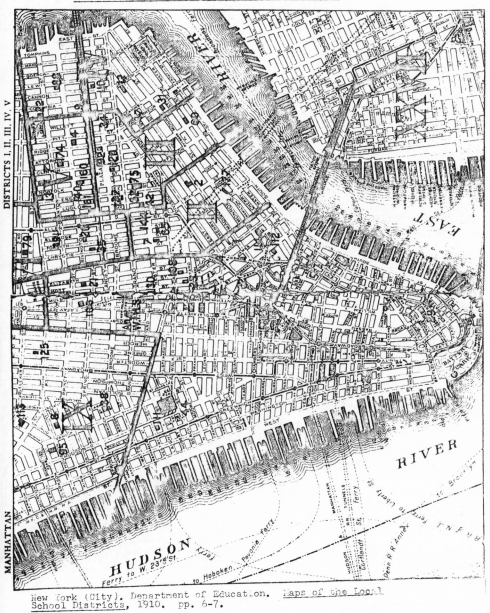

FIG. 6. SCHOOL DISTRICTS OF EAST HARLEM, 1910.

New York (City). Department of Education. Maps of the Local
School Districts, 1910. pp. 14-15.

FIG. 7. SCHOOL DISTRICTS OF WILLIAMSBURG, BROOKLYN, 1910.

FIG. 8. SCHOOL DISTRICTS OF BROWNSVILLE, BROOKLYN, 1910.

New York (City). Department of Education. Maps of the Local
School Districts, 1910. pp. 72-73.

CHAPTER IV.

THE EXTENSION OF THE SCHOOL

If Horace Mann, or another·educator of his generation had visited the headquarters of the Board of Education
in New York City in 1910, he would have been completely
astonished at the number and variety of school activities
being planned, activities which took place outside of the
classroom and which had very little to do with formal education, as he had known it.

To a degree never dreamed of by 19th century educators, the schools of New York City had extended their activities into recreational and social programs in an attempt to
help the masses of newcomers adjust to the pressures of urban
living. Mann and his fellows had won the difficult fight
for the tax-supported common school, expecting only that
it would provide the basic literacy a free people needed.
Never did they plan for the school to provide play opportunities, health services, low cost lunches and family counselling. Yet all these programs became part of the educational framework of New York City in the early years of the 20th
century, as the schools extended their function into many
different aspects of the children's lives.

The motivation for these new programs was not human-
itarianism alone, although that certainly was one consideration. Few people could see the ghetto during a sweltering
July and August without being stirred to compassion, and for
some it was equally painful to see young children with rickets
or tuberculosis due to malnutrition. But self interest on
the part of the power structure of both the schools and the
city also was involved. It was not difficult to see tha'
sick, tired and underfed children could not learn; that
the large number of school dropouts threatened to lower the
level of American life, and that, when the schools were
closed, the children of the slums roamed the streets, and in
their unsupervised idleness, committed crimes of vandalism
and violence which threatened the security of all the
respectable folk.

Adolescent gangs were not an invention of the 1950's,
nor was prostitution and theft. Mothers worked summer and
winter, and the crowding in the tenement apartments forced
the uncared for children to the city streets, often with
disastrous consequences. There were the empty schools,
expensive to build and useless after three p.m. and during
the summer, and there were the dirty, hot mischievous
children. It is no wonder that the settlement and charity
workers who could not absorb all of the youngsters into
their own group work programs, turned to the vacant schools
as the answer to the recreational problems of the poor

immigrant children.[1]

The programs urged on the schools were threefold, consisting of vacation schools for summer mornings, playground groups for summer afternoons and recreational centers for winter evenings. Other refinements such as open-air roof playground activities during the evenings of July and August were added as the years passed.[2] There were two legal prerequisites necessary to the establishment of these extension programs. Until the mid-1890's, most schools did not have grounds adjoining them or any space in their buildings suitable for recreational activities. Due to the efforts of Jacob Riis and the same reform groups that won the "school war", the State Legislature passed a law requiring every school built after 1895 to have provision for playgrounds. This gave the schools the physical space to work with and can be considered a direct response to the problems caused by increasing congestion in New York.[3]

---

[1]
The various extension programs were begun at different times during the years 1898-1912, as the chapter will make clear. Some of the new projects were noted as early as 1903 by Adele Marie Shaw in "The True Character of the New York City Schools", World's Work, VII (November, 1903) p.4206, but all of them, and the reasons why they had been established were discussed by William Henry Maxwell in "The City and the Child" XXVI, Publications of the National Recreation Association of America, n.d.,p.7 and in William Henry Maxwell, A Quarter Century of Public School Development (New York, 1912) p.323.

[2]
See Tables 7,8,9 which list the growth of the various recreational programs.

[3]
Jacob Riis, The Battle With the Slum(New York:1902) pp.289-290

It took some years before there were any large
number of schools built in accordance with this law, and in
the meantime, settlement workers and the Public Education
Association cast about for a way to utilize the space in
the already existing schools for recreational programs.
Until 1898, the Department of Education answered all requests
for permission to use school property by saying it was not
legally authorized to do so. Two residents of the University
Settlement, James K. Paulding, and Winifred Buck, joined
with Mariana Van Rensaleer, President of the Public Education
Association, and Charles C. Burlingham, then head of the
Board of Education, to push through an amendment to the
educational chapter of the Charter of 1897 which provided
that the schools could be used for "purposes of...recreation
and other public uses."[4]

This was accomplished in March of 1898, and in
June, the Board of Education appointed Miss Evangeline E.
Whitney to be the supervisor in charge of vacation schools
and recreational programs.[5] A better choice would have
been hard to find. Miss Whitney was dedicated to her task
of providing stimulating and healthful play for the children
of the slums and her verve and drive added much to the
program.

---

[4] Riis, p.387; Lillian Betts, "The Child Out of School
Hours", Outlook, LXXV (September, 1903), p.209; Sol Cohen,
Progressives and Urban School Reform (New York: 1964) p.51.

[5] New York (City),Department of Education,Journal
of the Board of Education, March 23, 1898, p.71; June 13,
1898, p.281.

She wrote long annual reports for Superintendent
Maxwell which were always refreshing to read. In 1906, when
the funds for her department were in danger of reduction,
she said:

> Could the taxpayers realize what these cool
> (school) buildings mean to the children banish-
> ed to the sweltering pavements, and the physical
> as well as the moral benefit conferred by keeping
> them happily busy, we are sure the cry against
> spending so much money would be changed into a
> demand for an extension of the work.   6

In this particular statement, Evangeline Whitney
was referring to the morning vacation schools which had
originated in Boston in 1866 but had not come to New York
City until 1894, when the Association for Improving the
Condition of the poor began to operate one. Finding that
the demand for places far exceeded their resources, the
Association petitioned the Board of Education to operate
the schools. Not until the passage of the permissive
law of 1898, however, was this done. In the following
year 15 vacation schools were opened in Manhattan, mostly
below 14th street. At first the staff was hired on a
haphazard basis; salaries were very low and applicants not
the best qualified, but after 1902, candidates for these
jobs had to be licensed by the Board of Examiners by passing an appropriate examination.[7]

6
    New York (City), Department of Education, Eighth
Annual Report of the City Superintendent of Schools, 1906,
p.352.
    7
    New York (City), Department of Education, The
Organization of the School Board of Manhattan and the Bronx,
February 13, 1901, p.129; Fourth Annual Report of the City
Superintendent of Schools, 1902, p.51.

Miss Whitney was not alone in her emotional attach-
ment to the work of the vacation schools. The President
of the Manhattan-Bronx School Board said in 1901 that these
schools had "...done a great work...for the people on the
East Side...much of the sunshine of the children's lives
comes from the teacher of the vacation school...". Jacob
Riis felt the same. "The way to fight the slum in children's
lives is with sunlight and flowers and play..."[8]

An expert on play schools was more specific:

> The need for play centers is caused by the
> crowded, cosmopolitan city. The lack of space
> for play (has) brought into existence a generation
> of children in New York who do not know how to
> play (and) whose knowledge of activity is express-
> ed in mischief... (thus) producing destructive
> and undermining effects on character and intelli-
> gence.[9]

Superintendent Maxwell put the idea succinctly when he said
"The boy without a playground is father to the man without
a job,"[10] and related it even more directly to the immigrants

---

[8]
Organization of the School Board of Manhattan and
the Bronx, p.110; Riis, p.364

[9]
Betts, Outlook, LXXV, p.209

[10]
Fourth Annual Report of the City Superintendent of
Schools, 1902, p.159.

in 1904. "In this city, where there are hundreds of
thousands of foreigners to be co..verted into American citizens
...this (school buildings) vast property ought to be utilized at all reasonable hours for the recreation and improvement of the pupils."[11]

To provide sunshine, "fun and games" while building
character, then, was the mission of the play schools. They
attacked the problem with many different weapons. In 1901,
at P.S. 1 on Henry St. 1,000 students were taught bandaging
and cooking if they were girls, and cane chairing if they
were boys. They also played games and to an observer, seemed to be having a great time.[12]   Two years later, in 1903,
judging from the equipment, another vacation school could
offer more. There was a game room, a gym for calisthenics
and dancing as well as a quiet room where clubs could meet.[13]
Even more progress was made by 1905 when another interested
reporter saw classes in "gymnastics, games, Venetian iron
work, basketry, bench-work, fret sawing, whittling (!),
chair caning, domestic science, sewing, embroidering, knitt-
ing, crocheting, and weaving."[14]

11
    Sixth Annual Report of the City Superintendent of
Schools, 1904, p.145.

12
    New York Times, July 9, 1901, p.7.

13
    Betts, Outlook, LXXV, p.211.

14
    Winifred Buck, "Work and Play in the Public Schools"
Outlook, LXXX, (July 22, 1905), p.730.

Adele Shaw had noted the educative purpose of the vacation schools in 1904. She said model rooms were used to teach cleanliness while personal hygiene and cooking were utilized in order to instruct in manners and good taste. Also once a week, every vacation school received the services of a teacher expert in the history of New York City who told the youngsters stories about the city and took them to visit historic places. Such activities were designed to Americanize and acculturize the immigrant children.[15] By 1906, some vacation schools had added classes in the three "R's" to prepare boys and girls who were almost old enough to apply for working papers and planned to do so.[16]

Similarly, a year later, English to foreigner classes were added for the newly arrived children. Miss Whitney was particularly enthusiastic about this part of the work. "If taken directly from Ellis Island and placed under the right teachers, these children could make rapid advancement during the summer session."[17]

15
Shaw, World's Work, October 1904 VIII, p.5406

16
New York (City) Department of Education, Minutes of the Board of Superintendents, June 7, 1906, pp 728,526.

17
Ninth Annual Report of the City Superintendent of Schools, 1907, p.520.

Remedial work for those "backward or foreign" youngsters
who were failing during the regular school year was included in the vacation school program in 1910.[18]   Superintendent
Whitney planned to establish school gardens, because she
felt it was important to get the city children "back to the
soil", but until 1911, she could not get the necessary funds.[19]
By 1912, the vacation schools were even offering lessons
to those youngsters able enough to complete advanced work
during the summer and thus be placed ahead when school re-
opened.[20]

Many children left the vacation school premises at
12 noon and returned for less organized activities in the
afternoon, thus filling their entire day. The activities
at the playgrounds were much more varied and often including swimming lessons if the school was equipped for them.
When a large number of children were present, the teacher
just led mass calisthenics; but in smaller groups, many
games and songs were taught. As part of this playground
work, Mother's clubs were formed. The meetings of these
groups were held while the children were at supervised
play and offered opportunities for relaxation and Americanization to the immigrant women.[21]

---

[18] Twelfth Annual Report of the City Superintendent
of Schools, 1910, p.477.

[19] Fifth Annual Report of the City Superintendent
of Schools, 1903, p.183.

[20] Fourteenth Annual Report of the City Superintendent
of Schools, 1912, p.171; Interview with Mr. Joseph Winick,
November 26, 1966.

[21] Shaw, World's Work, VIII, p.5413.

The content of the work done at the vacation schools and playgrounds was rarely criticized, although the management and expense of running them often was attacked. Like the kindergartens, these programs were popular with many different groups, and once the members of the Board of Estimate accepted the new idea that the schools were responsible for the children of the slums all the year round, appropriations were forthcoming.

The evening recreation centers won less universal approval. This may have been because they serviced an older group of youngsters who appealed less to the charitable instincts of the public. These centers were open from seven to ten p.m. during the months of October to May and were designed to offer play, remedial work and healthy recreation primarily to boys and girls who were obliged to work during the day.

> The discovery of the number of schoolboys who must work before and after school if they are to continue their education, and of boys who never hear English in their own homes and suffer in their grade work because of this and the over-crowded (condition) of their classes, led to the establishment of this particular (type) of center ...which marks a high degree of appreciation of the needs of the school children in our tenement house districts by the school authorities.

said social worker Lillian Betts, a close observer of the school extension programs.[22]

22
    Betts, Outlook, LXXX, p.213; A. E. Palmer, History of the New York Public Schools, (New York: 1905) p.288.

The idea of recreation centers for deprived adolescents was originally a development of the English settlement house movement and was brought to New York by social
workers who had been residents in London's Toynbee Hall.
In 1899, a group of East Side boys had organized a club and
were looking for a meeting place. The only location they
could find was in the backroom of a saloon. The social
workers of the area were horrified at this and asked the
Board of Education to open some classrooms at night for
the use of the clubs. The Public Education Association
assumed the responsibility for any property damage, and
in view of this, the Board approved, and one school on
Hester Street was opened for meetings, led by a volunteer
adult from a nearby settlement house.[23] The experiment
was a success and the number of recreation centers increased from the lone original to 62 in 1914.[24] Until 1908, the
centers were exclusively in schools located below 14th
Street. After that date, requests from other parts of
the city began to come to the Board of Superintendents and
centers were opened in Brooklyn, Queens and in Richmond.[25]

---

[23]
    Riis, p.372

[24]
    First to Sixteenth Annual Reports of the City
Superintendent of Schools, 1899-1914, passim, The growth
is shown by the following figures: 1899-1; 1903-23;
1906-30; 1911-43 and 1914-62.

[25]
    Department of Education, Minutes of the Board of
Superintendents, September 10, 1908, p.886; Ibid, January 3,
1901, p.25; Charles S. Bernheimer (ed.), The Russian Jew
in the United States (Philadelphia: 1905) p.197.

In accordance with group work theory, activities
at the recreation centers were varied. A list of supplies
ordered for them by the Manhattan Bronx School Board in
1901 indicated that games like author lotto, chess, dominoes,
and checkers were played and that gymnastics were encouraged
through the use of rings, climbing ropes, high jump boards
and parallel bars. The educational aspects were covered
by drill in literature, geography and "famous American
battles." [26] Some of the recreation centers held classes
in etiquette and how to apply for a job and maintained employment registers. [27]

The clubs that had provided the original reason for
the centers continued to meet and covered a wide range of
interests--from hobbies to politics. Folk and social
dancing were taught and classes in personal grooming were
held for the immigrant girls. This was a program identical
to that of the settlement houses and permeated with the
same philosophy, only held under public auspices and tax
supported. All of the work of the centers was directly related to the needs of the immigrant poor; the gym activities
to exercise the cramped muscles of the teenagers who sat at
sewing machines all day; the etiquette lessons for the girls
and boys who lacked "American" manners; the drill in

---

[26] Organization of the School Board of Manhattan and
the Bronx, p.220

[27] Eighth Annual Report of the City Superintendent of
Schools, 1906, p.363.

academic work to fill any educational gaps in the background
of the newcomers, and so on.

But the quiet rooms set aside for study were directly
related to the absence of privacy in the tenement flats which
prevented many school children from doing their home work.
These study rooms had a licensed teacher in charge who
could help the scholars who needed assistance. Many of the
older boys, ambitious for advancement, prepared for civil
service examinations at the centers as well. When all these
activities ended, in May, the roof playgrounds of the schools
built after 1895 were opened for recreational purposes only
although the clubs did continue to meet there. The evening
playgrounds also had band concerts and social dancing and
a change to get out of the sweltering apartments for a few
hours.

The social workers of the district felt these supervised activities prevented the boys and girls from engaging in
undesirable sexual activities and also protected them from
the "white slavers" and procurers who abounded in the area.
The best equipped schools were the most popular and widely
used. Indeed, the principal of P.S. 62 complained to the
Borard of Superintendents in 1908 that his school was being
overused; its playground and classrooms occupied all day
and all year.[28]   This worry about physical destruction of
school property was widespread, especially among the janitors,
who resented the additional labor created for them by the

---

[28]
Minutes of the Board of Superintendents,September 24,
1908, p.211

extension of the school. They often placed every obstacle
possible in the path of the supervisors of the center and
made conditions so unpleasant, the children stayed away.
Then, said the custodians, the centers were not really needed, because so few youngsters attended! It was a hard fight,
but the reform groups were finally able to make their point
-- the schools were for the benefit of the children, not
the janitors! [29]

Besides interference from the custodians, the recreation centers did have some other problems. Their dual
nature, while designed to appeal to a wide variety of
children, were also confusing. Were they for fun--or for
study? asked Mary Simkovitch, when she discussed the
functions of the enlarged public school. In spite of
her query, Mrs. Simkovitch, and others of her persuasion,
whole-heartedly supported the recreation centers and believed that they, and the other extension activities of
the schools, would bear much fruit in the regular classrooms, when the techniques of socialized education developed in the centers were used in the course of every day
school work. [30]

---

[29]
Riis, pp. 395-397.

[30]
Mary Simkovitch, "The Enlarged Function of the
Public School", Proceedings of the National Conference
of Charities and Corrections, 1904, pp 477-481.

Not every one was as sanguine. When the committee
of inquiry set up by Comptroller Grout in 1904, investigated the recreation centers, it found much to criticize. The
clubs, it appeared, were only successful when no work was
required and therefore the athletic clubs were well attended but the literary ones were short-lived. The committee
ridiculed the idea that teachers were necessary to supervise the play of children; such activities were natural
and needed no encouragement. It was in regard to the
study rooms that the criticism was most devastating. "Most
of the boys found in the study groups are either high school
or City College boys..." and not the working teenagers for
whom the rooms were intended.[31]

Even when allowance is made for the emphasis on
economy, which after all was the main reason for the
inquiry, it was probably true that the centers were somewhat less than perfect in their academic attempts, but
socially they were a great success, at least until 1910
or so, when the increasing availability of commercial recreation (movies, etc.) and the greater ability to pay for
such pleasures, diminished attendance at the public centers.
After 1914, they were no longer important in the extension
program of the schools. During their hey-day, however,
they   met the social and recreational needs of thousands

[31] New York (City), Board of Estimate and Apportionment, Report of an Investigation concerning the cost of
maintaining the public school system. (New York: 1904) pp.
177-179.

of immigrant boys and girls and therefore represented one
more innovation developed by the schools in response to
new pressures.

Although the children of the newcomers were a prime
concern of the schools, there was also much interest in
broadening the life of the immigrant adult and this need
was met by the extensive lecture program developed after
1889 and noted for its durability and popularity. After
a state law was passed in 1888 which authorized the Board
of Education to establish and maintain free lectures for
working men and women, $15,000 was appropriated with which
to start the program in Manhattan. It was extended to
Queens and Richmond in 1899 and to Brooklyn in 1901, under
the guidance of Henry Leipziger, a German Jew whose close
ties to the Educational Alliance undoubtedly influenced
his attitudes toward school extension work, because the
Alliance had pioneered in such programs.[32]   "In selecting
the subjects for the lectures...the known characteristics
of the neighborhood...are considered," wrote Superintendent
Leipziger in 1911, and the topics offered would seem to
indicate that the neighborhoods had very wide interests indeed.[33]

---

[32]
   Palmer, p.175

[33]
   "The City School as a Community Center", Tenth
Yearbook of the National Society for the Study of Education,
1911, p.9.

There were lectures on science, literature, history,
sociology and art; on geography, first aid, sanitation
and nutrition. Many were given in foreign languages
such as Italian, Yiddish and German and these had the
special purpose of preparing the immigrant for citizenship. The lectures alternated serious with lighter subjects
and often used stereopticon slides for illustrations.
Dr. Jacob Ross recalled earning $5. per night for lectures
he gave in music, and said the audience was most appreciative. [34]

Although not organized as courses and offering no
credit, the lectures were sometimes called "The People's
University". Possibly because the cost was low ($26.05
per lecture in 1911), the lectures were very popular, even
with the Board of Estimate. In 1909, Leipziger estimated
that 959,982 people had attended at least one lecture and [35]
the fact that none of the critics of the "new" schools
ever castigated these particular extension features, makes
it clear that much value was attached to them.

When Superintendent of Buildings, C.B. Snyder, was
planning new schoolhouses for the East Side he wanted the
auditoriums to be large and on the ground floor level,
so as to accommodate the lecture audiences. The Educational Alliance was so much in favor of these programs, it

---

[34]
"The City School as a Community Center", pp 10-11,
13; Palmer, p.175; Conversation with Jacob Ross, October
17, 1966.

[35]
Tenth Yearbook of the National Society of the
Study of Education, pp. 12,13,16.

wanted the Board of Education to extend them to adolescents
between three and five in the afternoon, but the Superintendents balked at this.[36]   The lecture series undoubtedly
had a tremendous influence on the growth of adult education
programs later in the 20th century and represent another
way in which the groundwork for a modern school structure
was laid in these early years.

The extended school was a significant change in
educational concept because it implied school responsibility for children of all ages after three p.m. and during
the summer, a theory not previously held by educators or
the public. In addition, the extension programs signified
a new departure in educational practice, as well as theory,
because the socialized techniques developed in the vacation schools and recreation centers were the origin of
new pedagogical methods, somewhat erroneously labeled
"progressive" when they came into widespread classroom use
in the nineteen thirties and forties.

The responses represented by all these activities
are part of a larger pattern, that is, school concern over
the whole child, his physical and emotional health, and
the relationship of these factors to his ability to learn.
Therefore, in addition to the extension programs, the movement to meet the needs of the newcomers led to developments
in health services, lunch programs, and counselling, some

36
Minutes of the Board of Superintendents, April 16,
1908, p.421

of which operated a bit outside of the school structure,
but which were encouraged, planned and partially supported
by the Board of Education.

In these social service areas, even more than in
the extension activities of the schools, the pressure of
the social workers who were in direct contact with the
immigrants led the way to Board of Education action. The
articles in their professional publications such as
Charities and The Survey abounded with reasons why the
schools must enter the welfare field. Jane Robbins wrote
that it was necessary for the school to assume a parental
role because the immigrant mothers and fathers were
unable to protect their young under urban conditions.[37]
Eleanor Johnson said that "...social service must come to
be regarded as a justifiable function of the schools..."
because no other agency could come in contact with so many
needy children.[38]

John Spargo was more vehement. Education was
necessary in order to have a literate population, essential
if our democratic government was to survive. But poor
children could not be educated because bad health and malnutrition prevented them from learning. Therefore, medical
care must be provided through the schools, for every
child, as a matter of right, if an educated citizenry was to

[37]
Jane E. Robbins, "The Settlement and the Public
Schools", Outlook, XCV, (August 6, 1910) p.785-787.

[38]
Eleanor H. Johnson, "Social Service and Public
Schools", Survey, XXX (May 3, 1913), p.174.

be attained.[39]   Robert Hunter, one of the first analysts
of poverty in the United States, spoke of the vicious
circle which entrapped the poor; slum children got the
least supervision, care, and food and therefore it was
harder for them to learn. Because of this, it was difficult for them to earn, and so they remained poor for
many generations.[40]

Not only social workers were concerned. Schoolmen
were also aware that physical factors in the child's life
interfered with the process of education. Superintendent
Maxwell pointed out how improper or insufficient feeding,
shortage of sleep and nervous tension due to congestion
and poor housing were blocking the learning ability of the
poor youngsters. He did not feel that destitution was the
most common lot of the children in the schools, but rather
that the immigrant families tended to hoard their money
or spend it unwisely which often led to deprivation.

Also, when mothers worked, the children were left
to shift for themselves and this caused unbalanced diets
and led to the neglect of physical ills. The need to
provide wholesome food at cost price was the "...most press-
ing of all school reforms" said Maxwell. The fact that the
Superintendent considered a better diet a school reform shows
how far educational philosophy had been permeated with social

---

[39] John Spargo, The Bitter Cry of the Children (New York: 1909) pp 58-59, 249

[40] Robert Hunter, Poverty, (New York: 1904) p.216.

service ideas, at the highest echelons, at least. [41]   Julia

Richman, District Superintendent of the Lower East Side,

cheerfully reported that the teachers were being trained

to look for what was wrong with the child physically and

socially, although her optimism was not shared by Robert

Hunter, who thought that the staff and the city fathers

did not appreciate "the new social needs" and that "teachers,

as a class, are lacking in a knowledge of industrial history

and social evolution." [42]

Of all the concerns of those interested in the

welfare of the immigrant school child, health came first.

Luther H. Gulick, the supervisor in charge of Hygiene for

the schools gave the reason for this when he showed that it

took a child with enlarged adenoids 9.2 years to complete

8 grades of school and that therefore retardation was

directly related to poor physical health. [43]   Maxwell went

deeper into the relation between the immigrant background

and the poor health of the children of such families:

---

[41]
    William Henry Maxwell, "Stories from the Lives of Real Teachers", World's Work, XVIII, (August-1909),p.11878.

[42]
    Julia Richman, "A Social Need of the Public Schools", Forum, XLIII, (February, 1910), p.169; Hunter, p. 209.

[43]
    Luther H. Gulick, and Leonard Ayres, Medical Inspection in the Schools, (New York: 1913) p.161.

> Every time a foreign parent is persuaded or
> compelled to do something for the improvement
> of his child's health, he moves a step nearer
> the American standard of living. Nor is the
> blame to be altogether laid upon the ignorant
> Pole or Italian or Russian, that he does not
> recognize at once, even when duly admonished,
> the necessity of a surgical operation on his
> child's throat, or of procuring glasses for his
> eyes. He has had no training or experience that
> would lead him to a realizing sense of the import-
> ance of such matters. Before he came to New York,
> he lived in the open country or in a small village,
> where the outdoor life was a powerful preventive
> against many of the ills to which children become
> heir when crowded in the slums of a great city... 44

Precisely because the immigrant parent had no

"training or experience" in matters of health care, it

was incumbent upon the schools to take action. Therefore,

in 1897 the Department of Health assigned 134 doctors to be

medical inspectors in the schools. They were to visit each

of their posts for one hour a day and be paid $30. a month.

All the physicians were expected to do was to examine the

children sent to them by the teachers and send home anyone

who might have a contagious disease.[45]   In 1902, as part of

the general improvement of the schools under the revised

Charter and the impetus of more money from the Board of

Estimate, doctors were required to spend three hours a day

at their assigned schools and were to be paid $100 a month.

---

[44] Ninth Annual Report of the City Superintendent of Schools, 1907, p.139.

[45] Wald, p.49; Gulick and Ayres, p.13

But whether for one hour or three, the examinations were perfunctory, concentrating especially on evidence of pediculosis, and no treatment of any kind was given. Since the object of the authorities was to have healthy children in school, not sick ones at home, obviously medical inspection alone was not enough. Therefore, the Board of Education and the Health Department began an experiment in school nursing in 1902 at four Lower East Side schools, using part of the staff of the Henry Street Settlement. Lillian Wald had been a prime mover in this project and was delighted to see it begin.

The examining doctor sent any pupil needing attention to the school nurse every day. She gave treatment on the spot, if suitable, gave instructions as to cleanliness (if lack of that quality was the cause of the trouble) and returned as many children as possible to class. Where the medical condition was more serious, the nurse visited the child's home and either told the mother about the availability of a dispensary, or took the child there herself. If the problem was lice, the mother was given a practical lesson in fumigation--using the child as a model.[46]

---

[46]
Wald, pp. 51-52.

The attempt to treat the child without compelling him to stay home was also an effort to cut down on truancy because previously, when a doctor sent a child out of school for a minor ailment, the youngster was likely to remain out permanently, partly because it was so difficult for him to catch up with his class when he returned.

The first nurse in charge of this experiment was one of Miss Wald's assistants at Henry Street, Miss Lina L. Rogers. She vividly described the working conditions of the school nurses at that time. The schools had no room set aside for a dispensary, so the nurses used a corner of the ground floor playground, which was rather cold in the winter. They wore long aprons and ankle length walking skirts and used simple supplies such as cotton, small basins, scissors for cutting hair, a spatula for applying vaseline and an alcohol lamp for heating water. The most common problem which they saw were eye illnesses, eczema, ringworm and pediculosis. Mostly, the nurses cleansed and disinfected the affected areas and tried to see the children daily in order to make the treatment continuous. They had to make out records for every school and home visit which was hard to do with damp hands and "when the names (might) belong to children of a dozen or more different national- ities".[47]

---

[47] New York Times, December 14, 1902, p.26. This article was the result of a personal interview with Miss Lina L. Rogers.

The experiment in school nursing proved so successful, especially in terms of improved attendance, that the
Board of Estimate voted $30,000 for the use of trained
nurses in the schools and the program continued to expand.
In 1903, there were 30 such women working for $75 a month
and doing a job that won them much praise.[48]   Evidently
the teachers did not cooperate very well with the nurses,
because in 1907 Superintendent Maxwell had to send a special
circular to the staff asking them to cooperate with the
Health Department, make especially sure overage children
were examined, and not frighten the youngsters when they
were about to receive medical attention.[49]

The scientific value of these check-ups was undoubtedly very great, but to the children involved, it was often
a terrible ordeal. The nurse's inspection visits were
purposely irregular and when she entered a classroom, "the
insides of the little immigrant daughters would begin to slide
--slide...", because the examination was done in groups of
five at the front of the class, and the public humiliation if
lice was found was almost unbearable.[50]   Directions to

---

[48] Shaw, World's Work VII, pp. 4208, 4209.

[49] Minutes of the Board of Superintendents, January 21,
1907, pp 86-87.

[50] Brody, The American Mercury, XIV, p.63.

remedy the situation were sent home in Yiddish and Italian
so no foreign born parent could be unaware of the cure.

Actually, pediculosis was the ailment most reported by the school medical staff--145,000 cases in 1910
alone. Impetigo, ringworm and scabies were a close second,
and eye diseases such as trachoma and the less serious
conjunctivitis were very prevalent. In addition, the
usual contagious diseases of childhood such as mumps and
measles were identified and isolated, and the diptheria
which was so dreaded in the families of the poor was
treated more promptly.[51]

By 1911, the school nurses and doctors were report-
ing physical defects among the children, not just contagious illness. They found that 59% of the youngsters examined needed dental care, 15% needed tonsillectomies, 11.9%
had nasal blockages and 10.6% required corrective glasses.
A smaller number had cardiac deficiencies, hearing impair-
ment, orthopedic defects while 2% had tuberculosis.[52]

---

[51] Gulick and Ayres, p.32; Harold McCormick, "The
First Fifty Years, Fiftieth Annual Report of the New York
City Superintendent of Schools, 1948, p.30. The prevalence
of trachoma may have been due to a loophole in the immigration laws which did not exclude persons with eye diseases.
Fourth Annual Report of the City Superintendent of Schools,
1902, p.112.

[52] Gulick and Ayres, p.40.

In spite of the clear advances in school medical
care, Superintendent Maxwell was not satisfied. In 1908
he recommended that the Board of Education provide free
eyeglasses to the poor children who needed them, and in
1912, 1913 and 1914 he urged that the Department of
Education recruit its own doctors because the physicians
of the Health Department were only reaching 1/3 of the
children in the schools.[53]   The inadequate efforts of
these medical practitioners must have continued, because
in 1916, the Director of Educational Hygiene of the
Department of Education, I.H. Goldberger, reported that
teachers were conducting simple tests for "defective
vision, hearing, teeth, nasal breathing and nutrition"
since so many children had these undiscovered and uncorrect-
ed defects.[54]

    There had always been sick and physically defective
children in the schools, but in the past they had been left
to nature and/or their parents. Now the problems were so
much more numerous, thanks to the great numbers of newcomers; and the awareness of the immigrant parents was so much
less, attention had to be paid in school, before contagion
spread and classes emptied. The motivation at first was
merely charitable and humanitarian, but continuing concern
and attention led to a search for causation, and malnutrition was seized upon as the prime reason for much of the

---

[53]
    Eighth Annual Report of the New York City
Superintendent of Schools, 1906, p.114; Fourteenth Annual
Report of the New York City Superintendent of Schools,
1912, p.179

ill health of the immigrant poor.

The remedies varied, ranging from the inclusion of lessons in domestic science and hygiene as part of the regular curriculum, to a prolonged battle for a nutritious school lunch program, which was carried on under private auspices, but with public school encouragement until 1919, when it became an official program of the Board of Education.

Proponents of school lunches argued that the large number of working mothers was the major reason why such a program was needed. The children of these mothers were "shut-outs", that is, locked out of the flat at the noon hour. Many were given a little money to buy lunch in a nearby shop, but instead spent their pennies on pickles and ice cream purchased from the "pushcarts and delicatessen stores (which had) grown up in the neighborhood of every public school."[55]

Possibly because of inadequate refrigeration facilities, it was not the custom to give the child a prepared lunch from home. The popularity of pickles was a great source of worry to the school and settlement people because they feared it presaged later addiction to other stimulants and would create new alcoholics! More seriously,

---

[54]
I. H. Goldberger, "The New York System of School Hygiene", National Education Association, Proceedings, 1916, p.781.

[55]
Burton Hendrick and Paul Kennaday, "Three Cent Lunches for School Children", McClure's, V, (October 1913), p.124.

investigations of the children's eating habits in two slum
schools, P.S. 21 and 51, indicated that many youngsters
came to school without breakfast, or had drunk only coffee
or tea for that meal. This, combined with a skimpy or
unhealthy lunch, led to malnutrition, especially when the
ignorance of the immigrant mothers about good nutrition
meant that supper might not be a balanced meal either.

The advocates of school lunches even found moral
reasons to bolster their cause. Some of the children did
not use their lunch money to buy food, but gambled instead,
while others ate on the run, standing on the curb outside
of the school building and eating without comfort or
grace. For reasons like this, the private committee which
supported the program in its early years claimed that
serving school lunches would teach manners and cleanliness
as well as good eating habits, all of which were so much
needed by the immigrant poor. Almost nobody believed that
the children were suffering from lack of any food; it was
rather the poor quality of their diet that caused concern. [56]

Like the recreation centers, school lunches at cost
had originated in England under settlement house auspices
and the idea had been brought to America by those social

56
     Hendrick and Kennaday, McClures, V, pp.122,123;
New York (City) Department of Education, Bulletin #3, 1914.
"he School lunch Service in New York City", p.10; Public
Education Association Bulletin #10, 1913, "Shall the Schools
serve Lunches?" p.2; Spargo, pp.88,104.

workers who knew of British developments. Philadelphia was the first American city to have such a program and New York saw the start of a very small scale project in the summer of 1908. Mabel Hyde Kittredge, an active figure in the charitable and reform movements of the day, had been a volunteer at a church in "Little Italy". She became convinced that one of the greatest needs of the tenement families was housekeeping knowledge and therefore she organized the first Practical Housekeeping Center in 1901 on Henry Street, in close cooperation with Lillian Wald's Henry St. Settlement.

The number of such centers grew and in 1908, Miss Kittredge began serving inexpensive lunches to the children of the vacation schools at P.S. 51. The principal of the regular school located there asked her to continue to do so during the rest of the school year. As a result of this successful experiment, Miss Kittredge broadened her group, changed its name to the School Lunch Committee, enlisted support from the Public Education Association, and began a program that continued from 1909 to 1919 when the Board of Education finally took it over. [57] The work of the Committee never blanketed the city but concentrated on the area below 14th St. and in Hell's Kitchen. By 1914, lunches were being served at 17 schools with a total

---

[57]
Morris. I. Berger, "The Settlement, The Immigrant and the Public School, (unpublished PH.D. dissertation, Columbia University), 1956, p.85; Hendrick and Kennaday, p.128; Spargo, p.110.

register of 24,087 children, although, of course, not all
the youngsters at any given school took advantage of the
[58]
program.

The School Lunch Committee had originally offered
a five, a three and a one cent lunch, but the children
resented the distinction and the Committee therefore adopted a standard three cent lunch. But this did not offer
enough variety, and since it was never compulsory to eat
lunch in school, the pickle stands continued to receive
large numbers of customers. Finally, the Committee adopted a one-cent-an-item plan, insisting only that every
child spend his first penny on soup and two slices of
bread. The boysandgirls could then use the rest of their
money on desserts like baked apples or custard, which were
also nourishing.

The cooking was done at a central building and
brought to the various schools where some of the children
served the food to their classmates and received free
lunch in return, although there was a paid supervisor in
charge at every lunchroom. Since the buildings were not
equipped for serving meals, the children ate standing up,
at portable counters which were set up each morning.
The foods which were prepared respected the preferences of
the various ethnic groups, so that at P.S. 20, the cuisine
was kosher and at P.S. 21, it was Italian, while meatless

---

[58]
"The School Lunch Service in New York City", p.9
Of these 17 schools at which lunch was available, 11 were
in areas of high immigrant population.

days were observed when appropriate.[59]

Good results were reported. One principal said he no longer needed to keep stomach remedies in his school, now that his pupils ate healthier lunches and the teachers saw improvements in learning ability, as well as manners.[60] The School Lunch Committee found the program a heavy financial burden and reported a deficit of $4,624, in 1914, even though by modern standards, the total cost of $17,889 was not very high.[61] Because of their difficulties in raising money, the Committee regularly appealed to the Board of Education to take over the program. They received some help from the Association for Improving the Condition of the Poor but in spite of much encouragement from school officials, they were unable to get the financial backing of the Department of Education until 1919, because the Board of Estimate would not appropriate the necessary funds.

---

[59] Hendrick and Kennaday, McClure's V, pp. 121,128; "Shall the Schools Serve Lunches?", p.2,4.

[60] "Shall Schools Serve Lunches?" p.4; Hendrick and Kennaday, McClure's V

[61] "The School Lunch Service in New York City", p.15.

Evangeline Whitney wanted a soup and milk program
in the vacation schools, hoping it might then be extended
to the regular schools. Elizabeth Farrell, alumnus of
the Henry Street Settlement and supervisor of ungraded
classes, urged that one cent a day be collected from the
children and be used for milk and whatever foods the
domestic science classes had prepared that day. Maxwell
strongly urged a publicly supported lunch program in
1906, 1910, 1912, and 1914, even collecting money personally from philanthropic individuals like Carnegie and
Guggenheim to help the School Lunch Committee,[62] but all
these suggestions came to nothing until much later.

Actually, a small sum _was_ allotted to the Committee by the Board of Estimate in 1913, but opposition to
the complete program was very great, due to the fear that
it would encourage destitution and further pauperize the
poor. Other opponents said the children would misbehave
create disturbances and engage in food throwing. Finally,
even people of humanitarian instincts, said these subsid-
ized lunches did nothing for the basic causes of malnutrition, but these individuals were answered by others who
said the schools must cope with the problems as they were;
not with their origins and thus should feed the hungry
children who faced them daily.

---

[62] Spargo, p.116; Fourth Annual Report of the City
Superintendent of Schools, 1902, p.63; Eighth Annual Report
of the City Superintendent of Schools, 1906, p.11; Twelfth
Annual Report of the City Superintendent of Schools, 1910,
p.207; Fourteenth Annual Report of the City Superintendent
of Schools, 1912, p.189; Sixteenth Annual Report of the City
Superintendent of Schools, 1914, pp. 174-175.

If tax-supported lunches seemed like carrying the
work of the schools too far into the realm of social
service, such arguments applied even more to another plan
originated by the settlement houses and urged upon the
schools, namely, the appointment of visiting teachers or
school social workers. This was a special project of the
Public Education Association, although suggested to them
by the settlement workers with whom they were so closely
allied. Actually, Hartley House and Greenwich House had
placed the first two visitors in Districts 9,10, and 11
as early as 1906, but the idea was not extended to other
areas until later.[63]

It was argued that visiting teachers were especially needed in New York City because/heterogeneous and
shifting population, ignorant parents, large and congested
schools and uniform curriculum for all children regardless
of background, made essential the services of a trained
visitor who would "discover...the causes of the difficulties which manifested themselves in poor scholarship,
annoying conduct and irregular attendance".[64]

In 1908, the Public Education Association convinced District Superintendent Julia Richman of the need for
school-home liason and at her request, the Association hired

[63]
    Hendrick and Kennaday, Mc Clure's,V, p.121; "Shall
the Schools Serve Lunches?" p.6.

[64]
    Mary Flexner, "The Visiting Teacher in Action",
Survey, XXX, (May 3, 1913, p.179; Harriet Johnson, The
Visiting Teacher in New York City (New York; 1916) p.xiv.

uch a visitor to begin an experimental program in one

chool in her Lower East Side district. The work of this

eacher was so successful, the Junior League offered to

ay the salary of four other visitors in different schools. [65]

Unfortunately, the ability of these charitable

rganizations to come up with the necessary funds was

imited. Therefore, Miss Richman and an associate, with

reat difficulty, raised additional money from the Russell

age Foundation, to support a total of seven visiting teach-

rs in the schools below 14th St., at the same time urging

upport from the Board of Education. [66] Although such support

as eventually forthcoming only for a special school for

motionally disturbed children, the various reform groups

anaged to keep the program going and by 1916 had visiting

eachers working in 33 schools in Manhattan and the Bronx,

ainly in areas of high immigrant population. [67]

The schools made most of the referrals to the

isitors, although they took cases brought to their atten-

ion by churches and settlement houses as well; providing

here were school aspects involved. A sample of the difficul-

es which came to their attention included poor grades,

ruancy, bad conduct, tardiness, ill health and "evil" home

---

[65]
Dorothy Whitney was an active member of both the
blic Education Association and the Junior League and was
e chief source of funds for this project. Cohen, p.77.

[66]
Richman, Forum, XLIII, pp. 163,164.

[67]
Johnson, p.vi.

conditions. The actions taken were highly individualized. First, the visiting teacher would take a detailed history of the child and his family. If indicated, the troubled youngster would be referred to one of the special classes set up in many of the schools. Sometimes just a transfer to another class or another school was successful. The visiting teacher always tried to make contact with the parents, explaining the school law and the opportunities available to their children. Many times, remedial physical care was the answer and the visitor would arrange eye examinations (free, with glasses, in some cases), take the children to the Manhattan Eye and Ear Hospital for hearing defect treatment, to dental clinics for their teeth and to orthopedic specialists for bone problems.

When all else failed, a recalcitrant parent or child could be threatened with legal proceedings or the possibility of the child's incarceration in the parental school. If dire poverty was discovered, direct relief was offered through donations of food and small ($1.50 to $3.00) weekly scholarships so that a child could remain in school. The visiting teacher was always flexible in her methods and with her time, and this was productive of success. One of the most interesting devices developed by these school social workers was group therapy sessions with adolescents, organized somewhat like clubs.

Superintendent Maxwell thought very highly of the work of these women, but was unable to persuade the Board of Estimate to appropriate the necessary funds. Therefore, he urged that regular teachers be required to make home visits to troubled children, but his suggestions were strongly opposed by the teacher organizations and except for the work of a few individuals, were never implemented.

With the growth of the social work profession, the activities of the visiting teacher became more and more separated from the schools, although the roots of the guidance programs developed later certainly lay, at least partly, in this early project. Although on a small scale, the visiting teacher idea illustrates the pattern of private charity and school cooperation which so marks the field of social service to the immigrant child. In most cases, the private agency was the initiator and brought pressure on the schools to take over the project, with varying degrees of success; total with the health services, eventual in the lunch program, and partial in regard to the visiting teacher.

68
    Flexner, Survey, XXX, pp.179-180; Johnson, pp.7, 25,65; Richman, Forum, XLIII, p.167; Fifteenth Annual Report of the City Superintendent of Schools, 1913, p.344; Twelfth Annual Report of the City Superintendent of Schools, 1910, p.197. The special classes were for the non-English speaking, the slow learners, the retarded, and the handicapped, all of which were developed during these years and are discussed in chapter five.

But even though the activities were limited and sometimes
slow to develop, the developing pattern of concern for the
children outside of the classroom became increasingly obvious.
Therefore programs arranged to meet the problems presented
by the immigrant poor were begun, to be expanded later as
money became available and techniques more polished.

As is clear from the names of the individuals
who have crossed these pages, many different reformers
were tremendously concerned with the school adjustment of
the immigrant child and the changes the schools needed to
make in order to cope with their new challenges. The
Public Education Association issued A Primer of Public
School Progress in 1914 in order to show how much had been
done, and Superintendent Maxwell wrote several articles to
show the achievements of the schools in the 25 years he had
been in their service.[69]

The underlying theme of all this was that the
schools of New York were bigger and better, in the sense
that they serviced more children in more ways by 1914, and
that this was how it should be. While not all the voices
who wanted the schools to limit themselves to the three
"R's" had been stilled, more and more, it came to be

---

[69]
Public Education Association, A Primer of Public
School Progress (New York, 1914) passim; William Henry
Maxwell, A Quarter Century of Public School Development,
passim; William Henry Maxwell, "School Achievements in
New York", Educational Review, LXIV, (October, 1912), passim.

expected that education would concern itself with the year round health and welfare of the pupil. The extension of the schools that had begun after the "school war" of 1895 and gathered momentum in the early years of the century became the normal pattern of school activity, accepted by pupils and public alike.

TABLE 7. NUMBER OF VACATION SCHOOLS   1899-1914

1899	15
1900	22
1901	27
1902	32
1903	54
1904	39
1905	33
1906	31
1907	31
1908	27
1909	30
1910	33
1911	32
1912	33
1913	33
1914	36

TABLE 8. NUMBER OF RECREATION CENTERS   1899-1914

1899	0
1900	5
1901	8
1902	12
1903	23
1904	23
1905	21
1906	30
1907	31
1908	22
1909	22
1910	32
1911	43
1912	48
1913	56
1914	62

TABLE 9. NUMBER OF PLAYGROUNDS   1899-1914

1899	0
1900	41
1901	58
1902	63
1903	64
1904	77
1905	67
1906	87
1907	99
1908	105
1909	246
1910	116
1911	236
1912	210
1913	203
1914	197

FIGURE 3. THE ORGANIZATION OF THE DEPARTMENT OF EDUCATION IN 1912.*

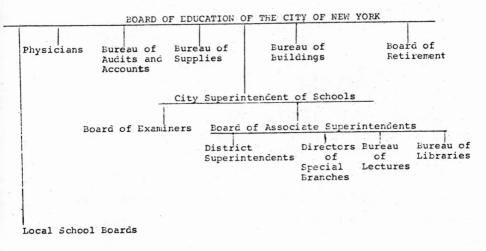

BOARD OF EDUCATION OF THE CITY OF NEW YORK

| Physicians | Bureau of Audits and Accounts | Bureau of Supplies | Bureau of Buildings | Board of Retirement |

City Superintendent of Schools

Board of Examiners   Board of Associate Superintendents

District Superintendents   Directors of Special Branches   Bureau of Lectures   Bureau of Libraries

Local School Boards

*Source: Directory of the Board of Education, 1912, p.5.

CHAPTER 5.

THE SCHOOLS TO FIT THE CHILD.

Ellwood Cubberly, distinguished Professor of education and commentator on the scholastic scene, wrote a book in 1909 in which he said (with some bitterness) that there was a "changing conception of the function of the school" and a new view of "the classes in society which the school of the future (was expected) to serve."[1] Cubberly was only one of many observers who saw that the conception of what education in the United States should be had changed enormously in the late 19th century.

While basic primary education had long been considered the right of an American child, and the "common school" (common to all the people) had been a hallmark of American society for generations, the vast majority of children had left the schoolhouse early in their life, and only the minority destined for college and the professions had remained to complete their elementary education.

---

[1]
Ellwood Cubberly, Changing Conceptions in Education (Boston: 1909), p.52.

In the decades following the Civil War, this pattern
had changed, mostly because of the upward revision of the
age at which a child could legally end his schooling, which
went from 10 to 12 and finally to 14 in 1903.[2]

Most of the children now required to remain in school
until adolescence were not bound for college and were unable
to cope with the difficult classical curriculum which made
up the studies of the grammar school at that time. Therefore, they lost interest, received failing marks and remained in the lower grades until they reached the school leaving age, profiting not at all from the additional years
they had been required to remain in the classroom.[3]   And
then the permissable age of 14 arrived--what then? Poorly
educated and totally untrained for positions in industry
and business, they took menial, dead-end jobs which added
little or nothing to their personal lives or to the economic
security of the families they soon began to raise.[4]

2
Raymond Callahan, Education and the Cult of Efficiency,
Chicago: 1962), p.15; I.L. Kandel, American Education in the
0th Century (Cambridge: 1957), p.24.

3
Lawrence A. Cremin, The Transformation of the School
New York: 1961), p.39.

4
William H. Kilpatrick, "Educational Philosophy" in
. L. Kandel. (ed.) Twenty-Five Years of American Education
New York: 1929) p.276.

Thus, a double challenge was presented to the schools of the 20th century--to simplify the entire curriculum in order to meet the needs of the average child, not merely the scholar, and to make provision for industrial and commercial education so that, after graduation, most of the children could find positions in the industrial and business world of the day. In the great cities, like New York, the influx of the immigrant children added urgency to the search for new methods and new subjects with which to reach the expanded school clientele.

The results of the quest were many and varied. The curriculum was revised by the inclusion of domestic science, manual training and physical education, and the three "R's" were brought up to date. Halting steps were taken in the direction of industrial education, and for the first time, efforts were made to educate the exceptional child, handicapped physically, mentally or by reason of foreign birth.

While the changing conception of education was a nationwide phenomenon and not unique to New York City, efforts here had an air of urgency about them because of the pressures of numbers and the greater complexity of the problems. Not only did basic skills and subjects have to be taught, but knowledge of the adopted country --its language, customs and laws had to be included in the already crowded course of study.[5] It was no wonder that so many immigrant children fell by the wayside and required remedial

[5] New York (City) Department of Education. Addresses delivered at the opening of the new Hall of the Board of Education, February 22, 1900, p.20

work to catch up with their classmates. The widespread difficulties led to continuing effort on the part of the educational authorities to determine exactly why so many of the children were failing.[6]

The first area which came under scrutiny was the basic elementary curriculum, because if primary education could not reach the youngest children, no other refinements would be very successful, and judging by the studies made of the number of overage children in the New York City public schools, a great many youngsters were not learning the necessary skills.

Superintendent Maxwell, who did not claim modesty as one of his many virtues, said that he was the first person in the world to call attention to the problem of the over age student.[7] Actually, in 1904, he did supervise the first age-grade statistical compiliation made anywhere in the United States which showed that 39% of all elementary school children in New York City were over age. The percent of retardation increased with the grade, so that 23.2% of all first graders were older than the standard six years, and 49% of the fifth graders were more than the normal age of ten. Interestingly, the percent of over age youngsters was

---

[6] New York (City) Department of Education, _Thirteenth Annual Report of the City Superintendent of Schools_, 1911, p.240.

[7] _Ibid._, p.59

lower in the seventh and eighth grades because the most retarded youngsters had dropped out of school by then.[8]
Maxwell's report stimulated the Russell Sage Foundation to
finance another survey into the problem. This was done by
Leonard Ayres, Director of Educational Research for the foundation, in 1908, and resulted in similar findings. Out of the
total of 20,000 children who were tested, 23% were found to
be above the normal age for their grade. 9,489 pupils were
examined intensively and it was determined that 5% of this
number progressed at a rate faster than normal, 55% were
promoted at the standard rate, and 40% were overage for
the grade in which they were.

Ayres reported finding "many children...who had begun
their school lives before their present classmates were born".
These must have been extreme examples because the study
determined that, on the whole, it took the average child
9.48 years to complete the standard eight grades of work
Finally, the report indicated that girls tended to be les.
retarded than boy students, possibly because the curriculum
suited them better.[9]

Many reasons were offered for the existence of the
problem. In 1904, Maxwell thought that the over-large classes,

---

[8]
Sixth Annual Report of the City Superintendent of
Schools, 1904, p.47. The exact percentages are as follows:

1st grade - 23.2%	5th grade - 49%
2nd grade - 38.1%	6th grade - 42%
3rd grade - 45%	7th grade - 32%
4th grade - 49%	8th grade - 25.3%

[9]
Leonard P. Ayres, Laggards in our Schools (New York:
1909, pp.107, 82,87,5.

part-time education, and late entry age on the part of the
immigrant children were the basic causes.[10]   The chief in-

vestigator for the Grout Inquiry, Mrs. Mathilde Coffin Ford,

thought the origin lay in the course of study which was both

too difficult and too crowded.[11]   By 1906, the Superintendent

said decisively that the late entry and paucity of educa-

tion of the immigrant child was the major reason for the

high percentage of retardation in the New York City elementary

schools.

> In this city-the chief center of immigration-- it
> it inevitable that there will always be found in
> every grade many children beyond the normal age.
> Tens of thousands of children come to our schools
> every year from abroad, the majority of whom cannot
> speak our language and a considerable proportion of
> whom (have) had little or no school instruction
> before they reached our shores. 12

Ayres agreed with this estimate of the causes, saying
that foreigners, regardless of age, always constituted a

larger proportion of the lower grades than they did of the

upper or the high schools. But he thought the most important

causes of retardation were that the course of study was fitted

only to the bright child, and that the teachers greatly in
varied

10
     Sixth Annual Report of the City Superintendent of
Schools, 1904, p. 48

11
     New York (City) Board of Estimate and Apportionment,
Reports of an Investigation Concerning the Cost of Maintaining
the Public School System of the City of N.Y., (New York; 1905)
p.64.
12
     Seventh Annual Report of the City Superintendent of
Schools, 1905, p.63.

competence.[13] Very likely the rapid growth in the number of school children combined with the inadequate school building program was at fault, as well as the frequent shifts of population within the city, because the content and methodology of the elementary school work varied greatly from school to school, although a uniform curriculum was always one of Maxwell's goals.[14]

After the publication of the Ayres Survey, the Superintendent appointed a committee of principals to study the causes of retardation. They reported in 1909 and said that truancy, due to the failure of the courts to enforce the compulsory education law; the lack of parental cooperation and the shortage of attendance officers was the major reason for the lack of normal progress on the part of so many children. In addition, the principals thought inefficient teachers, the overuse of substitutes, the lack of uniform standards for promotion, the part time sessions and, to a great extent, the poverty and anti-school attitudes of many of the foreign children were contributing causes of this problem.[15]

---

[13] Leonard Ayres, pp. 114,5,48.

[14] Harold McCormick, "The First Fifty Years" in the Fiftieth Annual Report of the City Superintendent of Schools 1940, p.30.

[15] McCormick, p.32.

While Maxwell did not deny that any of these reasons were operative, he still tended to place most of the responsibility on the late school entry of the immigrant child, saying, in an article entitled "The City and the Child" that there were more foreign children between 12 and 14 in grades one to six than in grades seven to eight where they belonged.[16] Maintaining his interest in the problem, which he called the greatest facing the schools, the Superintendent appointed still another committee of teachers, to study the causes in 1910.

The results of this inquiry indicated that irregular attendance due largely to poverty and poor home conditions, ignorance of English "due to foreign birth and to the fact that English is not the language of the home", physical defects on the part of a number of the children, prolonged and frequent absences of the teachers, and the slow mentality and emotionally disturbed background of many of the youngsters all contributed to the situation.[17]

The actual mechanism which had caused the problem of the overage child was non-promotion. When a child could

---

[16] William Henry Maxwell, "The City and the Child", Publications of the National Recreation Association of America, XXVI, no date, pp. 7-8.

[17] Twelfth Annual Report of the City Superintendent of Schools, 1910, pp. 80-81.

not do the required work, he was simply left back to repeat the grade. Promotion was semi-annual and very much at the direction of the teacher. Julia Richman was perhaps telling secrets out of school when she said the number of promotions often depended on the need for space in the grade below and not on the work done by the child.[18]

Miss Richman was in a position to know such facts because she had devoted considerable time and energy to the problem of non-promotion while she was principal of P.S. 77. No child was ever made to repeat a grade more than once, she pointed out, and therefore, whether the material had been learned or not, the slow child entered the next grade after repeating the lower one. These children, known as "holdovers", suffered from a system in which individualized instruction was not possible, because the "...teachers had not been trained to teach different grades or different parts of the same grade simultaneously" and the children were not used to doing work on their own.[19]

---

[18]
First Annual Report of the City Superintendent of Schools, 1899, pp. 113,114.

[19]
Julia Richman, "A Successful Experiment in Promoting Pupils", Educational Review, XVIII (June, 1899), p.24.

Because of the inadequacy of the staff and the lack
of equipment such as movable furniture, which might have
made individualized instruction practical, it was virtually
impossible for a failing child to receive remedial help
during school hours, and as a result, the "holdovers" repeated grade after grade until they dropped out of. school
entirely. Troubled by the waste and unfairness of this
arrangement, Miss Richman had taken several tentative steps
toward. classification of the children in the hope that this
might lead to some individualized teaching. At promotion
time she had been dividing the youngsters at her school
into "positively fit, positively unfit and doubtful."
There was not much question about what to do with the
children in the first two categories, but the doubtful
ones were numbered in "order of merit" and promoted in turn
until the grade above was filled to its extreme limit. This
had to be because "the inexorable pressure from without for
admission to the school absolutely forbade a vacant seat
anywhere..."[20]

Under the system of forced promotion, the bright
child suffered because his class had lots of dullards and
disciplinary problems .and the slow child was in even deeper trouble because the tasks were beyond his ability. Julia
Richman's sense of justice was offended by this situation
and therefore, in September, 1898, she formed "bright,

20
  Ibid.

medium, and poor" classes on the same grade level, and if
only two rooms were available, made at least two classes,
of the best and of the worst students. The "better or
more experienced teachers were placed in charge of the poorer material" in line with her belief that the slowest
children needed the most expert handling. This plan of
Julia Richman's was the origin of homogeneous grouping in
New York City, a concept to be developed and argued about
all through the next fifty years. The new scheme had an
additional feature which represented quite an innovation
for education in New York--flexible promotion.

The marking system was highly individualized and
so was the rate of advancement. A dull child was given
six months to complete a simplified version of the term's
work, while a bright one could be promoted in mid-term, if
his marks justified. Although Miss Richman admitted that
the shifting of pupils all year caused some disruption,
she felt this was a small price to pay because of the
good effects on the dull children when they lost their
sense of failure and began to grow "through self-help and
self-development." For the bright children, now stimulated
by being in a class with their peers, the benefits were also
considerable, and their apathy and laziness vanished. All
in all, the new system was a great improvement over the
uniform grading and promotion which had so displeased this
particular principal.[21]

[21]
Ibid., pp. 23-29.

The P.S. 77 plan could not have spread much beyond
the boundaries of that school for a number of years,
because when Leonard Ayres made his study of retardation in
1908, he reported city-wide conditions to be much as they had
been in Julia Richman's school prior to 1898. He said that
children who were left back simply stayed in their regular
classes, often with the same teacher who had denied them
promotion the previous term. New York City had one of the
lowest promotion rates in the nation, this study reported,
and spent 12.6% of its total school budget on repeaters.[22]
It is no wonder the educational authorities were concerned.
Ayres thought a combination of remedies would lower the
non-promotion rate. He recommended flexible grading, homogeneous grouping, a limit on transfers and that teachers
discontinue the practice of leaving children back as a
means of punishing them for poor conduct, which was evidently being done.[23]

In 1908, Maxwell drew some conclusions from the
part of Ayres' report which had indicated that the 43% of the

---

[22]
    Ayres, pp. 143,96.

[23]
    Ibid.,p.218.

children who were retarded were so because of late school
entry, and recommended that six years be made the compulsory age for entrance into first grade, hoping that an
earlier start would tend to reduce the possibility of
being left back.[24]

A table developed for the Superintendent's report of
1911 showed that the greatest number of non-promotions in
Manhattan occurred on the Lower East Side, while District
9, which was predominantly Italian had the largest number
of children repeating a grade. District 31, in the Brownsville area, had the greatest number of non-promotions in
Brooklyn, all of which would tend to indicate that the
immigrant children had the most difficulty keeping up with
their grade level.[25]

The child who was kept behind and became more and
more overage in relation to his grade level was most likely
to be a dropout long before completing the normal eight
grades. Maxwell gave an example of how harmful this could
be when he pointed out that a boy of 14 who had a fourth
grade education was "handicapped for life".[26]

---

[24]
Tenth Annual Report of the City Superintendent of
of Schools, 1908, p.64. Since 1902, children could enter at
six years of age, but did not have to attend school until
they were eight years old.

[25]
Thirteenth Annual Report of the City Superintendent
of Schools, 1911, pp. 78-79.

[26]
Eleventh Annual Report of the City Superintendent
of Schools, 1909, p.75

The completion of the sixth grade often coincided with the 14th birthday of many of the children and the event was often marked by an application for working papers and the end of formal schooling. The Superintendent asked teachers to pay special attention to this "dangerous" time in the children's school life, because the youngsters were totally unprepared for employment and should therefore remain to complete at least the eighth grade.[27]

Girls were less of a worry; in addition to being promoted more often, they tended to stay in school longer.[28] An incident related by a reporter for the New York Times in 1904 indicated one reason why boys left school. In a third grade class in Little Italy, 34 boys ranging from 11 to 15 years old were engaged in basting two pieces of cloth together evidencing great boredom all the while. The teacher explained that this kind of activity kept them busy and that they liked it because they were naturally artistic![29] Such an educational experience was not likely to reduce the number of dropouts.

In 1912, the Public Education Association conducted a vocational guidance survey of two Lower East Side school

---

[27]
Fifteenth Annual Report of the City Superintendent of Schools, 1913, p.43

[28]
Fourth Annual Report of the City Superintendent of Schools, 1902, p.40

[29]
New York Times, February 22, 1904, p.5

districts and reported their findings to the Board of
Education. It appeared to them that economic need was not
the main reason why children dropped out of school, although this certainly was a contributing factor. Rather,
it was apathy on the part of the youngsters, and a desire
to be free of the boredom and restraints of school that
caused them to leave at 14. No good results came of this
early school leaving, reported the committee, because the
boys and girls could get only very temporary, inadequate
and poorly paying jobs (if any) and soon tired of them.[30]

The problem, then, was real and obvious. For many
children, especially those with foreign backgrounds, the
course of study offered by the elementary school was
totally unsuitable, and the results of this were very
serious--both for the individual youngster and for society
as a whole. Here was a truly educational matter--not one
that could be blamed on poverty or bad housing. The
schools had to revise, adjust and experiment with their
curriculum in order to reach the greatest number of children
for the longest possible period of time. To this task
the educational authorities devoted themselves all through
the years 1902 to 1914, with varied results.

In Maxwell's very first report as City Superintendent

---

[30] Fourteenth Annual Report of the City Superintendent
of Schools, 1912, p.385.

he recommended that a survey be made of the children who
were mentally or physically unable to cope with the
regular school work, and suggested further that special
classes be set up for such youngsters.[31] This proposal was
made in a very low-key way; unlike some of the Superintendent's other ideas. It was almost as though he really
did not think the newly organized city school system would
pay much attention. Basically he was correct; most educational officials were just coping with the daily problems
of the schools, but a few were concerned enough to give
the problem of special classes some thought, and foremost
among this group was Julia Richman, the principal who had
been so disturbed by the uniform promotion system.

This remarkable woman had been born in the Chelsea
district of New York City in October of 1855, the third
child of Jewish immigrant parents who had emigrated to
the United States from their native Bohemia. The family
was middle class and included rabbis and teachers among
their European ancestors. Mr. Moses Richman, her father,
was a painter and glazier of some skill, later receiving
the contract for the glass work in the Peter Cooper Institute. When Julia was five, the family moved to Huntington,
Long Island and remained there for six years, returning to
the city in 1866. The future superintendent attended
elementary school at P.S. 50 on East 20th St. and then went
to the Normal College, from which she was graduated before
her 17th birthday.

---

[31] _First Annual Report of the City Superintendent
of Schools_, 1899, p.130,132.

Although her father objected, Julia obtained her
teacher's license a few months later and began her 40 year
pedagogical career with a boy's class at P.S. 59. She had
achieved this appointment with the aid of some prominent
Democratic politicians, but should never have been allowed
to teach at that age. Unable to cope with the unruly boys
in her class, she obtained a transfer to the girl's division of the same school and here achieved a marked success.
In 1882 she was made vice-principal of P.S. 73, and two
years later became the first woman principal of the Jewish
faith in New York City, having in her care the children
of P.S. 77 at First Ave. and 86th St. Miss Richman made
this institution a showplace and a "pattern" school, to
which visitors came from all over in order to see the
educational innovations she had begun. After 19 years as
principal, she was appointed district superintendent, the
first of her faith to be so honored. When the appointment
was offered, her male colleagues deferred to her womanly
status and gave her a choice as to which districts she
would supervise. To their great surprise, Julia Richman
chose the Lower East Side as her bailiwick, "because the
tremendous influx of immigrants had brought problems there
which no other section of the city faced."[32]

---

[32]
Bertha R. Proskauer and Addie R. Altman, Two
Biographical Appreciations of the Great Educator (New York:
1916), p.10.

She was fully aware of the dimensions of her job
in this congested area. Although not of the newest wave
of Jewish immigrants herself, she had worked for years
with the Educational Alliance, and her devotion to the
ideals of Judaism, shown in the temple affiliation she had
maintained over the decades, made it only natural for her
to choose the teeming East Side for her special province.
So complete was her dedication, she purchased a house in
the heart of the Ghetto and made it a Teacher's Settlement,
encouraging the personnel of the Lower East Side schools to
take up residence there in order to be closer to the
community they served. Miss Richman lived there herself
for some period of time, although maintaining a permanent
address at 330 Central Park West with her brother Daniel.
Her school office was at P.S. 65 on Eldridge St. and from
there she presided over the educational problems of the
23,000 children and 600 teachers who occupied the 14
schools of her district.

In addition to the great responsibilities of her
job, Julia Richman engaged in many supplementary activities.
Her role with the Educational Alliance was not honorary;
she was fund raiser, producer of Sunday afternoon plays
for children, member of half a dozen committees, and the
link between the Alliance and the public schools. In
addition, she was an organizer for the National Council
of Jewish Women, and utilized the services of this group

to obtain certain benefits, such as free eyeglasses, for
the deprived children in her care. Always an advocate
of healthful exercise, and aware of the limited opportunities for such activities available to the children of
the slums, she was a director of the girl's branch of the
Public Schools Athletic League from 1905 to 1910.

Energy like hers was truly remarkable, since while
she was engaged in all these peripheral activities, her
major work as superintendent was not neglected. By 1912,
she was very tired and on the verge of a physical break-
down. Hoping to regain her strength, she requested a
leave from the Board of Education and sailed for France
on the "Victoria Luise", planning to spend the summer at
Versailles, and resign as superintendent in September,
devoting "herself to educational work in the Russian-
Jewish quarter of New York", and to the writing of her
memoirs. Unfortunately, she was stricken with appendicitis
while the ship was on the high seas, and did not reach the
American hospital at Neuilly, France in time. Although an
operation was performed, peritonitis set in and Julia
Richman died on June 24, at the age of 57.[33]

The flags of all the school buildings of New York
flew at half mast when the news of her death reached the
city, and the eulogies about her from Superintendent

[33] Proskauer and Altman, pp. 7-27; The New York Times,
June 26, 1912, p.13; June 27, 1912, pp.11,13; June 29,1912,
p.11.

Maxwell, individual Board of Education members, the officers
of the Educational Alliance, and the National Council of
Jewish Women filled many columns of the Times. Maxwell in
particular, seemed very moved by her death and summed up
her contributions to public education in New York City in
these words:

> She was inventive and creative (and) an excellent
> executive and supervisor. Intellectually honest,
> she never made colorless or inaccurate reports.
> She...believed that...the home, the church and
> the school (should) cooperate to improve the
> child's environment. 34

The Superintendent's statement regarding her colorful
reports was certainly true. The minutes of the Board of
Superintendents for the years during which she was active,
are marked by frequent clear calls from her for all sorts
of projects which would improve the schools, in contrast
to her colleagues who usually limited themselves to dry
statistical statements regarding conditions in their
districts.

When her two sisters wrote their "appreciation" of
her, this social work ideology of Julia Richman was also
stressed. She was interested in welfare work from childhood on, said one sister, and the other quoted her as
believing that the curriculum was less important than the
condition of the individual child, using as an example
this thought:

34
Fourteenth Annual Report of the City Superintendent
of Schools, 1912, pp 266-267.

It is so much easier and so much prettier to
teach the oath of allegiance to the flag, than
to teach a community to keep the fire escapes
free from encumbrances, and yet which is more
important?   35

The clearest statement of her ideas on education
as she believed it needed to be in the 20th century was
found in an article she wrote for the social work magazine
Survey in 1904, when she was the district superintendent
in Lower Manhattan. Entitled, "What Can be Done in a Graded
School for the Backward Child", it explained in detail a
plan for the special classes which she had come to believe
were essential to the children of the slums. This article
was probably the stimulus for the program of new groupings
on which the school system embarked on at that time.

Miss Fichman explained that she had become a
superintendent just as a new and stronger compulsory education law had been passed, in 1903. She ordered an investigation into the records of the children into her district
who were applying for working papers and found that 1,719
youngsters were 14 but had not finished fifth grade, (as
the law required) which she thought was "appalling." Most
of these children were of immigrant backgrounds but not
recent arrivals in the United States. Therefore, she said,
the failure of these youngsters to go through the required

35
Proskauer and Altman, p.11.

grades could not be blamed on their late entry into the
schools alone, but must be considered the fault of the
educational system in New York.

She documented this idea by suggesting the reasons
why the mass of 14 years old was unable to meet the requirements of the law. Many of them had been "unwisely
classified and too slowly promoted". Others had been
turned away from school or kept for years on waiting lists
n the days when principals had that privilege". Some had
been expelled for unruly behavior while others had been
excluded for reasons of contagion and stayed out of school
longer than necessary. Never one to gloss over the defects
n the school system, Julia Richman said a number of these
youngsters were "children whose minds had been spoiled in
he days when only a substitute was placed in charge of the
afternoon part-time classes". Also, some of them were truly
defective in physical or emotional areas and had received
o special attention. Hearkening back to her earlier study,
he blamed the mass promotion system for much of the retardation.[36]

Having uncovered these facts, Miss Richman squarely
presented them to the Board of Superintendents and asked
will your board give me as district superintendent authority
o form for the benefit of these children special classes
whereever I deem it necessary"? If the answer was yes --

---

[36]
Julia Richman, "What Can be Done in a Graded
chool for the Backward Child", Survey, XIII (October, 1904
p. 129-131.

would the Board arrange a simplified course of study to
consist of just "...the absolute essentials demanded by
the compulsory education law?" She went on: "The omission
of paper folding, construction of paper boxes, knotting of
cord, sight reading in music, illustrative drawing and many
other requirements of our present course (even though they
have a distinct educational value to the normal child of
English speaking parents) will make it possible to cover
the work of two or more grades in one term" and thus bring
the children closer to fifth grade by age 14.[37]   As a by-
product of forming these advanced classes, children with
mental and physical weaknesses would be separated from the
normal, and special classes of a different nature could be
set up for them as well.

The Board of Superintendents referred Miss Richman's
request to their committee on compulsory education, which
reported favorably a few days later and ordered the
Associate Superintendents to confer with their District
Superintendents "with a view to organizing special classes in
the schools, to provide instruction for children who
are...far below...grade."[38]   By the following September,

---

[37] New York (City) Department of Education, Minutes
of the Board of Superintendents, December 14, 1903, p.1627.

[38] Minutes of the Board of Superintendents, December,
28, 1903, p.1682.

the districts in Julia Richman's care had 21 such classes
in 10 schools, with a total register of 652 youngsters. She
was delighted because she foresaw great benefits to both
the child in the special class and the one who did not need
additional work.

"The object of these classes is to fit the (overage
child) to become a decent, self-respecting wage earner and
a creditable member of society." The regular class would
be much better off without these older children because

> The boy or girl of 12 or 13 or 14 years who is
> placed in a class where the work prescribed and
> methods employed are designed for children from
> six to nine years of age, is almost without ex-
> ception, a burden to the teacher and a menace to
> the discipline of the class.   39

Superintendent Richman said that she did not know
to what extent these special classes were being established in other districts, but she was harsh on principals who
did not see the advantage in them.

> One can only pray that either God or the Board of
> Education may remove him or her before greater
> wrongs may come to the children. Until every
> principal and every teacher can be made to see
> that to save the soul and character of the child
> is a far higher achievement than to obtain a high
> average in arithmetic, grammar or spelling, it
> will be impossible to give every child a child's
> rights.   40

39
  Julia Richman, Survey, XIII, p.131.

40
  Ibid.

Although by far the most articulate and the earliest proponent of special classes, Julia Richman was not the only one. At P.S. 114 in an Italian district, the principal had established a "salvage" class, where boys were placed in a special group to work at subjects they had failed. Each was given a graph on which to record his personal progress. The results indicated considerable success--the principal report-ed a great decrease in truancy and a growth in the self con-fidence of the boys.[41]

By 1905, Associate Superintendent Meleney had ab-sorbed at least part of the idea of homogeneous grouping and recommended a two track course of study for the entire system; I for normal and bright children and II for all those who were not academically minded or who were re-tarded.[42] In the same year, Superintendent Maxwell added up the number of special classes in the city as a whole and found that 95 such groups with 2,677 children were in existence in Manhattan, two, with 67 youngsters were locat-ed in the Bronx, and eight with 209 children, were present in Brooklyn. Of the 77 schools which had some type of

---

[41] Mary Fabian Matthews, "The Role of the Public School in the Assimilation of the Italian Immigrant Child in New York City, 1900-1914" (unpublished Ph.d. disserta-tion, Fordham University, 1966), p.277.

[42] Seventh Annual Report of the City Superintendent of Schools, 1905, pp. 144-146.

pecial classes at this time, 44 had large immigrant popula-

ions which would indicate the close relationship between

he needs of the alien children and the response of the
[43]
chools.

As the figures indicated, Brooklyn had a comparative-

y small number of special classes and the Superintendent in

harge of a portion of that borough explained why in 1907.

> Owing to the large number of pupils on part-time
> in Division VI (Brownsville and South Brooklyn)
> it has not been deemed advisable to make an undue
> increase in this number by the organization of
> many small special classes...

The Superintendent did indicate that many of these
[44]
hildren received some after school help from their teachers.

y the next year, Meleney reported that a few more special

lasses had been established, but his superior, Maxwell,

as not satisfied, saying that the principals had not taken

hough advantage of their discretionary power to establish
[45]
ach special groupings.

The blame was shifted to the teachers by the

ssociate Superintendent for the Bronx in 1909, who said the

ason for the paucity of special classes in his district
[46]
as the laziness and inertia of the staff.

---

[43]
Ibid., p.384
[44]
Ninth Annual Report of the City Superintendent of
chools, 1907, p.201
[45]
Tenth Annual Report of the City Superintendent of
chools, 1908, pp. 204, 62.
[46]
Eleventh Annual Report of the City Superintendent
Schools, 1909, pp. 235-236.

Queens and Richmond were slow to establish these innovations, mostly because they had almost no immigrant children, although a few working-paper classes had been formed by 1911.[47] In the same year, Superintendent Meleney found himself discouraged by the opposition of "district superintendents, principals and teachers" to the idea of special classes. He said that in many schools "...the foreign and backward pupils have been allowed to remain in regular classes and have not been instructed according to their needs."[48]

It would appear that the formation of these classes, as with so much else in the school system, was erratic and variable. The area which needed them most, however, had the greatest number and achieved the most success in their use. This was Division I, where Julia Richman had begun her experiment in 1904. By 1908, her Division Superintendent, Gustave Straubenmuller, was able to report the existence of 150 special classes with about 25 children in each, most of whom were improving daily. Indeed, Mr. Straubenmuller said that many of the youngsters did so well in the smaller, less pressured classes, they abandoned the idea of leaving school at 14 and remained to prepare for high school![49]

---

[47] Thirteenth Annual Report of the City Superintendent of Schools, 1911, p.270

[48] Ibid., p.258

[49] Tenth Annual Report of the City Superintendent of Schools, 1908, p.168.

In 1910, Maxwell saw a decrease in the number of
overage children in the schools below 14th St. and he
credited the special classes for this improvement, since
they were enabling the large numbers of immigrant children
who entered school late to catch up and move ahead.[50]   It
was left, fittingly, to the Associate Superintendent for
the Lower East Side to develop the educational philosophy
behind the idea of special classes, some years after they
had been in operation. As with so many of the changes in
the schools in this era, the response preceded the formu-
lation of the theory, because, as in this case, the retarded 14 year olds clamoring for working papers could not
wait for pedagogical discussions.

In 1910, Mr. Straubenmuller stated that

> In large cities...the unprecedented inpouring of
> children of all ages from countries where they
> have had no educational advantages, imposes
> upon the schools the burden of teaching them the
> language, the task of overcoming their mental
> retardation, due to neglect, and the assumption,
> in many cases, of their entire mental and moral
> training...

These additional responsibilities required the schools to
abbreviate the traditional subject matter and to reorganize
the conventional grading system. The special classes were
a step in this direction, but Superintendent Straubenmuller
believed that homogeneous grouping, should be extended to
regular classes as well, so that the school system would

---

[50]
    Twelfth Annual Report of the City Superintendent
of Schools, 1910, pp. 77,103.

have slow, normal, and bright classes, as well as the special working paper and foreign language ones. He urged that the teachers recognize the individual needs of the children, which in a city as varied as New York could range from genius to mental defective.[51]

A year later he reported that he had been able to establish this three track system at P.S. 20 on Rivington Street with reasonable success. The achievement would have been greater if the teachers had been more able and cooperative. He put in a final plea for the need for special grouping in New York City at that time.

"Equal educational rights for all cannot be sustained until we give attention to the needs of the child and adapt courses of study and syllabuses to the physical and mental capacity of the children in our schools. We should be courageous enough to teach the child only what it is capable of learning and attempt to do no more".[52] Superintendents Straubenmuller and Richman must have worked well together, because they appeared to have shared a common educational philosophy, of which the immigrant children of the East Side were the beneficiaries.[53] Their efforts found

---

[51] Ibid. pp 227-236

[52] Thirteenth Annual Report of the City Superintendent of Schools, 1911, p. 240.

[53] Figure II indicates how Associate Superintendent Straubenmuller, who was in charge of Division I (Lower East Side), was the superior of District Superintendent Richman.

favor with the Public Education Association which urged the Board of Education to

> adopt as its working policy the principle that
> all children of whatever condition and capacity
> are entitled to as much education as they are
> capable of receiving and that the Board of
> Education, accordingly, shall include in its
> plans the children now lacking such provision. [54]

Since the lack of English of the alien children was the most obvious cause of all their other problems, it was only natural that the classes for non-English speaking children should have been the most developed. These groups were variously called "steamer", "vestibule", or "C" classes, but they all had the same function: to get the foreign child over the language barrier in the shortest possible period of time.

The origin of these classes lay in a unique settlement house whose influence on the Russian Jewish immigrants was incalculable-- The Educational Alliance. It was organized in 1890 as one of the beneficiaries of the Baron de Hirsch Fund, an endowment established by a wealthy European Jew to aid his suffering co-religionists emigrate from Russia. One of the first activities of the De Hirsch Fund in New York City was to establish English classes for the immigrant children, where arithmetic, penmanship and geography were taught, as well as the essential new language. As soon as a child learned enough English, and an opening for him was

---

[54]
Sol Cohen, Progressives & Urban School Reform, (New York; 1964), p. 55, 69

found, he was entered in public school, because the intent
of these classes was not to replace the regular educational
structure but simply to prepare the immigrant child for
entry into the schools.[55]

The Fund classes became so popular, it was necessary
to restrict admission only to the totally non-English speaking but even so, the drain on the resources of the organization was very heavy and the Board of Directors sought to
shift the burden to the public schools. Prior to 1904,
however, there was no comparable facility in any tax-supported school, and the De Hirsch Fund classes continued.[56]   In
1901, there were 506 children in these units with an excellent attendance rate of 94%.[57]

By 1905, Superintendent Maxwell's interest in the
problem of the non-English speaking child had grown to the
point where he discussed it in an address he made before
the National Education Association.

---

[55]
Samuel Joseph, History of the Baron de Hirsch Fund,
(New York: 1935), pp. 9, 253, 255.

[56]
Ibid. p.257

[57]
Educational Alliance, Ninth Report, 1901, p.17.

> It is absurd to place the boy or girl, 10 or 12
> years of age, just landed from Italy, who cannot
> read a word in his own language, or speak a word
> of English, in the same class with American boys
> and girls five or six years old.   58

Special classes, such as those developed at the Educational

Alliance, were essential. A few such groups had been

started on the Lower East Side during the previous year

and by 1905 there were 250 "C" classes in existence.

As the Superintendent described the work, it appear-

ed that during the first five or six months the children

spent in one of these classes, they devoted their time

"almost exclusively" to learning to speak, read and write

English. "As soon as they...acquired the linguistic medium

they (were) transferred to the grades where they appropriate-

ly belonged". Maxwell contrasted this with the previous

custom, which "was to place all of the children, no matter

what their age, in the lowest or next to the lowest grade.

This arrangement was the most ineffective possible for the

immigrants, and seriously retarded the progress of the
                                   59
regular first year children".

By the following year, the Board of Superintendents

got around to publishing a syllabus for the use of "C"

classes. First discussing organization of the group, the

Superintendents suggested the following order of preference:

58
     William Henry Maxwell, A Quarter Century of Public
School Development (New York: 1912), p.378.

59
     Seventh Annual Report of the City Superintendent
of Schools, 1905, p.64.

First, children over eight with no European education
were to be admitted, then partially educated children over
eight, and finally children under eight, if there was enough
room. The aim of these classes, said the Superintendents,
was to give the youngsters enough English quickly so that
they could enter a normal class.

Only the language of their adopted country was to
be used in the classroom and the teacher was to begin with
oral training, using concrete objects and illustrating verbs
by her actions. There was to be drill "en masse" on pronunciation and when a class had mastered this part of the work,
they were to move on to written lessons using "child centered"themes. The teacher was asked to praise the children
liberally and talk conversationally with them, using ges-
tures and smiles until the pupils could understand her
words. She was cautioned to go slow, review often and to
teach the phrases and directions the youngsters would need
in their regular classes later. All in all, the syllabus
was most specific, even providing model lessons and a
daily routine, and it was noteworthy for its emphasis on
individual attention and the need to draw from the children's
apperceptive basis, techniques not adopted in general teaching until years later.[60]

---

[60] New York (City) Department of Education. A Syllabus
for the Teaching of English to Grade "C" classes in the
Elementary Day Schools, 1906, pp 3-8.

A member of the Child Study Committee of the Normal
College Alumni conducted a three month investigation into
the operation of these "C" classes in 1906 and reported
favorably. The children, she said, were chiefly Russian
Jews and Italians, and the aim of the teacher was to get
them to express themselves in English. "They learn the
names of objects, occupations and allied words and how to
apply them properly". Many children spent only six weeks
in these classes and those who were literate in some language,
predictably did the best.[61]

At various times, it was suggested that additional
subjects be added to the curriculum of the "C" classes,
such as sewing for girls, shop for boys and hygiene for all,
but the Board of Superintendents resisted these ideas, insisting that the "C" class was only a "vestibule" to the
regular class where all such subjects would later be learned.

In 1906, the Division Superintendent for the Lower
East Side could report at least one "C" class in nearly
every school in his area; no mean achievement for a program
only two years old. In the city as a whole, 1,458 children
were in these "steamer" classes, the greatest number of
course, being in Manhattan.[62] By the following year, 1,616

[61]
     Jessie Rosenfield, "Special Classes in the Public
Schools of New York", Education, XXVII, (October, 1906), p.99.

[62]
     Eighth Annual Report of the City Superintendent of
Schools, 1906, p.137,55.

youngsters were getting this kind of help, and the number
increased to 1.742 in 1908.[63]   The organization of these
classes, while far smoother than many other new projects
the schools undertook, was not without its problems.
Sometimes two "C" classes had to occupy the same room
with two separate teachers, due to a shortage of space,
and many schools, especially in Brownsville and Williamsburg, although they had large numbers of foreign born
children, had no such classes at all.[64]

The Board of Superintendents appointed a committee
consisting of Messrs. Straubenmuller, Meleney and Haaren
to evaluate the "C" classes in 1909, using a questionnaire
to be filled out by the teachers of these pupils.[65]   The
results were satisfactory and in addition, the New York
City "C" classes won praise from the New York State Commission set up to investigate immigration problems in 1909.[66]

---

[63]
    Ninth Annual Report of the City Superintendent of
Schools, 1907, p. 56; Ayres, p. 197; Tenth Annual Report of
the City Superintendent of Schools, 1908, p.58

[64]
    Ninth Annual Report of the City Superintendent of
Schools, 1907, p. 60,188

[65]
    Minutes of the Board of Superintendents, March 25,
1909, pp. 280-281

[66]
    New York (State) Report of the Commission on
Immigration, 1909, p. 98.

By the following year, the Educational Alliance was finally
able to close down its "vestibule" classes because of "the
adoption by the Board of Education of its policy of giving
instruction to immigrant children in special classes".
It was freely admitted by all concerned that the contribution of the Alliance classes had been very great, both
because they had shown the advantages of segregating non-
English speaking children and because they had, by experimentation, developed the methods later used with success
in the public schools.[67]

In October, 1913, the "C" classes were almost a
decade old, and fortuitously, at that time the North
American Civic League for Immigrants of New York City held
a conference on the problems of the immigrant at C.C.N.Y.
members of the Board of Superintendents dominated the
discussions of the section on the "Education of the Immigrant
Child", because they were, through no fault of their own,
experts. William Maxwell spoke first and said "It is the
great business of the department of education in this city
...to train the immigrant child from the shores of the medi-
terranean Sea to become a good citizen" and this noble object
was being accomplished through the teaching of health education, citizenship, and English.

---

[67]
Joseph, pp. 263,266.

Superintendent Haaren said the problem of the
immigrant child became serious in New York City around 1900.
"The despair of the teacher charged to instruct large classes
in which were a number of pupils unable to understand a word
of English may easily be imagined". The troubles of the
teachers were equalled by those of the immigrant child himself since first grade work for a 12 year old was quite
dreadful. The establishment of the "C" classes, therefore,
was a boon to all. Mr. Haaren was justifiably proud of the
syllabus he had worked out (with Messrs. Meleney and Straubenmuller) and said it was a model for educators in the rest
of the United States to follow. District Superintendent
Cevil A. Kidd explained the methodology of these classes to
the group, emphasizing especially the use of phonics, music,
(patriotic) "memory gems" and the use of concrete objects.[68]

Although many individual children were helped by
the "C" classes, the number reached never exceeded two
percent of the total school enrollment, mostly because of
the inertia and opposition of the teachers and principals,
and the ever present problems of overcrowding and lack of
funds. Their greatest importance lies instead in the
impetus they gave to the techniques of individualized instruction and the influence they exerted on later methods
of teaching English, speech and civics.

[68] United States, Bureau of Education, Bulletin 51.
"Report of a Conference on the Education of Immigrants in
the United States" (Washington: 1913), pp.18,19,22.

The designation "C" for the English to foreigner classes was similar to the use of "D" for the working paper classes which were also begun in 1904. The pupils in these classes were approaching their 14th birthday and were either not motivated to stay in school, or needed the income a job would produce. For a variety of causes, primarily late entry into school due to their arrival in the United States when they were older than ten, they had not yet reached the fifth grade. The "D" class offered them a "cram" course so they could meet the requirements of the compulsory education law.

The Educational Alliance had pioneered the development of classes like these, as well as the "C" variety, beginning in 1903. There was universal agreement about the need for this kind of service because immigrant parents, aware that 14 was the permissible age for working paper application, simply would take their children out of school at that time, whether or not the youngsters had reached fifth grade. This created much difficulty for the officials charged with enforcing the Compulsory Education Law, and sent poorly educated boys and girls out on the labor market.[69]

---

[69] Joseph, p.261; Educational Alliance, _Twelfth Report_, 1905, p.38; McCormick, p.31; Ayres, p.197.

The "D" pupils were taught some American History
and geography and remedial work was done on the three
"R's". There were 4,590 children city-wide in these
classes in 1906, 4289 in 1907, and 3,523 in 1908. In some
schools, especially those on the Lower East Side, an effort
was made to prepare the about-to-leave youngsters for the
outside world, by giving them training in homemaking and
machine sewing, but generally, the classes represented a
small scale "last ditch" effort to give these working class
children a tiny bit of education. It would have been far
better to have classified and trained them from the start
of their school life, but like part time education, these
cram classes were better than nothing. The decline in the
number of students in "D" classes was probably due to the
growth of continuation schools, which were organized in
1913. Since so little could be done for the almost 14
year olds, even in special classes, it seemed better to
let them get jobs and to pick up their education on a part
time basis while they were working.[70]

The last type of special class was designated "E"
and was designed to be a rapid advancement group for
bright boys and girls who had entered school late, but
who intended to complete at least the eighth grade and
possibly go further. Because they were able to do the

[70]
Eighth Annual Report of theCity Superintendent of
Schools, 1906, p. 56; Ninth Annual Report of the City
Superintendent of Schools, 1907, p.57; Tenth Annual Report
OF THE City Superintendent of Schools, 1908, p. 59.

work quickly, and were overage, it seemed best to allow [71]
them to accelerate their learning in these special classes.
The "E" Groups served the additional purpose of clearing the
lowest grades and were popular with everyone. In 1906,
two years after they had first been organized, 12,974
youngsters were in such classes, (city-wide) 13,769 were in
them in 1907, and 14,997 by 1908. [72] "E" classes helped
many a bright immigrant child get ahead faster in his
educational career, and were noteworthy for this reason
alone, but in addition, they further influenced the schools
to accept flexible promotion, acceleration and homogeneous
grouping, all of which have remained part of the educational
framework today.

In sum, "C,D, and E" classes represented change and
flexibility in a school system noted for great rigidity
prior to 1900. A similar trend could be seen in the
curriculum, changes which occurred during the same period.
Since the bulk of the pupils did not enter special classes,
it was actually the changes in the course of study and the

71
   Ayres, p.197; McCormick, p.31.

72
   Eighth Annual Report of the City Superintendent of
Schools, 1906, p.56; Ninth Annual Report of the City
Superintendent of Schools, 1907, p.57; Tenth Annual Report
of the City Superintendent of Schools, 1908, p.59.

introduction of new subjects which most affected them. When
Angelo Patri, Italian immigrant and later a "Schoolmaster
in a Great City" went to elementary school in 1887, he
found that the content of the work was most unstimulating
and that the methodology consisted of drill and rote learning in which the children simply repeated everything after
the teacher. It was essential to sit still and even "calls
of nature" had to be accomplished in a set period of time
--one minute, and that was permitted only if a child was
good![73]

   Conditions were no better six years later when Dr.
Joseph Mayer Rice made his survey. Insisting that a
particular lesson in arithmetic which he observed was not
atypical, Rice described a recitation in which the children
bobbed up and down so rapidly in giving answers that "the
class presented the appearance rather of traveling pump
handle than of a large number of human beings". The principal of this school (and many other supervisors as well)
believed in saving time, above all, and therefore encouraged the greatest possible speed in recitation. Answers were
screamed rapidly and the children were not permitted the
time to think. In toto, Rice saw the typical New York City
school of the period as one which was "...hard, unsympathetic
and mechanical..." with drudgery as its outstanding quality.[74]

---

[73]
  Angelo Patri,A Schoolmaster of a Great City,
(New York: 1917), p.2,3
[74]
  Joseph Mayer Rice, The Public School System
(New York: 1893), pp. 32,38.

Three years later, another future principal,
Leonard Covello, detected no improvement. In his elementary
school, all subjects were learned by rote, and arithmetic,
penmanship, spelling, grammar and geography were recited
in unison and learned by repetition. He found the constant
drill, great loads of homework and the "...pressure of
memorizing" very unpleasant, and was at the point of dropping
out many times. [75]

It was not only the unfortunate pupils who were
aware of the defects in methodology and curriculum in the
schools at the time of consolidation. Superintendent
Maxwell, in his second report, pointed out the inadequacies
of rote work and memorizing, and hoped for "more intelligent
ways of learning and teaching". He was particularly critical
of poor English teaching, which he said spent too much time
on grammar exercises and not enough on creative writing. He
also thought teachers had been wrongly trained to put on a
show, and not to teach for lasting understanding. [76]

As a result of his recognition of these deficiencies,
the years during which Maxwell was active were marked by
constant efforts in the direction of curriculum revision,
in order to make the course of study less rigid and more
easily learned. In 1901, the Teachers Association of

---

[75]
     Leonard Covello, The Heart is the Teacher,(New
York: 1958) pp. 25,41.

[76]
     Second Annual Report of the City Superintendent of
Schools, 1900, pp. 80-82.

Manhattan-Bronx offered its suggestions for improvements in
the curriculum. First, said this faculty group, the course
of study must be made flexible enough to be adapted to any
neighborhood because the city varied so much from district
to district, and the needs of the children differed so
much. For example, there should be no foreign language teaching in areas with large immigrant populations, although
French and German were of value to the native born child.
This procedure should be followed because to the foreign
born youngsters, "...English itself is a foreign language..."
The elementary school course should include less mythology and
more history; the amount of manual training and physical
education being taught should be increased, and the teaching
of "temperence physiology" should be discontinued. In
addition, music and art should be made subjects of appreciation rather than skills to be mastered.[77]

In 1902, when the revised Charter gave him additional power, Maxwell was able to make changes in the elementary
school curriculum in the direction he favored at that time.
The course of study was made uniform for all the boroughs
and the teaching of science, nature study and drawing was now
required of all the schools. In its overall emphasis, the
new syllabus was designed to make school work more interesting,

---

[77] Third Annual Report of the City Superintendent of
Schools, 1901, pp. 89-92.

and this was done partly by eliminating some of the difficult mathematics and foreign languages previously taught. German, French, Latin, Elementary Algebra and Geometry were made electives and the Superintendent specifically recommended that they not be offered in neighborhoods where children of foreign background predominated. It had previously been the custom for certain teachers to go from school to school and give twice a week lessons in German or French. This type of enrichment would no longer take place in the ghetto schools. Hygiene was now to be taught in its more practical aspects and not limited to the evil effects of alcohol, as previously.

So did Maxwell attempt to simplify and make more flexible the elementary school course of study, but he resisted the inclusion of some of the new subjects which were suggested to him. The Superintendent was not sure it was practical to add such subjects as cooking and shop work to the curriculum, both because the schools lacked the equipment and the trained staff to teach them properly and because of the time element. Since it was still necessary to teach the "three R's", where would the staff find the time for new areas of study?[78]

He also turned his attention to pedagogy in the hope of improving the methods of teaching and was able to report

---

[78]
Fourth Annual Report of the City Superintendent of Schools 1902, pp. 78; Fifth Annual Report of the City Superintendent of Schools, pp. 65-67.
1903

some success in 1907.   Methods of teaching arithmetic,
reading and handwriting were now more skillful, he said,
and in particular, he rejoiced over the use of the Palmer
system of penmanship, which, by encouraging large; free
movements would make for better writing and give much needed exercise.[79]   What it was like to have "large, free movement" drill when youngsters sat three to a seat, defies the
imagination. Probably, as with many other innovations, it
was taught only in certain schools.

In spite of what seemed to Maxwell like substantial
changes in the previously rigid curriculum, others demanded
further progress.   In 1912, the President of the Board of
Education, Thomas Churchill, attacked the 1902 revisions
as inadequate.   He said the course of study was still inflex-
ible and did not allow for individual differences. Churchill
related the problem particularly to the needs of the immigrant
child in this way:

> It (the 1902 course of study) came into the
> school of the immigrant child of Rivington St.
> who hears no English in the thoroughfare or in
> the home (and) who, at the stroke of the clock
> that declares him of legal working age, must
> take his place in the ranks of toilers for a
> wage. It came as well, into the school of the
> well-bred child of Washington Heights whose
> home life is a liberal education (and) who looks
> with practical certainty to a career in high
> school and college.

---

[79]   Ninth Annual Report of the City Superintendent
of Schools, 1907, p.162; Interview with Dr. Jacob Ross,
October 17, 1966.

Obviously, said Mr. Churchill, the two groups needed a very different kind of education and the Board of Superintendents needed to make further changes in the course of study in order to accomplish this.[80]

In the same year, the Ladies Home Journal attempted another expose of the schools, in the earlier tradition of Joseph Mayer Rice and Adele Marie Shaw and came up with conclusions similar to those of Mr. Churchill. Commenting on the lack of domestic science education, the magazine said that when New York school records were examined in the future, investigators would conclude that Americans were educated for celibacy, because no trace of preparation for marriage or parenthood was in the elementary school curriculum. The magazine used the term "lock-step education" to describe the methodology that taught every child in the same way, and explained that "...conditions have changed since the establishment of the public school idea and (yet) the public school has not changed with them." The series ended with a call for more and better domestic and manual arts training,because the need was very great.[81]

---

[80] Thomas Churchill, The Board of Education, (New York, 1915), p.107.

[81] Ella F. Lynch "Is the Public School a Failure" Ladies Home Journal, XXIX (August, 1912), pp.3-5.

Partly in response to attacks like these, Andrew
S. Draper, New York State Commissioner of Education, included
some ideas on the subject in his widely read book, American
Education. Dr. Draper placed himself in the ranks of those
who opposed further simplification of the curriculum for
the benefit of the non-academic child. "If the time comes
when the common schools are sustained only or mainly to keep
the slums from destroying us, then the chief character of
the schools and the chief glory of the American plan of
education will be gone". He felt the middle class and
academic values of education must be retained and that the
course of study should not be geared to the lowest common
denominator.[82]   Draper also opposed the use of the school
for social purposes. "The schools are not asylums...If the
conditions of life are specially hard in some places, they
must be met by private and public charity". Finally, the
schools were not laboratories either, and projects in
experimental education belonged in the universities and
not in the lower grades.[83]

---

[82]
    Andrew S. Draper, American Education (Cambridge,
1909) p.77.

[83]
    Ibid., p.130.

Perhaps reinforced by the opinions of an educator
he knew very well, Maxwell also came out against further simplification of the curriculum in 1912. He said it was terrible
to reduce the teaching of history only to American History
(as had been advocated) and then "reduce that to a series
of interesting stories". It was also wrong to eliminate
everything of difficulty in arithmetic or "take out of grammar
that which gives it a vital force as a training in elementary
logic."[84]

The attitudes expressed by Maxwell in 1912 contrast a bit with those he held in 1902, and yet the educational dilemma the two sets of ideas represented was very real.
It took no special insight to see that a classical education
was no longer possible to achieve with the new mass clientele
of the schools. And yet, to reduce the subject matter to a
level the non-academic child could master, would leave the
course of study with little of enduring value. What was to
be done? The Department of Superintendence of the National
Education Association made a study of this problem in 1915
and came out on the side of the modernists. The elementary
school curriculum must minister to the needs of "ordinary
American children"...Subject matter too difficult for the
majority...must be excluded."[85]

---

[84]
Fourteenth Annual Report of the City Superintendent
of Schools, 1912, p.123

[85]
"Minimum Essentials in Elementary School Subjects
Standards & Current Practices, National Education Associa-
tion", Fourteenth Yearbook of the National Society for the
Study of Education, 1915,p.15.

In the end, this had to be the conclusion of a man
like Maxwell as well, if only because he was Superintendent
of Schools in New York City where the school population was
including more and more non-academically inclined children.
If the public schools were going to educate the masses, they
could not use a curriculum of value to only the middle classes.
As Professor Cubberly summed it up: "Education must turn away
from its aristocratic nature and...become more democratic
in character."[86]

Cubberly related this change directly to the needs
of the immigrants from Southeastern Europe, and Maxwell did
the same when he finally accepted the need for new subjects.
Physical education was essential for the health of slum
children who have no access to play opportunities; sewing
was indispensable to poor girls; manual training was equally
important to poor boys; and cooking most important of all
because:

> If the standard of living in the tenements is to
> be raised from that of the poorest classes in
> Italy and Russia to the American standard--a con-
> summation to be desired for the good of a society
> in general...it will be done through the teaching
> of homemaking in the public schools.   [87]

---

[86]
Ellwood Cubberly, Public Education in the United
States (Cambridge; 1919) p.504.

[87]
Maxwell, A Quarter Century of Public School
Development, pp. 58-62.

And so it went. Every new subject added, every old one
dropped, was related in some way to the needs of the alien
poor. Even so unlikely a field as nature study was so
connected.

The first school gardens had appeared in 1905,
mostly in rural Richmond and Queens, where land was available. By 1908, a School Garden Association had been formed
by a group of charitable, nature loving ladies, who believed a return to the soil would greatly benefit the poor city
child. A year later, the Association was able to point
with pride to the existence of over 80 school gardens carried
on by the voluntary efforts of some teachers and these philanthropic women. The benefits of these gardens were many,
according to Miss M. Louise Greene, a leader in the movement. They would make nature study more real, teach color
and design, make literature more concrete, give practical
work in arithmetic, teach elementary science, be of value
in teaching good nutrition, and altogether "answer the
present day appeal for an education that will educate for
every day living...[88]"

The idea of nature study as a public school subject
had originated with Professor L. H. Bailey at Cornell

---

[88]
M. Louise Greene, Among School Gardens (New York:
1910), pp. 254-258.

University as part of an attempt to rejuvenate agricultural education, but because it seemed to fill a gap in the city child's experience, it was eagerly seized upon as a device for practical education for the children in urban schools.[89] Unfortunately, however, it was very difficult to find land for a garden, or to teach the beauties of nature in a slum school, although many teachers tried through such devices as window boxes, house plants, Arbor Day tree planting, and occasional park excursions. Because of the practical difficulties, by 1911, Maxwell was suggesting that nature education be redirected to economic geography and instead of discussing the non-existing trees in the congested districts, classes study the commodities brought to the greatest seaport in the world--New York![90] This might be called making a virtue out of a deficiency, but presumably it partly answered the need.

Nature study, then, because it was so far removed from the lives of the tenement children, was not a great success, but other new subjects did better, and Physical Education was one of these.

---

[89] Lawrence Cremin, Transformation of the Schools, (New York: 1961) p.73

[90] Thirteenth Annual Report of the City Superintendent of Schools, 1911, p. 190

As early as the 1880's, teachers were performing "Swedish calisthenics" with their classes, but lacking facilities or equipment, not much physical development resulted. As long as New York was partly rural, and children had access to open space, the educational deficiency was not greatly felt. But where could a child get healthful exercise on Eldridge St.? or Mott? Again, it became part of the school's responsibility to provide opportunities for physical training, and so by 1899, physical culture instruction and a supervisor of that subject appeared on the roster of special teachers at the Board of Education.[91]

In 1902, the first city wide director of Health Education was appointed and the change in his title indicated a new direction for the subject. Not only gymnastics, but hygiene was to be part of the course of study. The syllabus for this program stressed personal cleanliness, nutrition and healthful leisure time activities, matters not previously considered subjects for education, but essential to the new school population. In accordance with progressive educational thought, exercise was accomplished through the use of games, not just calisthenics, and, perhaps in response to settlement house pleas for cultural

---

[91] First Annual Report of the City Superintendent of Schools, 1899, p.49.

pluralism, the folk dances of Italy, Germany and Bohemia
[92]
appeared in the curriculum.

Superintendent Maxwell heartily approved of physical
education, because he said it lessened the disadvantage
[93]
the city child bore in comparison with his "country cousin".
Because of his approbation, the teaching of hygiene and
health education spread rapidly and became an enduring part
of the work of the schools. By 1914, the revised hygiene
syllabus had a definite relation to the out of school life
of the children. Anti-tuberculosis instruction was given,
of great value on the Lower East Side, where the "white
plague" was so destructive; home hygiene was taught, including measures against vermin, health problems of hot
weather (how well the children of the tenements knew about
that!) and industrial hygiene, so important to those young-
[94]
sters about to get working papers.

---

[92]
McCormick, p. 29.

[93]
Fifth Annual Report of the City Superintendent of
Schools, 1903, p. 67

[94]
Twelfth Annual Report of the City Superintendent
of Schools, 1910, p.428

An offshoot of this subject was an after-school program that was also organized in response to the problems posed by urbanization. In the autumn of 1903, the Public Schools Athletic League was formed by a group of principals, physical training experts, social workers and philanthropists. Its purpose was to organize competitive sports for schoolboys in New York City (it later developed a girl's branch as well) and the organization also maintained afternoon gym and track practice using school facilities. The teachers who supervised these activities were not paid an extra salary, although the Board of Examiners gave them credit for the work if they took promotional tests. In the words of one of its founders: "The Athletic League was formed to bring back into the lives of our children their birthright of competitive play, and to weld it into the educational procedure of a great city."

It accomplished both objectives, because inter-school athletics became very important in the lives of school children, and remained an integral part of the school's work.[95]

Much attention was lavished on domestic science. This was natural because the need for such instruction was even more obvious than the necessity for physical education. It was no longer as easy for a girl to learn housekeeping skills from her mother, although many probably did. The division of labor and the distractions of urban life all

[95]
C. Ward Crampton, "Organized Athletics" in Tenth Yearbook of the National Society for the Study of Education, 1911, pp. 33-38.

combined to make the home less of a school than it had
been for earlier generations. Indeed, often the immigrant
mothers were in need of such instruction themselves. Life
in a tenement presented household problems which were very
different from those which had existed in the villages of
the old country. The harried, puzzled mother, even if not
weighted down with the burdens of poverty, could have given
little guidance to her daughters, but considering the harsh
circumstances of her life, training in domestic arts would
have to come to her children from elsewhere. That "elsewhere", of course, was the public school.

In 1902, the School Journal reported a demand that
cooking and nutrition be taught to the daughters of immigrants
because their food habits were so poor. Mabel Hyde Kittredge
may have read this call for action, because she was the
person responsible for the organization of the first model
housekeeping center that year, at 226 Henry St. The center
taught vermin removal, baby care, methods of laundering
and economical marketing; all matters which Miss Kittredge
thought essential to the immigrant girls. Without such
instruction, the poor eating habits of the foreign born
families would result in feeble minded children
and tenement house reform would be useless because the
poor would not know how to make use of their improved
quarters. This outspoken reformer therefore urgently requested that the public schools establish model housekeeping

flats and teach domestic arts in all the elementary
        96
grades.

Actually, cooking had been authorized, but not

mandated by the schools in 1887, and in 1899 teachers of

both cooking and sewing appeared in the school directory.

By 1903, the subject was important enough to warrant a

place in the appendix of the Superintendent's annual

report for the first time, and in 1907, it was being taught
        97
in 157 schools.   The program must have been successful,

because Maxwell considered its extension in 1909, and by

1914, Miss Kittredge's pleas had been heeded and the first

model housekeeping flat was opened at P.S. 2 on the Lower
        98
East Side.

The success of the domestic arts program was more

apparent than real, not for any lack of enthusiasm, because

everyone (even tax-conscious politicians) favored it; but

because of the lack of equipment and trained teachers.

From 1900 through 1913, each of the Superintendent's reports

mentioned more and better domestic training, but the very

repetition of his demands indicated the extent of the

failure.   Teachers in this subject were the most poorly paid

---

96
        Mabel Hyde Kittredge,"The Needs of the Immigrant",
Survey, XXX, (April, 1913),p189-192.
        97
        McCormick, p. 12; First Annual Report of the City
Superintendent of Schools, 1899, p. 49; Fifth Annual Report
of the City Superintendent of Schools, 1903, p. 235; Tenth
Annual Report of the City Superintendent of Schools,1908,
p. 491.
        98
        Twelfth Annual Report of the City Superintendent
of Schools, 1910, p.207.

in the system, and very few schools had the necessary
stoves, sinks, refrigerators, etc., to say nothing of all
the furniture and linens Miss Kittredge's plans required.
All of the new schools were so equipped and many poor girls
did learn some household management, but the programs were
never sufficiently well-financed to have the impact its
adherents desired.[99]

Much the same sad evaluation could be made regarding manual training, the boy's companion to domestic arts,
except that this program led to the establishment of vocational schools, a very important development in the educational history of New York. The long range success of
manual training was probably due to economic reasons, because,
while a girl might struggle through housekeeping one way or
another, a boy had to become a wage earner, and without
training, his income was likely to be very low indeed.

Variously called industrial education or manual
training, the program first began to appear in some United
States schools in the 1880's although it made its greatest
advances in the nineties. Opinion as to the merits of this

---

[99] Second Annual Report of the City Superintendent of
Schools, 1900, p. 40; Fifth Annual Report of the City
Superintendent of Schools, 1903, p. 65; Eighth Annual Report
of the City Superintendent of Schools, 1906, p.95; Thirteenth
Annual Report of the City Superintendent of Schools, 1911,
p.371; Eleventh Annual Report of the City Superintendent of
Schools, 1909, p. 532; Ninth Annual Report of the City
Superintendent of Schools, 1907, p. 99.

kind of training always differed greatly. Businessmen liked
it as an anti-union device, because it might free them from
the apprentice system, while some educators felt it to be a
necessity in an industrialized nation like the United
States. Labor unions were usually hostile because they
thought it might be a source of non-union, low paid workers,
while some pedagogues opposed industrial training because
they feared it would destroy liberal arts education. The
debate lasted for several decades and was settled nationally
by the passage of the Smith-Hughes Act of 1917 which gave
federal funds for vocational education.[100] In New York
City, the question was decided earlier, and in favor of such
a program, subject only to the usual limitations of money
and equipment.

Under the leadership of a dynamic heiress to a
copper fortune named Grace Dodge, the Industrial Education
Association had been formed in New York in 1884. An influential and energetic woman, Miss Dodge became the first
woman member of the New York City Board of Education in
1886 and promptly pushed her favorite project. As a
result of her efforts, the Committee on the Course of
Study, of which she was a member, recommended the addition
of manual training to the curriculum in 1887. A syllabus
for teachers was published in the following year which
urged the use of manual methods in drawing and art work,

---

[100]
Cremin, pp. 33-41, 56

rather than study <u>about</u> such matters. This was the level
at which the subject remained for many years--merely an
extension of drawing. The reason for this was related,
once again, to finances. It cost almost nothing for
"artistic" manual training, but real industrial educatio[n]
required a great deal of expensive equipment and for this
reason, no one except Miss Dodge and her cohorts considered it seriously for a long time.[101]

In 1899, teachers of the subject were listed under
manual training and drawing, and were active only in
Manhattan-Bronx and Brooklyn. The advocates of the program
argued that industrial education was essential to the city
boy because he could not learn such skills from his parents
as did the rural child or even the city boy of years past.
At the same time, the demand for skilled workers, and the
lack of opportunity for unskilled ones was becoming more
obvious all the time. The need was especially great for
the bulk of the new immigrants. The Italian workers, being
largely possessed of agricultural skills, had difficulty
finding other than unskilled jobs. Although many of the
Jews already possessed urban skills, knowledge of additional
trades might be useful and enable the newcomers to broaden
their fields of endeavor.

---

[101] Charles A. Bennett, History of Manual and Industrial Education (Peoria, Illinois; 1937) pp. 414-416; Abbie
Graham, Grace H. Dodge, Merchant of Dreams (New York: 1926)
p. 159.

So went the reasoning which favored manual training and proponents like John Spargo even thought it would be of value in "regenerating" the children who created discipline problems for the schools because they were not touched by the academic subjects. Those concerned with truancy believed that the children could be made to stay in school longer if they saw the prospect of a better job with the acquisition of new skills. Above and beyond all other considerations was the fact that a new kind of education was essential if the public schools were going to cope with the masses of working class youngsters of varied ability.[102]

Regardless of the high hopes for the program, in actual operation it was an arts and crafts type of subject, as an exhibit viewed by an interested observer in 1906, indicated. He said he saw a great array of objects connected with the study of "Hiawatha"; tepees, pipes and baskets; aquariums, pendulums, and water clocks that were correlated to science study; and an entire miniature replica of New York City, made in connection with a study of transportation.[103]

---

[102]
John Spargo, "The Regeneration of Ikey" Craftsman, XII, (September, 1907), pp. 642-646.

[103]
Colin A. Scott, "The Manual Arts in the City of New York", Educational Review, XXXI, (April, 1906), pp. 413-415.

These were all very commendable enrichments to the
course of study, but bore very little relation to the
practical needs of working class children. In addition to
lack of trained personnel and equipment, there was a theoretical basis for keeping manual training on the level of drawing.
As Maxwell was to reiterate constantly, the job of the
school in this area was to be only pre-vocational, that is
to say, to lay the foundation on which the employer would
build when a boy actually became a wage earner.

But even when viewed within these limitations, paper
box folding and Indian tepees could hardly be called technical training and a host of people interested in the subject
pressured the schools to change, partly on the assumption,
later to prove erroneous, that duller children could profit
from a vocational education. This was an idea that became
demonstrably false as industry became more and more technical
and the vocational schools were left further and further
behind, to become the "dumping ground" of the school system.

But in 1900, vocational education seemed a very good
idea to people such as Superintendent Gustave Straubenmuller,
a leader in the movement within the Department of Education.
He called it "learn and earn" education and his influence
led Maxwell to hesitantly suggest the establishment of a 7th
and 8th grade pre-vocational school in his second annual
report, relating the need for such an institution directly
to the boys of "our crowded tenement house neighborhoods." [104]

104
        Second Annual Report of the City Superintendent of
Schools, 1900, p.89.

One trade school under private auspices was functioning in New York City by 1902. This was the Manhattan Trade School for Girls, organized and presided over by Mary Woolman who firmly believed in the value of vocational education for girls of working class families. Her school remained private for eight years, but the Department of Education was cognizant of the methods she used and later adopted them to their own schools.

Girls of 14-17 only could be admitted, and they had to have a fifth grade education and at least one reference. Even with such qualifications, the new student served a one month apprenticeship and if satisfactory, remained for the year course, which was tuition free. The school taught the trades most important in New York; "needlework, pasting and designing". English, arithmetic and civics were also given and related to the vocational aims of the girls.

Hygiene was offered as well, because Miss Woolman thought it essential to the welfare of her students. She also tried to maintain a liason with the businessmen of the city in order to keep the trades she was teaching in line with the actual needs of the job market. The girls filled orders from businessmen while they were still students, earning the prevailing wage rate, and were given a one month trial on a job the school found for them, before they graduated.

There were 159 fortunate girls at the Manhattan
Trade School at any one time, with a long waiting list
composed of those who wished to enter. , Only a, girl who
could afford to stop earning money for a year was able
to take advantage of the course, and this provided a
natural limit on the number of applicants. But, all in
all, Mary Woolman thought her school a success, and it
evidently was, because the Board of Education took it
over in 1910 when it became part of the Vocational
Division.[105]

Still somewhat unsure about the merits of industrial education, in 1905 Maxwell coupled a second recommendation for the establishment of an intermediate pre-
vocational school with a suggestion that New York educators
needed to study European trade schools, in order to learn
more about this kind of education.[106] By the following
year, however, he had made his decision and strongly urged

---

[105] Mary Woolman, "The Manhattan Trade School for
Girls" Educational Review, XXX, (September, 1905), pp. 178-
187.

[106] Eighth Annual Report of the City Superintendent
of Schools, 1906, pp. 123,125

the Board of Estimate for an appropriation which would

enable the Department of Education to begin a pre-vocation-

al school for boys.

> Because of its enormous foreign population....
> New York City stands sorely in need of trade
> schools. There are tens of thousands of child-
> ren leaving our schools every year at 14 years
> of age to go to work who have not completed the
> elementary school course and who, under present
> conditions, have not acquired any art by which
> to earn a livlihood. They are turned loose on
> the community either to make their living by
> their wits or to eke out a miserable lielihood
> by unskilled labor. 107

No closer connection between the new immigration

and the pressure on the educational authorities to establish

trade schools could be drawn.

Possibly because of this fervent plea, Maxwell was

able to say in his next report that plans for the first

pre-vocational school were being made. He coupled this

announcement with a reiteration of his earlier statements

about the need for more manual training in the elementary

schools, because he recognized that many of the boys who

might profit most from the intermediate school would not

be able to continue their education past the fifth grade. 108

It took two years more, but in 1909, the Vocational

107

     Ninth Annual Report of the City Superintendent of
Schools, 1907, p. 147

108
     Tenth Annual Report of the City Superintendent of
Schools, 1908, p. 128

School for Boys opened its doors at 138th St. and Fifth Ave.
as the first of its kind in New York. It was to serve boys
14 and over who had graduated from elementary school or
passed an equivalent examination. The school was organized
like a factory, on a nine to five basis for eleven months
of the year. The instructors were skilled workmen who
taught the boys woodworking, plumbing, the electrical
trades and sheet metal work, as well as machine tool use,
forging, printing, bookbinding, and drawing. There were
also related subjects offered, such as trade mathematics,
English, industrial history, applied science, simple
bookkeeping and commercial law. The boys who were admitted
to the two year course were on probation for the first five
months and were not permitted to stay if they did not work
hard.[109]   By 1910, there were 600 boys enrolled in the
school, and Superintendent Straubenmuller, who had been a
prime mover in its organization, was exultant.[110]

The courses offered were good, and the staff carefully selected, but deficiencies in the operation of the
new vocational school were noted by 1912. It was found to

---

[109] McCormick, p. 128

[110] Gustave Straubenmuller, "Industrial Education",
Education, XXX, (April, 1910), p. 520

be very difficult to teach new trades to the students because
of the great gaps and variations in their elementary school
background. Also, the pupils often did not remain to
complete the course, either because they could get a good
job after only a year's training or because of sudden economic
need.[111]

In spite of these drawbacks, the Superintendent still
thought industrial education was essential because the
school census of 1910 had indicated what poor jobs were
available to the adolescents who lived below 14th St. who
were untrained. By far the largest number (3,091) were
errand boys and messengers, while a sizeable group of girls
were houseworkers and a smaller number machine operators.
The boys were office boys and sometimes clerks, but none
had established themselves in a trade. Perhaps out of dis-
couragement, Maxwell began to think about the possibility
of an agricultural school so that New York children could
earn a living outside of the city, when depression struck.[112]

His main objective, however, was to obtain funds
for more pre-vocational schools. He set the number needed

111
   Fourteenth Annual Report of the City Superintendent
of Schools, 1912, pp. 343-344

112
   Thirteenth Annual Report of the City Superintendent
of Schools, 1911, pp. 140, 324-325.

at 20, and in pursuit of this goal he was joined by the
powerful Public Education Association.[113]   As a result,
the Murray Hill Vocational School began operations in 1913,
with hours of study and a curriculum much like that of
its predecessor. Drafting and advertising were taught at
Murray Hill, although they had not been included in the
original vocational school and general science was added
to the list of academic subjects. Interestingly, the
pamphlet which announced the opening emphasized that a
boy who graduated from this school could still go on to
high school, which was probably an attempt to reach a
higher caliber student. It would appear that vocational
educators were already learning the sorry truth that a
dull student did no better in trade subjects than he had
done in academic ones.[114]

The matter was still fraught with controversy in
1914, when a stormy hearing was held at the Board of
Estimate, attended by Mayor Mitchel, Maxwell, Churchill,
numerous Associate Superintendents, the principals of the
three vocational schools, and Abraham Flexner, Secretary

---

[113]
Fourteenth Annual Report of the City Superintendent of Schools, 1912, pp. 167,397.

[114]
New York (City) Department of Education. The
Murray Hill Pre-Vocational School for Boys, no date,
pp.3,4.

of the General Education Board, a non-profit foundation

established with Rockefeller money to encourage educational

progress in the United States. The tenor of the meeting was

critical of the vocational policies of the Department of

Education, mostly because it appeared that graduates of

the two existing schools had not been placed in jobs, or

has been taught trades impossible for them to enter due

to union regulations regarding apprenticeship.

Flexner was most outspoken, and attacked the Board

of Superintendents in particular, saying that they were

largely ex-elementary school principals who knew nothing

about vocational education. Maxwell cautiously defended

his associates and pointed out that three pre-vocational

schools, specialized high schools like Manual Training

High School and Washington Irving, plus all the manual

and domestic training in the elementary schools was

not such a poor record for a school system which had to

battle the Board of Estimate every year for funds. The

Mayor tried to pacify all sides and the hearing adjourned

inconclusively.[115]

115
    New York (City) Board of Estimate and Apportion-
ment. Minutes of a Hearing on a Report of the Sub-Committee
...of the Board of Education on Vocational Guidance,
June 16, 1914, pp. 1-3, 14,20.

In the same year, a new aspect of industrial education was begun. The Board of Education was experimenting with the Junior High School or Intermediate School, thinking of it as a holding operation which might keep children off the labor market an additional year, and began to offer a pre-vocational course in a few of these schools, so that a child could decide whether he wished to attend a regular high school or a vocational school after eighth grade.[116] A good number must have chosen the latter, because in his 16th report, (1914) the Superintendent noted that relatively, the vocational school population was increasing faster than any other division in the school system.[117] Even Brooklyn was to get such an institution in the following year.

The real transformation in vocational education took place, however, after 1918, when large four year high schools were organized which utilized many of the devices and subjects of the earlier pre-vocational schools so favored by Maxwell, but kept close to the normal school day and year. The growth of this kind of education was due partly to the availability of funds under the Smith-Hughes Act and partly because Maxwell's successor, William Ettinger, was an

---

116
   McCormick, p. 61

117
   Sixteenth Annual Report of the City Superintendent of Schools, 1914, p. 30

ardent advocate of trade high schools. For better or worse,
since the first appearance of a large number of dull
students in the schools, the die had been cast. If they
could not learn Latin, let them learn lathing, and the construction of an entire division of schools began on this
premise, as part of the answer to the problems posed by
industrialization and immigration.

Because of the basic fact that a child could leave
any kind of education behind him at 14, and therefore did
not have to attend a vocational school if he chose not to,
it was apparent that this kind of training would not reach
a large number of adolescents. Therefore, while the search
for the best industrial education was going on, the schools
were also experimenting with the continuation of work-
study type of program.

This idea had originated with the 1903 Compulsory
Education Law which required a 14 year old who had not
completed eighth grade to attend evening elementary school
for 16 weeks each year until he reached his 16th birthday.
The provision was virtually unenforceable, and from 1907 on,
Maxwell urged the establishment of day continuation schools
for these drop-outs. In 1911, he waxed eloquent on the subject:

> Are employers to have the best of the child's
> day at toil that is often grinding and poorly
> remunerated and leave him little, if any chance
> to cultivate those functions of mind and body
> upon which success and happiness in after life
> depend?   118

118
    Thirteenth Annual Report of the City Superinten-
dent of Schools, 1911, p.144.

A year later, he thought such day continuation schools were what New York City needed the most, and believed they should be arranged so that the children attended six to eight hours a week on the employer's time.[119] The passage of a permissive state law on the subject, in 1913, encouraged the Superintendent to carry his plan further, and later that year it bore fruit with the start of the first continuation school classes in New York City. In the next few years the system was refined and adjusted and it appeared that Maxwell had won his point about the duty of the school to reach all the children, even those who rejected education at an early age.[120]

In the process of making some kind of education available to all, the school system extended its services to what has euphemistically been called the "exceptional" child; meaning the youngster defective in some way, physical or mental, which set; him apart from his peers. Associate Superintendent Andrew Edson gave some of the reasons why such children should be educated in an article in Education in 1910. First of all, he said, education is the right of every child, and the state is obligated to provide it. But

---

[119] Fourteenth Annual Report of the City Superintendent of Schools, 1912, p.167

[120] McCormick, p.67

even if this duty did not exist, public education of the
defective youngster was desirable because, if such
children received training, it was less likely they would
remain dependent and a continuing burden on the state. [121]

Although Edson emphasized the responsibility of
the public school for the handicapped, in actual fact, the
first classes for crippled children had begun in a private
school on Avenue E in 1899, under the auspices of the
Association for the Aid of Crippled Children. [122] Superintendent Maxwell, however, was aware of the need for such
education and recommended the establishment of more classes
like these in 1905 and 1906. [123] His suggestions were implemented in the latter year, when the Board of Education
opened a unit for crippled children at P.S. 104, although
the Association continued to provide for the transportation
of the youngsters out of its own funds. [124]

---

[121] Andrew Edson, "Instruction of Exceptional Children
in the New York City Public Schools", Education XXXI,
(September, 1910), p. 1

[122] McCormick, p. 33

[123] Seventh Annual Report of the City Superintendent
OF Schools, 1909, p. 119; Eighth Annual Report of the City
Superintendent of Schools, 1910, p. 114

[124] McCormick, p. 33

Maxwell maintained his interest in the matter, urging the establishment of an entire school for the handicapped in his Ninth Report, (1907) and such an institution was established a year later on Henry St. The pattern of cooperation with private charity was continued in the lunch program of the school, which was provided for out of Association funds. Such classes were extended to Brooklyn at the same time and increased to 25 in that borough by 1910.[125] In the years that followed, classes were established in many schools, as well as continued in the central one on Henry Street and by 1910, there were 48 such units in the city as a whole.[126]

Simultaneously with the development of education for the handicapped went the growth of classes for the ill. In 1904, the Bellevue Hospital Ladies Auxiliary had raised money for a class for tubercular children to be held on a ferryboat moored in the East River. This unique educational establishment was still in existence, supported by the Board of Education in 1909, and in that same year, a doctor working

---

125
    McCormick, p. 33; Ninth Annual Report of the City Superintendent of Schools,1907, p. 145. Although Maxwell recognized the initiative of private organizations, he always wanted control over special programs to remain with the Department of Education and classes for crippled children were no exception.

126
    Edson, Education, XXXI, p. 5

for the Charity Organization Society and the Department of
Education began an experimental open air class for anemic
children at P.S. 21 on Mott St.[127]

The need for such classes evidently extended beyond
the limits of Little Italy because a doctor at Gouverneur
Hospital recommended to the Board of Superintendents in 1912
that open air classes be established in every school in the
vicinity of the hospital, which meant most of the East Side.[128]
Eventually such classes came to be part of many schools in
all the boroughs and the sight of children bundled up to
their eyes in layers of clothing while absorbing the three
"R's" in the fresh air that was considered so beneficial,
became familiar to parents and teachers all over the city.
Whether the classes ever did much to prevent tuberculosis
or arrest anemia is hard to judge, but they did represent
a continuing concern with the atypical child, which was
further manifested by Maxwell in 1912 when he suggested
that the Department of Education establish a boarding
school for tubercular children in the country; an idea not
acted upon by his superiors.[129]

127
        McCormick, p. 34; Twelfth Annual Report of the
City Superintendent of Schools, 1910, p. 104

128
        Minutes of the Board of Superintendents,
September 12, 1912, p. 519

129
        Fourteenth Annual Report of theCity Superinten-
dent of Schools, 1912, p. 176

Also in the focus of concern was the child with limited sight and hearing. The Superintendent had spoken of the need for classes for such children in 1905 and three years later the education of blind children was begun, with six units in existence by 1910. Similarly, deaf children came under the wing of the school in 1908 and 160 youngsters with this type of handicap were receiving training by 1910.[130]

Even stutterers and lispers came within the all pervasive notice of the schools. An experimental speech therapy class had been organized by the principal of P.S. 2 in 1907 and Maxwell encouraged the establishment of more such units in his 11th and 13th reports.

Although the documents do not so indicate, it is possible that speech correction originated at P.S. 2 with its totally foreign student body precisely because those children needed extra help in pronouncing English words. From such small beginnings, the teaching of speech and the correction of speech defects grew to become a major part of the school's work.[131]

---

[130] Seventh Annual Report of the City Superintendent OF Schools, 1909, p. 119; Eleventh Annual Report of the City Superintendent of Schools, 1909, p. 192; McCormick, p. 34; Edson, Education, XXXI, p. 5

[131] Eleventh Annual Report of the City Superintendent of Schools, 1909, pp. 469, 188; Thirteenth Annual Report of the City Superintendent of Schools, 1911, p.151.

Of even greater importance was the development of classes for a different kind of defective, the mentally retarded child. As early as 1899 a few experimental centers for the identification and possible instruction of this type of youngster had been established, but in 1902, the first official ungraded class was organized at P.S. 1 under the care of Elizabeth Farrell, a young elementary school teacher who had become interested in work with such youngsters, partly under the influence of Lillian Wald, whose friend she was. The class on Henry Street was unique and won much praise. Miss Farrell achieved considerable success with her first group of boys who she reached through individual attention and the use of definite objects in her teaching. Maxwell praised her work, and indicated that he favored the extension of it by asking for additional funds, and for a staff to assist her. By 1909 there were 86 Classes for Children of Retarded Mental Development in the city, and they have remained an enduring testimonial to the concern of the schools for the exceptional child.

Elizabeth Farrell herself was quite exceptional She never favored the segregation of the retarded child in a separate school, but always thought he would do best by maintaining some contacts with normal children. She paved the way for the present day Bureau of Child Guidance when she established the Psycho-Educational Clinic in her office at Board Headquarters in 1907. At the same time, she was able to achieve the appointment of Dr. Isabel Smart, the first doctor with psychiatric training to serve in a public school. When she found a shortage of personnel to teach the CRMD classes, she undertook to train teachers herself and gave a course on the subject at the Brooklyn and New York Training Schools.[132]

Miss Farrell then, was part of the small coterie of educational pioneers whose efforts to change the schools to fit all the children so marked the educational history of New York City during the early years of the 20th century. Like Julia Richman, Evangeline Whitney, Luther Gulick and Gustave Straubenmuller, Elizabeth Farrell worked to implement the "changing conception of the function of the school" noted by educational theorists like Ellwood Cubberly. In the continuing search for quality education, it became apparent that the schools would have to offer a greater variety of learning opportunities or bypass completely a

---

[132]
Mimeographed document about Elizabeth Farrell found in Board of Education vertical file 902; Helen Clark Phillips, "Elizabeth Farrell", Review of the International Council for Exceptional Children, I, (February, 1935), pp. 73-76; Fourth Annual Report of the City Superintendent of Schools, 1902, p.108; Fifth Annual Report of the City Superintendent of Schools, 1903, p.110; Ninth Annual Report of the City Superintendent of Schools, 1907, p.144; Eleventh Annual Report of the City Superintendent of Schools, 1909, p.187; Thirteenth Annual Report of the City Superintendent of Schools, 1911, p.148.

larger and larger segment of the population. Since the
increasing complexity of urban life demanded more, not
less education, continued failure to reach a substantial
portion of the children would be disastrous. Thus,
cooking, shop, "C,D, and E" classes, as well as vocational
education and CRMD classes became the tools by which the
school would fit the child and the benefits of education
could be extended to the greatest possible number of
children.

CHAPTER 6

TO REACH MORE SCHOLARS

The "...best of all ways to abolish truancy is to
make the public school so attractive (the) children will
not willingly be absent..."[1]   So pronounced Superintendent
Maxwell in his Fourth Annual Report (1902), while discussing the problems of poor attendance in the schools of New
York. Unquestionably, the statement was true, but in order
to demonstrate the attractive features then being developed, the schools had to get the children to attend in the
first place. Attempts to accomplish this took up much of
the time and energy of the educational administrators who
were in charge at the turn of the century.

In view of the shortage of seats and money which
so troubled the public schools of New York in this period,
it is surprising to note the extent of the efforts that
were expended on the children who evaded education. The

---

[1]
New York (City) Department of Education, Fourth
Annual Report of the City Superintendent of Schools, 1902,
p. 87

reason lay in the only partially acknowledged fear and mistrust the middle classes felt toward the immigrant poor. The reasoning of the "stable" elements of society went somewhat as follows: If left uneducated and ignorant, the foreigners would be an easy prey for unscrupulous politicians and could be misled into voting for candidates and legislation injurious to "American" institutions. It was therefore essential to expose all the newcomers to the English language, and American culture, history, and geography so they could become good citizens and not remain the dupes of the machine bosses. If the children and their parents could not be forced to obey the compulsory education laws, American democracy, at least in the big cities would be greatly weakened.[2]

Unfortunately, however, the legal framework with which to compel school attendance, left much to be desired. Although both Brooklyn and Manhattan had a small number of truant officers as early as the 1880's, enforcement of the

---

[2]
Rush Welter, Popular Education and Democratic Thought in America, (New York: 1962), p.157; Paul Klapper, "Bureau of Attendance and Child Welfare", Educational Review, L (November, 1915), p. 380-381; Robert A. Woods (ed.) Americans in Process (Cambridge: 1902), pp. 243-244.

weak compulsory education statute which demanded attendance
from ages eight to twelve was very inefficient. Both
cities also had unsavory truant homes for boys who were
repeated offenders, but the capacity of these institutions
was small and their reputation very bad. More than the
truant, it seemed that these schools confined the adolescent
criminal, under brutal physical conditions which were periodically exposed and criticized, to little avail.[3] The
combined efforts of the ineffectual enforcement staff and
"Dickensian" truant schools were inadequate to the task of
reaching the large number of reluctant scholars, and this
lack of success was a source of great concern to humanitar-
ians and educators alike.

The sixteen truant officers in New York City and
the nine in Brooklyn were simply not able to locate the
great bulk of the children who were illegally absent from
school. Jacob Riis estimated that 50,000 such youngsters
were untouched by education in 1892, although Superintendent Jasper of New York thought only 8,000 fell into this
category. Regardless of which figure was correct, it was
certain that a large proportion of these boys and girls
not attending school were holding working papers which had

_____

[3]
A. E. Palmer, History of the New York City Schools
(New York: 1905), pp. 181, 193, 227; Jacob Riis, Children
of the Poor (New York: 1892), pp. 92-93.

been acquired through evasion of the law. A parental
affidavit, certifying that a child was twelve years old,
was the only step necessary to obtain permission to work.
It was therefore easy for the parent to negate the intent
of the law by stating that his child was of age, and
unless the youngster was demonstrably younger than twelve,
the officials in charge blinked at the deception, and
issued the work permit.[4]

The varying estimates of the number of truants
made it clear that some enumeration was necessary, before
any defects in the law could be remedied. In the wake of
the reform victory of 1894, and the "great school war",
the State Legislature passed the school census law of
1895. The Police Department was to be responsible for
getting the facts on the number of children between eight
and sixteen who lived in New York City, and the Department
of Education was to tabulate the data. When the census
was actually taken, the results were startling. In
Brooklyn, it was found that 96,229 children between the
stated age limits were not in any kind of school; while
50,119 New York children were similarly untouched.[5] The
census was very inefficiently done and the results could
not be considered accurate, but the figures were an

---

[4] Riis, pp. 119, 121, 106

[5] Palmer, pp. 194, 234

indication of the extent of the problem. Even when the permissible working paper age of twelve was taken as the upper limit, at least 40,000 children who should have been in school, were not. The school authorities believed that the majority of these thousands"...came from the poorer, foreign born, non-English speaking families who exploited their children to supplement the family income." [6]

An attempt was made to correct at least some of the abuses in working paper administration in the Compulsory Education Law of 1897 which said a twelve year old could not receive a work permit unless he had attended school for eighty days prior to his twelfth birthday. [7] This new legislation, although a step in the right direction, could not have made a tremendous difference in the number of children reached, because five years later, school officials were still wrestling with the problem. One method which offered some promise was increased cooperation with the Society for the Prevention of Cruelty to Children whose president, Elbridge T. Gerry, was a member of the Manhattan-Bronx school board in 1901. Fear of the

---

[6] Harold McCormick, "The First Fifty Years" Fiftieth Annual Report of the City Superintendent of Schools (New York; 1948) p. 13.

[7] New York (State) Laws of 1897 Chapter 415, sections 70-76.

"Corrys" was a real deterrent to truancy on the East Side,
because the agents of the Society took the children to
their shelters when they found evidence of exploitation
or neglect. Among the immigrant poor, family ties were
strong, and therefore the agents were greatly feared,
mostly by reputation, since the number of families they
actually reached was never very large.[8]

In the same year that the Board of Education voted
increased cooperation with the Society for the Prevention
of Cruelty to Children, the attendance officers of the
Department of Education gave an indication of the major
causes of truancy in New York at that time. The largest
number of children (703) had been absent during 1900-1901
because of illness, but this number was closely followed
by those whose parents kept them home for purposes unknown.
(639). 319 youngsters illegally held jobs and 374 had
given wrong addresses and could not be found.[9] This report,

---

[8]
New York City Department of Education. Organization of the Manhattan-Bronx School Board. February 3, 1901,
p. 109, Other causes included poverty (69); transfers to
other schools who never appeared (88) & emigration out of
the city (40)

[9]
Ibid, p. 117.

of course, covered only those cases known to the schools,
but from these statistics, it would appear that it was a
combination of parental opposition and poor record keeping that lay behind most of the truancy.

In spite of the fact that the educational authorities were having trouble enforcing the law of 1897,
Superintendent Maxwell wanted more extensive legislation
and recommended that age limits of six to fourteen be
constituted the range for compulsory education, even though
he admitted that he would have to keep every child in the
city on split session until enough schools were built, if
this were done.[10]   The Superintendent was being somewhat
unrealistic, although commendably energetic, in this recommendation which he repeated in 1902, although the second time,
he coupled his suggestion with a request for additional
truant officers and for stiffer fines on parents, thus
recognizing the causation made clear by the report of 1901.

Maxwell's desire for a better compulsory education
law was shared by a large number of other "social progressives". These men and women organized a campaign during
1902 and 1903 which resulted in the passage of a strong
statute in the latter year. The first move came from

---

[10] First Annual Report of the City Superintendent of
Schools, 1899, p. 135.

Lillian Wald and Florence Kelly, co-workers at the Henry
Street Settlement. Mrs. Kelly had previously been a factory
inspector in Illinois and was the secretary of the National
Consumer's League, an organization which was trying to win
better working conditions for women in industry and retailing. Miss Wald and Mrs. Kelly influenced residents in
other houses on the Lower East Side to take up the child
labor problem as a social settlement responsibility. As a
result, early in 1902, the Association of Neighborhood
Workers appointed a Child Labor Committee with Robert
Hunter of the University Settlement as chairman.

Hunter raised $1,000 and was able to employ Miss
Helen Marot as chief investigator of the Committee. Miss
Marot and a group of volunteers supplied by the settlements
discovered over 1,000 violations of the Child Labor Law.
Hunter therefore urged the formation of a larger and more
influential committee in order to pressure the legislature
into passing a stronger law.

His efforts were successful, and a committee repre-
sentative of the wealth and social conscience of the city
was formed in late 1902. The committee members included
Felix Adler, leader of the Ethical Culture Society of
New York; George W. Alger, a prominent attorney; William H.
Baldwin, President of the Long Island Railroad; James K.
Paulding and W. English Walling of the University Settlement;
Lillian Wald and Florence Kelly of Henry Street; and

William H. Maxwell, the Superintendent of Schools. Robert
Hunter continued as Chairman.[11]

The cases uncovered by Miss Marot were published
in a pamphlet entitled "Child Labor, Factories and Stores"
edited by Hunter's assistant at the University Settlement
Leroy Scott, A city-wide labor organization joined with the
Child Labor Committee to push for the passage of a stronger
law, and Samuel Gompers gave his personal support. The
Committee used lobbying, letter-writing, and political
pressure in an attempt to convey to the legislators the
idea that public opinion was strongly behind it. The task
of the reformers was made easier because Governor Benjamin
Odell and the New York State Department of Labor favored
the passage of a law which would extend the age and educational requirements for working papers.[12]

---

[11]
    Fred S. Hall, Forty Years, 1902-1942, The Work
of the New York Child Labor Committee, (New York: 1942),
pp. 8,9.

[12]
    Irwin Yellowitz, Labor and the Progressive Move-
ment in New York State, 1897-1916 (Ithaca; 1965) pp.90,
49,86,91. Professor Yellowitz points out that child
labor restriction was one area in which unions cooperated
fully with middle class reformers because they desired to
keep low paid child workers out of the job market.

The most important provision of the new statute was
the one which raised the permissible age for working papers
from twelve to fourteen. Furthermore, it was made more
difficult to obtain a work permit. Documentary proof of the
child's age, such as a birth certificate, passport, or
baptismal certificate were the only acceptable papers; a
parental affidavit was not permitted. Even if the proper
papers were presented, the child had to fulfill a much more
extensive educational requirement. If he had completed the
eighth grade, the law had no further hold on him. But if
he had not, the recipient of a work permit had to attend
evening elementary school for six hours a week for sixteen
weeks a year until he reached the age of sixteen. No
child who had not reached the end of the fifth grade could
even apply for working papers. [13]

The latter provision regarding evening schools,
because it was virtually unenforceable, weakened the law
greatly, although the extension of the compulsory schooling age to fourteen, and the necessity to present documentary evidence of age were important advances. As a
result of attempts during the next decade to strengthen
further the compulsory education laws, a good deal of
attention was devoted to studying the question of causation.

---

[13]
    New York (State) Laws of 1903, Chapter 184,
Sections 70-73.

Why did so many children fail to attend school? It appeared that the causes were multiple, and included parental evasion as well as pupil hostility. In regard to the former, immigrant parents, especially Italians, came in for a great deal of criticism. The Associate Superintendent in charge of Division I (the Lower East Side) said in 1904, that the parents were his greatest problem, while Maxwell castigated them further in 1909;

> Thousands of the illiterate parents of these children have no right appreciation of the meaning or importance of an education for their children, and much prefer to place them at work. 14

In spite of this harsh statement, the Superintendent did recognize that parental attitudes were not the only cause of truancy, and that the part time system contributed to the problem. By permitting the child to spend his morning at leisure, the system made it more difficult for him to put aside play and enter school in the afternoon. Many such youngsters simply evaded school entirely, and if questioned by an attendance officer, lied about which session they were supposed to attend. Maxwell was also aware of "temporary necessity" cases in which a girl was kept at home to deal with a family emergency. Such an absence

---

14
        Sixth Annual Report of the City Superintendent of Schools, 1904, p. 101; Ninth Annual Report of the City Superintendent of Schools, 1907, p. 333.

as entirely excusable, but it was often prolonged past
he time that real need existed because the child, having
issed a good deal of work, was reluctant to return to
chool even when the emergency had passed.[15] Teacher hos-
ility to the returned truant was also cited as an aggrava-
ion of the problem, for which Maxwell chided his staff.[16]

In 1909 a principal's committee set up to study
he causes of truancy said retardation was the major
eason for the difficulty. Because of a number of factors
hich included late entry into school, poverty, frequent
ransfers, physical and mental defects, oversized classes,
oor teaching, and harsh discipline, many a child fell
urther and further behind his normal grade. This increased
is dislike of school and tended to encourage his truancy.[17]

15
    Ninth Annual Report of the City Superintendent of
nools, 1907, pp. 336, 337.

16
    Tenth Annual Report of the City Superintendent of
hools, 1908, p. 352

17
    McCormick, p. 32.

A teacher who was later to establish herself as
one of the most progressive members of her profession,
Elizabeth Irwin, analyzed the causes of poor attendance
as follows: low I.Q., broken homes, physical defects and
poor teaching. She criticized the schools for failing
to connect education with life and pointed out that the
major stimulus which kept children in school was good
marks which, under prevailing conditions, many youngsters
were not able to achieve.[18] The Director of the Bureau
of Attendance cited similar reasons: nagging teachers,
lack of clothing, poor physical conditions, incomplete
families, squalid homes, drunken parents, and the attrac-
tion of the streets. In regard to this last, the school
authorities seemed to think the newly established "penny
movies" contributed to absenteeism and conducted an unsuccessful campaign to close them during school hours.[19]

Even if all these causes were operative, it was agreed
that better enforcement by attendance officers would cut

---

[18]
    Elizabeth Irwin, Truancy, A Study of Mental,
Physical and Social Factors of the Problem of Non-Attendance at School (New York: 1915) pp. 15,20,33,42,46.

[19]
    John Davis, "Truancy in New York City", National
Education Association, Proceedings, 1916, pp. 858-859.

down on truancy. The search for this improvement was long
and arduous. First of all, there were never enough truant
agents for the city. The illegal employment of children
by factories and the constant movement of population in
search of cheaper or better housing made the officer's
job very difficult. Maxwell's reports routinely requested
the appointment of more enforcement officials, and the
corps did grow, but never large enough. [20]

In those situations where the agents were able to
do a good job, other factors often intervened. There was
no truant school for girls, so they were rarely brought
to court. Judges often did not impose heavy fines on
parents when attendance cases came before them and so the
threat of legal action lost some of its effect. Principals
frequently discharged a troublesome child after a brief
five days absence without waiting for the truant officer's
investigation, and similarly recommended a disciplinary
case for working papers at the first opportunity. The
whole administration of the working paper law was fraught
with difficulty. The child was supposed to apply to the
Board of Health and produce proof of age and a school
record certificate stating he had attended classes the
required number of days prior to his birthday. When the

---

[20]
Seventh Annual Report of the City Superintendent
of Schools, 1905, pp. 97,98.

children were refused permits because they lacked either
of these papers, they went to work illegally or played
truant. This situation, which Jacob Riis had noted in
1892, had not changed, in 1908. [21]

Attendance officers worked out of the offices of
the District Superintendents who felt overburdened by the
need to supervise this aspect of the school's work. Consequently, a principal soon learned not to send too large
a number of names to his superintendent's office "...for
there was a general feeling...that a long list from any
school reflected on the efficiency of its supervisor." [22]
These Superintendents were also responsible for the enforcement of another child labor statute passed in 1903,
called the "Newsboy Law" which prohibited any boy under
14 from selling papers without a permit and badge from his
District Superintendent. Boys under 10 or girls under 16
were not to sell at all, but the law was very difficult to
enforce and many a young child spent long nights on the
street and slept instead of attending classes the next day. [23]

[21] Irwin, p.11; Fifth Annual Report of the City Superintendent of Schools, 1903, p.34; Twelfth Annual Report of the
City Superintendent of Schools,1910,p.194; Fourteenth Annual
Report of the City Superintendent of Schools, 1912, p.233;
Tenth Annual Report of the City Superintendent of Schools,1908
p.364. The proof of birth provision was particularly hard on
Jewish girls, few of whom could produce a certificate. This
requirement was softened in 1907 by an amendment which provided
that working papers could be issued if a child had tried for
90 days to get proof of age and failed, and if three doctors
certified that the applicant was really 14 years old.Hall,p.20.

[22] Klapper, p.370.

[23] Ninth Annual Report of the City Superintendent of
Schools, 1907, p.333; New York (State) Laws of 1903, Chapter
151, Sections 174,179a.

As though their regular duties were not enough, attendance
officers were also responsible for truants of the corporate
(charity) and parochial schools in their district, giving
them a totally impossible load to carry.

While all the defects in the schools themselves,
and the inadequate enforcement procedures undoubtedly contributed heavily to the problem of truancy, the widespread
use of child labor also had to be considered. Because a
boy's work could add two or three dollars a week to the
family income, the temptation to evade the child labor law
was very great. In the case of girls, if they did not hold
a job themselves, they could free their mother to work by
taking over her baby tending chores. In either case, many
children did not attend school because they were otherwise
employed, and the educational authorities were able to compel very few to enter the classrooms. [24] The basic element
in child labor was economic, since Robert C. Chapin in his
investigation of the standard of living among New York City
workingmen, estimated that $900 "permitted the maintenance
of a normal standard, at least so far as the physical man is
concerned," for a family of five. Since most immigrant families in the

---

[24] Kellog Durland and Louis Sessa, "Italian Invasion
of the Ghetto", University Settlement Studies, I, (January,
1906), p.110.

city had incomes far lower than this, economic necessity,
coupled with inadequate enforcement procedure, made
truancy a way of life among the immigrant poor.[25]

To rectify this overwhelming array of causes,
Maxwell and others made a number of recommendations over
the years 1903-1914. In order to cope with the problems he
was having with Italian parents, the Superintendent suggested the appointment of three or four Italian truant officers
because "only those who speak the Italian language can deal
properly with Italian parents, who, as a rule, distrust
English speaking officers."[26]   Six years later, Maxwell was
less inclined to mollify the immigrant parent.

> The large number of Italian parents brought
> before magistrates for failing to send their
> children to school, leads us to believe that
> these foreign parents especially need the
> lesson of a fine in court. The fines imposed
> on Italian parents in Manhattan for such
> neglect have been published many times within
> the past ten months in the several Italian
> newspapers, and such publication has served
> to improve conditions. It will be remembered
> that children in most rural districts in Italy
> are not compelled to attend school after their
> ninth year of age, hence it is not easy to
> teach their parents the law which exists here.   [27]

25
       Robert C. Chapin, Standard of Living Among Work-
ingman's Families in New York City, 1909 (New York: 1909)
p. 246.

26
       Fourth Annual Report of the City Superintendent
of Schools, 1902, p. 29-30

27
       Tenth Annual Report of the City Superintendent of
Schools, 1908, p. 356

Different members of the Board of Superintendents had different remedies. One thought a better census would help locate the truants, another thought each child should carry an identification card so the truant officer could know where he belonged at any given time of the day. Superintendent Meleney believed only a trade education would keep a difficult boy in school and Julia Richman suggested that the provisions of the child labor law be pasted in the text books of every child in the fifth grade or over, so the boy or girl would know the legal requirements regarding school attendance.[28]

Other ideas reflected a different approach; namely the need for improved confinement of incorrigible truants. The deficiencies of the existing truant schools were widely known and in his very first report, Maxwell day dreamed about an ideal "parental" school for disturbed boys. It should be out of the city, he said, and well-equipped for manual training, gardening, farming, trade education, and the regular three "R's". A child should be committed for more than one year, and there should be at least two such schools for the city.[29]

---

[28] New York (City), Department of Education. Minutes of the Board of Superintendents, November 18, 1909, p. 1135; Seventh Annual Report of the City Superintendent of Schools, 1905, p. 280; Ninth Annual Report of the City Superintendent of Schools, 1907, p. 337.

[29] First Annual Report of the City Superintendent of Schools, 1899, p. 133-134. The term parental school referred to a boarding or cottage type of institution for delinquent truants, in which the cottage parents stood in lieu of the natural mother and father.

It took eight years, but in 1907 the school system
finally got at least one school very similar to the one
Maxwell described. It was located in Flushing, and covered ten acres with room for 600 boys in eleven sturdy stucco
cottages with red tile roofs. There were 60 boys in each
cottage, while one was reserved for the principal and his
assistant. Each cottage was a self-contained unit with a
house mother and father; called a matron and a master. The
boys of the school learned various trades and did a good
deal of farming, the harvest of which was used in the
city's charitable institutions.[30] It would seem as
though this institution might have accomplished some real
rehabilitation, although the emphasis on hard work and
discipline was perhaps too harsh for the disturbed boys
who were sent there. The Queens parental school function-
ed until September 30, 1934, when it was converted into
Queens College which currently occupies the site.[31]

_____

[30]
        "New York's Parental School", Harper's, LIV,
June 8, 1910, p.13.

[31]
        Thirty-Eighth Annual Report of the City Super-
intendent of Schools, 1936, p.60.

Another type of institution for "incorrigible truants" was the probationary school, first established under the auspices of Julia Richman at P.S. 120 on Broome Street in 1905. Miss Richman described her motivation for organizing such a school as being composed of equal parts of concern for the classes which had to suffer from the disruption of the disturbed boys and for the boys themselves who got nothing but abuse from their regular teachers. She felt that the truant schools were no answer at all and instead proposed a special day school to which every principal in her district would send her most serious disciplinary cases, numbered in order of "badness"! From these lists, 60 boys were chosen to start classes in the "small, old-fashioned building" the Board of Education had given her.

So tough and profane were these pupils that when Miss Richman first saw them, she thought she could not bear to inflict them on the staff, all of whom were volunteers, of P.S. 120. She forced herself to continue the experiment with eventual good results. The teachers did not try to do any academic work until they had won the respect and affection of the boys which they accomplished by giving them individual attention and treating them with a mixture of tenderness and firmness. Athletics, which the students liked very much, were used a great deal, and the staff was instructed never to "holler" at the boys and

to give them a great deal of freedom of movement, because
Miss Richman was convinced that it was earlier restrictive
and unsympathetic handling that had aggravated the problem
of these troubled youngsters.

After a year, the results of the experiment were
tabulated. Out of the total number of boys admitted (60
was only the first group), five were able to return to
regular school, thirteen reached the age of 14 and received working papers, 18 were found to be mentally retarded,
13 were sent to reform school, and the rest remained at
the probationary school where their attendance and work
habits were greatly improved, although they were not yet
ready to return to a normal class.[32] The school was much
praised and visited, and by 1910, similar institutions
were being organized in other parts of the city.

In spite of these efforts, which of course, touched a relatively small number of truants, successive attendance reports indicated a continuing problem. The report
for 1905 showed that 143,471 cases had been investigated,
while the one for 1910 indicated that 175,785 cases had
been examined. A small drop to 162,124 cases was noted
in 1912, but the number increased again to 181,063 in

---

32 Julia Richman "The Incorrigible Child" Educational
Review, XXXI, (May 1906), pp. 489, 490, 491, 496.

33
1914.

Perhaps because of these figures, a Teacher's
Council on Truancy was established in 1914 to study the
problem and make practical recommendations. In addition
to a number of familiar suggestions, the teachers thought
deep investigation into each truancy case was a desirable
procedure, but only possible if the number of attendance
officers was apportioned according to the needs of the
neighborhood, a procedure not then being followed. All
districts had the same number of truant agents, although
many sections of the city had practically no attendance
problems, while other areas, especially below 14th Street,
had a great many. The teachers also believed that attendance notices which were mailed to parents should be
printed in Italian, Yiddish, and German so the family would
be aware of the child's truancy. This faculty group
heartily endorsed the establishment of more schools like
P.S. 120 because it felt incorrigibles and truants should
34
be separated from regular classes.

33
    Seventh Annual Report of the City Superintendent
of Schools, 1905, p. 280; Twelfth Annual Reportof the City
Superintendent of Schools, 1910, p. 194; Fourteenth Annual
Report of the City Superintendent of Schools, 1912, p. 233;
Sixteenth Annual Report of the City Superintendent of
Schools, 1914, p. 430.

34
    New York (City) Department of Education. Report
of the Committee on Truancy, and Delinquency of the
Teachers Council, March 17, 1914, pp. 2,3,5,9.

In 1913, the Child Labor Committee, feeling that the schools, pupils, and parents had adjusted sufficiently to the changes brought about by the law of 1903, instituted pressure for the upward revision of the age and educational levels required for working papers. Their efforts were strongly opposed by the Male and Women Principals Associations who did not agree with the Committee on the value of keeping non-school minded youngsters in the classroom. The dispute between the Committee and the school staff was of long standing because the reformers had frequently accused the principals of issuing fraudulent school records to troublesome children, certifying that the child had completed fifth grade, in order to get them out of school. The quarrel grew so bitter, the Public Education Association had to moderate the differences by forming a group composed of the Child Labor Committee, Charity Organization Society, Association for the Improvement of the Condition of the Poor, and the Principals Associations.[35]

The Public Education Association's efforts were successful because all these groups did come to work together for the passage of the Compulsory Education Law of 1913 which required school attendance between ages seven

---

[35] Hall, p. 26; Sol Cohen, Progressives and Urban School Reform (New York: 1964), p.68.

and sixteen and permitted working papers at fourteen
only if the child had completed the sixth grade.
Youngsters in this latter category had to attend day or
evening continuation school until they completed eighth
grade or reached sixteen.[36]   This statute would greatly
extend the school life of many children if it was properly enforced and consequently, there was also an attempt
made to improve the administration of the compulsory
education laws at this time.

Previously, in 1909, a Permanent Census Board consisting of the Mayor, Superintendent of Schools, and
Police Commissioner had been established to take a yearly
school census, with special reference to immigrant children,
who were to be enumerated by the police from names sent
to them by the New York State Department of Labor, direct
from Ellis Island.[37]   This Board was absorbed by the
Bureau of Compulsory Education which was established in
1914 and finally lifted the burden of enforcement from
the District Superintendents.

---

[36] New York (State) *Laws of 1913*, Chapter 748, Section 622.

[37] Mary Fabian Matthews, "The Role of the Public School in the Assimilation of the Italian Immigrant Child," (unpublished Ph.d. dissertation) Fordham University, 1966, p.339.

The city was divided into 13 attendance districts, each of which was in charge of a supervisor to whom the staff reported directly. The forbidding image of the truant officer was to be banished; now he was to be a "social investigator for the school system" and take remedial as well as punitive action. The Bureau attempted to match its personnel to the ethnic background of the district and insisted on a psychiatric examination before committing a child to the parental school. This administrative apparatus, advanced by the standards of the day, remained the basic framework for the regulation of truancy in the city schools for many years.[38]

By 1914, then, New York City children were required by law to attend school full-time for three years longer than they had in 1897. The new seven-year span, coupled with better enforcement procedures, guaranteed a larger pupil population, different in quality as well as quantity from the students who had spent a shorter length of time in school in earlier decades. Previously, a child who remained to complete the elementary grades was very likely to be a "good" student, highly motivated and probably of middle class background. Now, however, everyone had to stay in school longer, whether dull or bright, poor or

---

[38]
Klapper, p. 371

comfortable, alien or native born. This basic change required the schools to undertake tremendous revisions in policies and practices, in order to cope with the mass of youngsters, so many of whom were foreign in background, as well as poor. The extension of compulsory education can thus be viewed both as a cause and a result of the "transformation" of the schools.

Because the needs of the industrialized, urbanized, cosmopolitan society required more education, it was necessary to lengthen the number of elementary school years regardless of the desires of the immigrants. But because this expansion changed the nature of the school population, it was essential that the schools alter their methods and content. Taken together, the increase in the number of years required for schooling and the changes which occurred during the longer span, led directly to the modern schools of today.

At the same time that efforts were being made to keep children in school longer, the evening schools, traditional route for the Americanization of the immigrant adult, were also undergoing basic changes in an attempt to reach those newcomers who were too old for the day schools. Innovations of educational importance emerged from the attempts of the Department of Education to rejuvenate the Evening Division and better fill the gaps in the older immigrant's lives.

The evening schools of New York City had a very
long history existing as far back as the 18th century.
Such classes had been organized by the Public School
Society in 1823. The major target of this type of
schooling was the illiterate native born male adult.
When the Board of Education was established in 1842,
the evening schools became a part of its responsibilities.
By 1866 there was sufficient interest to form evening
secondary schools, which meant that these schools actually
predated day high schools in New York City.[39]   In 1880
the arrangement was refined to the point where children
of thirteen to eighteen went to the junior division of
the evening schools while those 16 or over, whose prior
education justified it, attended the senior unit.[40]

39
     McCormick, p. 12; The Public School Society, a
privately run, but tax financed charitable organization
controlled education in New York City until the establishment of the Board of Education in 1842. William O. Bourne,
History of the Public School Society of New York (New York,
1873), p. 614

40
     Palmer, p. 177.

In the same year, the city of Brooklyn organized
two evening high schools, even though its two previously
established elementary schools were failing from lack
of funds and students. From these humble origins, the
school system of the consolidated city had managed to
assemble 61 evening schools in 1898, with a total enrollment of 49,734 students, although not more than thirty
percent of these attended regularly.[41]   The evening
schools grew with the school system as a whole. In 1904,
there were a total of 82 night schools in the city, 10
of which were on the secondary level.[42]   A substantial
increase occurred in the next few years, and there were
97 evening schools in the city by 1908, and 119 in 1911.
By 1914, the total number had dropped to 114, but the
number of high schools had greatly increased. Midway
in the period 100,000 students, 30,000 of whom were
foreigners learning English, were enrolled in the program

---

[41]
   First Annual Report of the City Superintendent of
Schools, 1899, pp. 126-128. All the boroughs had some
evening schools, although only Manhattan-Bronx and
Brooklyn had both high schools and elementary schools.
The number of night schools for each borough is as follows:
Manhattan-Bronx, 34; Brooklyn 16; Queens, 7; Richmond, 4.
The bulk of the students (62%) were in the elementary
schools.

[42]
   Palmer, p. 310

with 1,600 teachers to instruct them.[43]

The evening elementary schools which ran from October to May, offered four different types of courses. There were classes in the three "R's" for people who had never completed the regular elementary school curriculum, and for boys and girls who were not yet 16 but held working papers. There were classes in homemaking and in a few trades but these were on a very small scale because of lack of equipment. There were a few apprentice classes for the printing, construction and photo-engraving trades, but the largest single group of pupils were the foreign born who wanted to learn English.[44] The diversity of subjects offered looked imposing, but in fact, the evening schools suffered from a number of deficiencies. The gap between enrollment and attendance was very large, due to a variety of causes, only some of which were within the school's power to correct. The students had to attend five nights a week after a long days labor and often without time for supper. Fatigue, illness, and

---

[43] Tenth Annual Report of the City Superintendent of Schools, 1908, p. 535; Thirteenth Annual Report of the City Superintendent of Schools, 1911, p. 20; Sixteenth Annual Report of the City Superintendent of Schools, 1914, p. 18.

[44] McCormick, p. 43; Walter Ballard, "Adult Education in New York City" Journal of Education, LVXIII, (November 18, 1908), p. 540.

travel difficulties were great obstacles to good attendance. The gas-lit classrooms were hard on the eyes and
the child-sized seats added to the discomfort.

In addition, the teaching was very poor. Until
1902, evening school instructors did not need to be
licensed by the Board of Examiners and were appointed
on the recommendation of their borough superintendents.
When the schools were truly unified by the Charter of
1901, evening school teachers came under the merit
system, but the problems did not end there. A teacher
accustomed to dealing with young children all day had
great difficulty adjusting her methods to adults, and
yet almost all the evening school teachers were day
school personnel in need of the small sum the position
paid. Maxwell tried to reserve the jobs for men, taking
women only when absolutely necessary, but regardless of
sex, the teachers were not very satisfactory. The
pattern of ethnic similarity of pupils and teachers
noted in the day schools was present at night as well.
Evening elementary school #2 at 116 Henry St. for example,
had a totally Jewish staff. Considering the overwhelming
number of foreign born students at this school, it was
probably essential to have some Yiddish speaking teachers,
although the experts never could decide whether having
a teacher who spoke a foreign language hindered or helped

45

the student.

The Superintendent always considered the evening schools the weakest part of the system, mostly because of the appalling attendance statistics. He begrudged the money this division cost, and was constantly trying to find a way to improve conditions in this area. He suggested that teachers be trained in methods of instructing adults; that the evening school week be cut to four sessions, so that Friday night could be used to instruct the teachers; that the hour for the opening of classes be changed to seven-thirty instead of seven thus enabling the students to get some supper; that evening "socials" be held instead of classes, every so often; that students who registered be made to pay a nominal fee for supplies so they would have a stake in regular attendance; and that specialized kinds of evening schools be developed to attract and hold the students.

46

In spite of this barrage of suggestions, made over the years, most of which were accepted, the Superintendent was still unable to report success. In 1911 he said the

45

Ballard, Journal of Education, LXVIII, p. 540. Tenth Annual Report of the City Superintendent of Schools, 1908, p. 557; Palmer, p. 310; Third Annual Report of the City Superintendent of Schools, 1901, pp. 44-45; Minutes of the Board of Superintendents, June 1, 1908, p. 693

46

Seventh Annual Report of the City Superintendent of Schools, 1905, p. 353; Third Annual Report of the City Superintendent of Schools, 1901, p. 26; Fifth Annual Report of the City Superintendent of Schools, 1903, p. 144; Twelfth Annual Report of the City Superintendent of Schools, 1910, p. 526.

evening schools were a failure, except for the English
to foreigner classes.[47]   Although the New York City
evening schools ranked among the best in the nation in
attendance, and were considered second only to Boston in
quality, the Superintendent was not satisfied.[48]

In an attempt to improve this division of the
Department of Education, several diversifications were
begun. Evening vocational schools were organized in 1904
at the Manual Training High School in Brooklyn, and the
Bryant High School in Long Island City. Three years
later, a similar unit was opened at Stuyvesant High
School. All of these proved very popular and had to turn
students away, for lack of room. In 1905, an Industrial
Evening School for adults with little education was opened at P.S. 89 in Manhattan, followed shortly by one at
P.S. 5 in Brooklyn.[49]   This latter type of school was

---

[47]
Thirteenth Annual Report of the City Superintendent of Schools, 1911, p. 19.

[48]
Frank V. Thompson, Schooling the Immigrant
(New York: 1920) p. 32

[49]
McCormick, p. 44, P.S. 89 had a largely Negro
population, day and evening.

designed to meet a need described by Associate Superintendent Matthew Elgas who was in charge of the evening school
division:

> We must recognize the necessity of an educational
> system that will enable the pupil to earn his
> living and not merely be fit for admission to
> the high school or college. 50

Vocational education, especially for adolescents
attending evening schools in order to fulfill the requirements of the Compulsory Education Law, was the major
interest of an organization formed in New York City in
1906, called the National Society for the Promotion of
Industrial Education. The co-founders were Dr. James P.
Haney, director of art and manual training for the public
schools of the city, and Charles E. Richards, formerly
director of Cooper Union, and now professor of manual
training at Teachers College.

These two pioneers arranged a meeting of thirteen
prominent business-men and educators which was held at
Cooper Union on June 9, 1906. The group discussed the
widespread interest in industrial education then spreading
through the United States, and decided to form a permanent
organization which would pressure both the state legis-
latures and Congress for funds to develop this type of

50
Fifth Annual Report of the City Superintendent of
Schools, 1903, p. 155

schooling. Five of the thirteen men present at the June
meeting were designated an organizing committee and
succeeded in attracting 250 people from 20 states to an
assembly, again held at Cooper Union, on November 16, 1906.

A constitution was adopted, and Henry S. Pritchett,
President of the Massachusetts Institute of Technology
was elected President, M. W. Alexander of Ceneral Electric
was chosen Vice-President, F. Everitt Macy of New York
City was made the Treasurer, and Richards became the
Secretary of the new group. On the Board of Directors
were a number of manufacturers, educators, representatives
of organized labor, and social workers, including Jane
Addams. President Theodore Roosevelt, Felix Adler of
the New York Ethical Culture Society, Charles W.Eliot
of Harvard, Jacob Riis, and Dr. Elmer E. Brown, the
United States Commissioner of Education, all expressed
approval of the aims of the organization.[51]

The National Society, operating mostly through
Haney and Richards in New York State, organized public
opinion and applied pressure on the legislature in an
attempt to get state aid for evening industrial high
schools, because the costs of operating such units were
high, and the Board of Estimate was always unwilling to
appropriate much money for the purpose. In 1913, the
efforts of Haney, Richards, and the National Society were

---

[51] Charles A. Bennett, History of Manual & Industrial
Education,(Peoria, Ill.: 1937), pp. 517-518

successful. State aid was now extended to the teaching
of trade subjects in the evening schools, and from that
point on, evening industrial education expanded considerably.[52]

Still another way in which the schools tried to
reach the potential student who was also a worker was
through factory classes. This was an attempt to teach
English to the foreign born on the employer's premises
and at least partly on his time, with teachers and
supplies furnished by the Board of Education. Only one
such school was successful enough to graduate any
students by 1914. On June 4th of that year, 40 women
received certificates attesting to their ability to
read and write English. This training had been received
at the D. E. Sicher Co., a large manufacturer of muslin
underwear, where classes had been held during the previous
two years, taught by teachers from nearby P.S. 4. Although
Superintendent Maxwell hailed the event, saying it was a
first for New York City and possibly for the world, and
"...the beginning of a great movement to hasten the assimilation necessary to national unity...", employers generally
resisted the idea, and factory classes did not become widespread until the Americanization movement of 1917-1919.[53]

[52] Fifteenth Annual Report of the City Superintendent
of Schools, 1913, p.115; Bennett, p.540.

[53] Sixteenth Annual Report of the City Superintendent
of Schools, 1914, p.442; McCormick, p.44.

In spite of efforts which expanded and diversified
the work of the evening schools, the most important area
of their labor remained the teaching of English to foreigners. Even in 1899, one third of all the students in the
evening schools were foreigners learning English, and two-
years later, the percentage was closer to one half. In
1905, over 50% of the evening school pupils were primarily
aliens receiving instruction in English and citizenship,
and this figure remained about the same throughout the
period.[54]   The growth of this part of the school's program
did not go unnoticed.   "The teaching of English to foreigners in our evening schools has come to be justly regarded
as perhaps their most important branch of instruction" said
Maxwell proudly, in 1906.[55]

As would be expected, these evening "C" classes
were located "...mostly (in) the crowded schools on the East
side of Manhattan where the foreign non-English speaking

54
    First Annual Report of the City Superintendent of
Schools, 1899, p.128; Third Annual Report of the City
Superintendent of Schools, 1902, p.50; Seventh Annual Report
of the City Superintendent of Schools, 1905, p.352; Ninth
Annual Report of the City Superintendent of Schools, 1907,
p.544; Twelfth Annual Report of the City Superintendent of
Schools, 1910, p.519

55
    Eighth Annual Report of the City Superintendent of
Schools, 1906, p.380.

element (was) enormous".[56] The work of these classes followed the lines laid down in a special course of study adopted by the Board of Superintendents in 1902. Prior to that time, the instruction had not been systematized at all. According to the "Directions of the Board of Superintendents to Evening Schools for the Teaching of English to Foreigners", classes were to be organized on the basis of 1) Nationality, 2) General Intelligence and 3) Age.

The teaching was to be oral, objective, in English only, and to utilize "subject matter...taken mainly from scenes and experiences of (the) daily life of the pupil".[57] The order of instruction was spoken English first, then reading, and finally American History and Civics. A special course of study in the latter area was developed in 1914 which discussed the following topics. "What the government does; how the city, state and nation work; the chances for a foreigner in the United States; (and) American History".

---

[56] Fifth Annual Report of the City Superintendent of Schools, 1903, p.153.

[57] Fourth Annual Report of the City Superintendent of Schools, 1902, p.178.

he object of this instruction was "...to give the (immigrant)
[58]
n ardent and loyal devotion to the country of (his) adoption".

In spite of these efforts to improve the curriculum,
he attendance figures of the English to foreigner classes,
lthough higher than those of the evening schools as a
hole, were discouraging. In 1909, the State Immigration
ommission Report, while praising most of the work of the
ew York City evening schools, said that summer evening
chool classes were essential, since, at the moment, the
vening schools were closed during the months of heaviest
[59]
mmigration, namely May through September.   The Educa-
ional Alliance, pioneer in the field of alien education,
ad realized this years earlier and had been conducting
[60]
ust such summer evening classes.   Superintendent
axwell endorsed the recommendation of the State Commission

---

[58]
    Gustave Straubenmuller, "The Work of the New
ork Schools for the Immigrant Class", Journal of Social
cience, XLIV (September, 1906), p.178; Fifteenth Annual
eport of the City Superintendent of Schools, 1913, p.254.

[59]
    New York (State) Report of the Immigration
ommission, 1909, p.100

[60]
    Paul Abelson, "The Education of the Immigrant",
ournal of Social Science, XLIV, (September, 1906), p.167;
inutes of the Board of Superintendents, March 10, 1910, p.248.

and in May of 1910, an experimental unit was opened at
P.S. 22 at Stanton and Sheriff Streets.

In the following year, two more such schools were
opened at P.S. 25 on Fifth Street and at P.S. 2 on Hester
Street. By 1912, there were a total of seven such schools,
including three in Brooklyn, in the Williamsburg and
Brownsville areas.[61]   These May to September classes were
predictably popular, both because it was easier to attend
school in the summer and because, just as the Educational
Alliance and Public Education Association had said, the
bulk of the immigrants _did_ arrive during these months and
needed some English immediately, in order to find work.

The search for more ways to reach the foreigner
did not end with these summer classes. In 1914, Maxwell
recommended that evening schools be established near the
shops and factories in which the aliens worked in order
to attract more immigrant students, and in the same year,
the Board of Education did incorporate the day classes
which the Educational Alliance had been holding for those
of the foreign born whose work prevented them from attending at night.[62]

---

[61] Eleventh Annual Report of the City Superintendent
of Schools, 1909, p. 48; Twelfth Annual Report of the City
Superintendent of Schools, 1910, pp. 192, 514; Fourteenth
Annual Report of the City Superintendent of Schools, 1912,
p. 26.

[62] Sixteenth Annual Report of the City Superintendent
of Schools, 1914, pp. 163, 436.

It is very likely that the large amount of energy
spent by the Board of Education on the teaching of English
to foreigners was stimulated by the great interest in the
subject displayed by various outside groups during the
period. Foremost among these organizations was the New
York Committee of the North American Civic League for
Immigrants, which had been established in 1909 for the
purpose of assimilating, protecting, and easing the adjustment of the immigrant. In an attempt to reach these goals,
the Committee sponsored a Conference on the Education of
the Immigrant in May, 1913 at C.C.N.Y.[63]

In general, the Conference had considerable praise
for the New York City program, but at a symposium directed
by Superintendent Albert Shiels, who was in charge of the
New York City evening schools at that time, the discussion
made it clear that there was still much room for improvement.
Shiels himself criticized the teachers who failed to draw
from the student's own experiences and often patronized
them. The Secretary of the Board of Examiners said that
evening school instructors were paid three dollars a night,
and for that salary, no great teachers could be expected.
All of the principals and supervisors at the meeting agreed

---

[63] Edward Hartmann, The Movement to Americanize the
Immigrant (New York: 1948), pp. 38,56. Clarence Abbott
"On the Education of the Immigrant", American Leader,III
(June 12, 1913), p. 698.

that better trained evening school teachers were essential,
and that this could only be accomplished if more money was
paid them. The discussants further indicated that the bulk
of the evening school faculty had little interest in
helping the students with any supplementary activities and
tended to teach only when they needed money, which resulted[64]
in many changes in staff and prevented continuous learning.

A few years later, a specialist in immigrant
schooling for the U.S. Department of Education, H. H.
Wheaton, said nothing regarding the qualifications of the
teachers, but praised the New York City immigration education program, because it made an effort to classify the
students according to prior education and nationality,
held summer and winter sessions, and attempted to mix
socialization with the learning of English.[65]

A teacher in the evening schools at the time,
however, was much less enthusiastic. In an article which
he wrote for the Jewish Immigration Bulletin in 1916,
Samuel Strook faulted the night schools for the "merest
pretence" at classification, uncomfortable physical arrangements, for unsuitable texts and "capricious and unduly
exacting teachers". Understandably, Mr. Strook wanted the

[64]
    United States, Bureau of Education. Bulletin 51,
"Report of the Conference on the Education of Immigrants
in the United States", (Washington: 1913), passim.

[65]
    H. H. Wheaton, "Survey of Adult Immigrant Educa-
tion", Immigrants in America Review, IV, (June, 1915), p.48.

evening schools to be upgraded and the teachers to be
professionalized, and felt the high drop out rate would
continue until this was done.[66]

The aims of this teacher were shared by the
supervisory personnel of the evening schools. Dr. Morris
E. Siegel, who served as teacher, principal, and eventually
Director of Evening Schools for the Board of Education,
said the greatest problem his division faced was getting
well-prepared teachers and keeping the students who registered. Dr. Siegel, however, felt that the evening schools,
in general, _did_ succeed in their job and that, through
improved courses of study, better teaching and supervision,
as well as many extra curricula activities, a very large
number of immigrants were helped to adjust to American
life.[67]

Although it might have been true, as a 1916
National Education Association Report put it: "The night
school attracts only the most ambitious (because) it must
compete with the appeal of the moving picture entertainment,
the parks and dance halls", it is/clear that, in an attempt
still
to reach as many aliens as possible, the evening schools of
New York City improved their methods considerably, and that
this type of experimentation made them a model for the rest

[66]
Samuel Strook, "The Night School and the Immigrant",
Jewish Immigration Bulletin, VI, (August-September, 1916)p.6.

[67]
Interview with Dr. Morris E. Siegel, November 20,
1966.

of the United States during the later Americanization movement.
Books on the subject, written in 1919, urged the adoption
of many of the programs which were already a decade old in
New York City, especially the year-round evening schools
and the use of daily experiences in the lives of the immigrants
as a device for learning English.[68]

After the furor to Americanize the alien had
passed, and the great immigration flood had decreased to a
trickle, the evening schools continued to grow, although
their role in assimilating the immigrant was much less important. Instead, they reverted almost to their original
function--to further the education of the native born
worker. The framework set up for the schooling of the
immigrant adult was used, beginning in the late twenties
and early thirties, for the education of all adults.
Thus, in New York City, the Division of Immigrant Education
became the Division of Adult Education, and the National
Education Association's Department of Adult Education grew
out of the Department which had been concerned with the
immigrant. American education was enriched, therefore, by
the efforts to assimilate the alien adult, efforts in which

---

[68]
Elsa Alsberg, "Education of the Immigrant",
Proceedings of the National Education Association, 1916, p.790;
Thompson, p.215.

he New York City schools were leaders, mostly because
hey felt the immigrant impact stronger and earlier than
id other American cities.

There must have been many occasions in the course
f the years 1898 to 1914, when the educational authoritie
f New York, bewildered at the vast variety of activities
hey had undertaken, and discouraged by the ever present
hortages of money and materials, wished the immigrant im-
act had struck elsewhere and that the schools could return
ɔ the simpler pattern of earlier decades. Such retro-
ression, of course, however appealing, was not possible,
ɛcause of the changes which had taken place in American
ɛban life by the turn of the century. The millions of
ᵢmigrants, children and adult, required services both
ɨucational and social, which the schools were called
ɔon to deliver. With many false steps, and often grudging-
ɤ, the educational system of New York did rise to the
ɔcasion and succeeded in offering more knowledge to more
ɛople. The efforts of individuals as diverse as the
ᵣuant officer and the night school teacher resulted in
ᵢfluencing the lives of many boys and girls and men and
ɔmen who might otherwise have been less touched by American-
ɨng influences.

In the course of these endeavors, however halting
ᵢey were, the content, organization, and methodology of
ᵢe schools changed, and the framework for the school of
ᵈay was constructed.

PART III. CONCLUSIONS

CHAPTER 7

TOWARD THE SCHOOLS OF TODAY

"Quality education is the only way to break the vicious cycle of poverty, unemployment and other social problems besetting a city as large and complex as ours".[1]

So spoke Dr. Bernard E. Donovan, Superintendent of Schools of New York City, in 1966, in the budget request he presented to the Board of Education in December of that year, and the words could easily have come from any one of the educational leaders who were active in the schools of New York a half century earlier. Of note also was the Superintendent's easy assumption that the schools should and could bear the responsibility for easing the problems of social change, a concept established with much difficulty in the earlier period and now taken as a fact of educational life.

Elsewhere in his statement, Dr. Donovan gave the details of the programs for which he was requesting a record one billion, one million dollars. An expanded kindergarten plan, a five instead of a four hour day for first graders, additional guidance personnel, extension of services to the handicapped, and improved summer school, after school,

---

[1] The New York Times, December 12, 1966, p. 1.

and recreational programs were all part of the steps the
Superintendent thought were necessary to achieve the
"Quality education" so badly needed in New York City in the
second half of the century.[2]

Although the cost of the programs and the methods
of financing them were vastly different, the proposals
themselves could have been found in many of the reports
of Dr. Donovan's predecessor, William H. Maxwell, sixty
years earlier. Indeed, in 1966, plans like these were
really continuations of programs which were brand new
in 1906. It was the decade 1902-1912, after all, that
saw the start of kindergartens, counselling services,
classes for the handicapped, and after school recreational activities, and these devices have evidently proved
viable enough to be considered of use today.

But are they really so? Can the remedies for the
ills of an era when the impact of industrialization, urbanization, and immigration were creating new social problems
be of use in the city of today? The educational authorities
seem to think so. Are these officials merely coasting
along on the plans developed by earlier school leaders,
demonstrating once again the inertia and uncreativity of
which their critics have so often accused them? Or can it

---

[2]
Ibid.,p.51

be that the programs developed by the pedagogues of the
Progressive Era, under the spur of the problems presented by the great influx of immigrants, were of such great
value they can be used to help the schools of today adjust to the truly massive difficulties confronting them?

In order to better answer this question, it is
necessary to evaluate the changes in the schools which
occurred between 1898 and 1914. Such an evaluation was
performed by a distinguished group of educational experts,
under the chairmanship of Dr. Paul Hanus, between 1911 and
1913. The circumstances which led to the establishment of
the Committee on the School Inquiry, as it was formally
known, were the familiar compound of educational and financial difficulties which had previously led to investigation
of the schools of New York. The enormous growth in the
number of pupils, (57% between 1901 and 1911) and the
desire to implement a number of new programs to combat
retardation and better meet the social ills of the day,
led the Department of Education, in 1910, to request a
very large sum for the use of the schools.

The Board of Estimate, always reluctant to embark
on new expenditures, which usually meant heavier taxation,
responded by asking the Board of Education for detailed
data on school population shifts, which the educational
authorities were unable to supply. Irked by this, the
Estimate Board refused to appropriate the additional funds

and instead, on October 26, 1910, launched a full scale
inquiry into the public school system, suspecting that
curriculum inadequacies and administrative difficulties
were as much a cause of school problems as were the shortages of money which were blamed by the Department of
Education for all of its troubles.[3]

A committee of the Board of Estimate, composed
of John Purroy Mitchel, President of the Board of Aldermen,
William A. Prendergast, City Comptroller, and Cyrus C.
Miller, the Bronx Borough President, was placed in charge
of the inquiry. They engaged Professor Paul Hanus, head
of the Department of Education at Harvard University to
oversee the investigation, and he in turn, chose eleven
educational experts to assist him and they began work in
June, 1911.

They were: Frank P. Bachman, Assistant Superintendent of Schools in Cleveland, Ohio; Edward C. Elliott,
Professor of Education at the University of Wisconsin,

---

[3]
    Frederick Shaw, Fifty Years of Research in the
Board of Education, Publication # 226, Educational Program,
Research and Statistics (New York: 1964), pp. 1-2; New York
(City), Board of Estimate and Apportionment, Report of the
Committee on the School Inquiry, (New York: 1913), Vol. I,
pp. 59-60.

Frank McMurray, Professor of Elementary Education at
Teachers College, Jesse D. Burks, Director of the Bureau
of Municipal Research in Philadelphia, Herman Schneider,
Dean of the College of Engineering of the University of
Cincinnati and specialist in work-study programs; Frank
W. Ballou, Assistant Professor of Education at the Univer-
sity of Cincinnati, Ernest C. Moore, Professor of Educa-
tion at Yale; Calvin O. Davis, Assistant Professor of
Education at the University of Michigan, Frank V. Thompson,
Assistant Superintendent of Schools in Boston, Massachusetts;
Henry H. Goddard, Director of the Department of Psychological
Research of the New Jersey Training School for the Feeble
Minded and Stuart A. Courtis, head of the Department of
Science and Mathematics at the Detroit Home and Day School.[4]

    All of these men had rather impressive backgrounds
in their chosen fields. Hanus, for example, had taught
at both the high school and college level, had founded the
Graduate School of Education at Harvard, and was a member
of the Massachusetts State Board of Education. Bachman
held a Ph.D. from Columbia University, had been a high
school principal and professor of education at Ohio State.
Elliott also was a Ph.D. from Columbia and had been a
school superintendent in Colorado before coming to Wisconsin. After his work on the Hanus survey, he went on to

----

[4] Education, XXXIII (May, 1913), p. 573.

become the president of Purdue University. McMurray had
earned his Ph.D. at the University of Jena in Germany and
had been the dean of a teachers college in Buffalo before
his appointment to Columbia.

Schneider, who held a Sci.D. from the University
of Pittsburgh, became the president of the University of
Cincinnati after his work for Hanus. Ballou, who had
earned his degrees at Columbia and Harvard, had taught
at every level from the elementary to the graduate school,
and eventually became the superintendent of schools in
Washington, D.C. Goddard had won a reputation as an expert
in the psychology and education of gifted children, after
he had adapted the Binet intelligence test for American
schools. Moore had received his Ph.D. at the University
of Chicago and specialized in the philosophy of education
at the University of California, after being at Yale.
Courtis, like Goddard, was known extensively for his work
in tests and measurements and held a doctorate from the
University of Michigan.[5] Hanus, McMurry, Goddard, Courtis,
Burks, and Schneider were to deal with the educational
aspects of the schools, while the other men studied the
administrative and financial side.[6]

---

[5] J. McKee Cattell (ed.), Leaders in Education (New York: 1932), passim

[6] Report of the Committee on the School Inquiry, p. 1; Shaw, p.2.

The Chairman of the Board of Estimate Committee
and moving force behind the investigation, John Purroy
Mitchel, stated that he wanted the experts to provide
him with information on: the number of teachers really
needed, the number of part-time classes in existence;
the advisibility of establishing intermediate schools,
the value of special and visiting teachers, the size of
high school classes, the work of attendance officers, the
extent of teacher absences and the cost of substitutes.[7]
As the inquiry proceeded, even more information was demanded, all of it in areas in which the Board of Education had been much criticized.

For example, in May of 1911, Craftsman magazine
published an interview with James Creelman, a journalist
and official of the Bureau of Municipal Research, who had
been appointed to the Board of Education by Mayor Gaynor
and had resigned after one month, because he found himself
unable to exercise any influence at all on the schools.
Creelman maintained that the Board of Superintendents, not
the Board of Education made all the decisions and that
three quarters of the members of the latter body were
totally uninformed on school matters. The remaining portion
of the Board, who dominated the committees through which
that body did its work, depended on Superintendent Maxwell

---

[7]
Report of the Committee on the School Inquiry,
p. 122.

for all their information.

The Superintendent and the Board of which he was
the chairman were overworked and overwhelmed with detail,
and as a result, they were not planning for the real needs
of the city's cosmopolitan population:

> ...although there are a few special classes to
> take care of the exceptional pupils, the
> curriculum of the elementary school...is an
> ironbound, inflexible system of study enforced
> throughout the city, regardless of the fact
> that the metropolis had become more or less
> an aggregation of foreign colonies...   8

Furthermore, said Creelman, 94 out of every 100
public school children got only an elementary education
and went to work at 14. Therefore, they should get
vocational training early in their school lives, instead
of the formal, academic education they were presently
receiving. Creelman ended his devastating critique with
a recommendation for a paid, full-time Board of Education of six or seven members who would take control of
the schools away from the Board of Superintendents, leaving those officials to execute, not make, policy.   9

8
    Isaac Russell, "Is our Public School System Behind
the Times?", Craftsman, XX (May, 1911) p.143. Creelman's
Bureau of Municipal Research was a private watchdog
committee which examined the financial affairs of the city
periodically, and commented on waste and inefficiency. The
Department of Education was one of its special targets.

9
    Ibid., pp. 142-145. This proposal was incorporated
in the McKee Bills which were passed by the Legislature in
1913, but vetoed by Governor Sulzer.

As frequently happens, the Hanus Committee was
unable to investigate all of the many areas demanded by
the critics of the schools. The eleven specialists worked
only part time for the committee and coordination of their
reports was very difficult. Also, Mitchel and his group
were constantly asking Professor Hanus for immediate
answers to their questions, being unwilling to wait for
the results of the thoroughgoing inquiry the Professor was
attempting to achieve. The officials at the Board of
Education were, understandably, most uncooperative, the
Board of Estimate was somewhat dilatory in its appropriations, and as a result, the Committee had to limit its
work to those educational and administrative problems which
they found most susceptible of investigation and remedy.[10]

Its final report began by establishing the importance
of the schools to the city's budget, a not unreasonable
place for a committee of the Board of Estimate to start.
24.83% of the city's total expenditures went for education,
reported Professor Hanus, and it therefore behooved the
people to know how this large sum of money was being spent.
It appeared that these public funds were not being expended very well at all. The Committee found that almost one
half of the children who entered the first grade in New York

---

[10] Report of the Committee on the School Inquiry, p.128.

never remained to complete the eighth, and the extent of
retardation in all the grades was shocking.

Contrary to what Maxwell said, the large number
of part time classes was not the major reason for the
overage problem. Rather, the real cause was the lack of
flexibility in the curriculum, due to the school's un-
willingness to respond to individual and social needs.[11]

As an example of this rigidity, Professor McMurry
said "In spite of the fact that four-fifths of the
children in some schools hear only foreign languages at
home, while few in other schools hear anything but English,
all are expected to spend approximately the same amount
of time in the study of English."[12]

The experts found that the dead hand of bureaucratic
inertia due to overcentralization lay heavy on the entire
system, destroying creativity and lowering the morale of
teachers, principals, and district superintendents alike.
The Board of Superintendents came in for special disapproval
because it was too cumbersome and overburdened with detail
to properly supervise the schools, and inadequate for its
administrative responsibilities. In an attempt to control

---

[11] Ibid., pp. 54,19,151.

[12] Ibid., p.19.

every aspect of the school's work, it was accomplishing
little, and was even unaware of its own successes or
failures, due to a lack of evaluative machinery.[13]
Professor Elliott had an additional criticism regarding
the district superintendents. "The existing method of
selecting district superintendents too narrowly confines
choice to those whose education, training and experience
have been entirely within the city."[14]

One of the very few bright spots in the system,
reported the investigators, were the kindergartens, which
were adequately fulfilling their function. The small
number of intermediate schools, serving grades seven and
eight were likewise approved, as was the speed with which
the city school children could do arithmetic problems. On
the other hand, these same youngsters placed below
national standards in accuracy and reasoning ability, which
led Stuart Courtis, the mathematics expert, to question the
value of their speed.

The schools were also faulted for the paucity of
their facilities for mentally defective children, and for
the fact that the new two year vocational schools were not

---

[13] Ibid., pp. 27,183.

[14] Ibid., p.37.

reaching enough youngsters. The high schools were likewise severely criticized because they were too scattered,
too large and too classical in their orientation, emphasizing mathematics and languages to the exclusion of the
commercial subjects, which, when taught at all, were of
very poor quality.[15]

Various administrative entities of the educational
structure were also found wanting. The district superintendents were not well qualified, and like their superiors,
too engrossed in routine detail. The Board of Examiners
was honest, but too far removed from classroom realities
to know a good teacher from a poor one. The local school
boards, in their present position, were of no importance
whatever and should be either dropped, or utilized properly. As to the Superintendent of Schools, the Committee
was ambivalent. Maxwell was called a courageous and able
leader, but criticized as being too autocratic, so that
he got obedience, but not cooperation from his staff,
and stifled any display of the initiative so badly needed
by the school system.[16]

---

[15] Ibid., pp. 142,146-148, 145, 156, 162-164, 170, 176.

[16] Ibid., pp. 180, 182-183, 184, 186, 193.

When it came to making recommendations to correct this wide assortment of deficiencies, the Hanus Committee found itself in an awkward position. As professional educators, they knew very well that any improvements they might suggest were bound to cost more money. Yet--the very reason for their existence lay in the fact that the school budget was already considered to be too high. Faced with this dilemma, the Committee emphasized those features which were likely to cost the least; but honesty compelled them to say, albeit quietly, that larger appropriations would do the schools much good.

Their first recommendation, however, would entail no additional expenditures at all.

> The course of study in all schools should be
> organized around human problems and made simple
> and elastic enough to permit of differentiation
> to meet the needs of different nationalities
> and groups.   17

To develop such a curriculum in New York City was not difficult, the report pointed out, because "the different nationalities live for the most part in compact groups..." Professor McMurry suggested that the principals be given the power to develop their own curricula in accordance

---

17
Ibid., p.18.

with the needs of their community, so that the immigrant
children of the Lower East Side would not have to learn
the same items that were taught to the middle class
youngsters of the Upper West Side.

Other members of the Committee suggested that
committees of teachers and principals draw up different
courses of study for the various neighborhoods, while
Stuart Courtis demonstrated how even the teaching of
arithmetic could be used to fit the needs of the different
nationalities in New York.[18]

The Committee's interest in adapting the school to
the community extended to after school programs. They
said a comprehensive plan should be "worked out for the
wider use of school buildings for purposes of recreation,
for public assemblage, and for civic and social gatherings,"
and that the work of all the different agencies concerned
with school extension should be coordinated. In addition
to meeting the needs of the community in these ways, the
Committee said attention should be paid by the schools to
developing a course of study which would emphasize commercial, industrial, and vocational education.

In the same area of curriculum, they thought the
use of teachers of special subjects should be discontinued

---

[18]
Ibid., pp. 21,20,139.

and that <u>all</u> the faculty should have the training necessary
to teach music, drawing and physical education. If this
were done, no critics of the schools could say such
subjects were frills or fads and the content could be
better integrated with the traditional subjects. Regarding the basic studies of the elementary schools, Hanus and
his associates asked that arithmetic be simplified and made
less formal and that only that part of world history that
had relevance to the American experience be taught.[19]

Because they thought the three intermediate schools
were doing a good job, the Committee urged that more be
built, and that they be called junior high schools, since
they bridged the gap between the elementary grades and the
high schools. Dean Schneider recommended that cooperative
vocational programs be established in these junior high
schools, programs which would enable students to alternate
work and school.

Although they found the ungraded classes to be
an important part of the school, the experts suggested
that they be expanded and place more emphasis on manual
work and less on the three "R's". They also saw a great
need for better testing and classification of mental
defectives. Here they were advocating programs which would

---

[19]
Ibid.,pp. 41, 21, 25, 139.

cost more money and they trod this dangerous ground a
little further by saying the Board of Estimate should
make larger appropriations for the purpose of reducing
the number of part time classes.[20]

The high schools were an area which interested a
number of the consultants. They were not sure whether
small specialized high schools or large mixed ones were
better and suggested that the Board of Education consider
the question. If more large, centrally located high
schools were constructed, the Committee thought the school
system should pay the transportation costs of the children
who would have to travel long distances to reach them.
It was further recommended that the academic high schools
teach more manual training, civics, commercial subjects,
and homemaking, so as to better meet the needs of the
students. This progressive idea was followed by a re-
actionary one, which excited much discussion. Professor
McMurry advocated the use of corporal punishment, because
he felt the large number of non-school minded children now
forced to stay in school could only be controlled in
this way.[21]

20
  Ibid.,pp. 22,23,143,151.

21
  Ibid., pp. 28, 162, 163-164, 34.

A large portion of the Committee's recommendation
ealt with changes in the structure of the schools. First
f all, they thought it essential to establish a Bureau of
nvestigation and Appraisal so that the Board of Education
ould have a factual basis for its decisions. This Bureau
ould have the prime responsibility of accumulating educa-
ional statistics, vital in planning school affairs. A
eachers Council, to have a voice in school administration,
nd make reports and recommendations to guide the Board of
uperintendents, was another great need of the schools. In
he same category, the Committee urged that attendance
rocedures be revised, making enforcement of the compulsory
ducation law the province of a special Bureau of the
epartment of Education, which would also oversee the
ensus Board, the probationary and parental schools, and
he visiting teachers.

Headquarters should also be reorganized, especially
he Bureau of Supplies, and the Bureau of Buildings. The
ccounting system of the Board was in very bad shape and
as the reason for some of its financial difficulties.
n entirely new system of audit and control was suggested,
o that the Board of Estimate could get a clear picture of
he fiscal affairs of the schools.[22]

22
Ibid., pp. 29, 39, 54, 43.

Some really revolutionary suggestions followed.
Abolish the Board of Superintendents, said the Committee,
for it is a hindrance, not a help to the schools, and
reduce the Board of Education from 46 to 16 members (some
of the experts said six to nine men would be enough),
because in its present large size it was too unwieldy to
accomplish anything. Having cut the Board by more than
50%, and eliminated its chief executive arm, the Hanus
specialists offered it some support, saying that the
Department of Education must have greater financial
flexibility and not have to go to the Board of Estimate
for every penny it needed, and that, in the long run,
educational affairs in the city should be conducted by
an independent body with taxing powers of its own.[23]

Predictably, the Hanus Report was extremely unpopular with school officials, at all levels. Maxwell had
indicated his displeasure as soon as the investigation had
begun, saying that the Inquiry was causing the schools a
great deal of trouble and that he wished the Committee
would leave him alone for a while![24] When the report was
published, the Superintendent gave it a brief, bitter,
review which was particularly harsh on Professor McMurry.
He differed with Hanus regarding the cost of the Inquiry;

23
   Ibid., pp. 184,52,190-191.

24
   New York (City), Department of Education, Thirteenth
Annual Report of the City Superintendent of Schools, (New York:
1911), p.231.

the chairman had said the bill came to $95,139 but Maxwell
placed the charge at $100,000. and said the schools could
well have used this large sum for educational, rather than
investigative purposes.[25]

Not wishing to carry the ball of criticism alone,
the Superintendent had asked his associate, Dr. Meleney,
to answer some of the Hanus charges. That gentleman chose
to discuss the section in which the Committee had recommended that principals be empowered to make curriculum changes
in accordance with the needs of their neighborhoods. The
Associate Superintendent said that principals already had
that power, and that the Board of Superintendents required
only a basic minimum of studies which was needed by all
children, native and foreign born alike.[26]

Shortly thereafter, a committee of teachers and
superintendents issued a bitter attack on McMurry, Thompson,
and Courtis, emphasizing particularly the former's controver-
sial recommendation regarding corporal punishment.[27]

25
     Fifteenth Annual Report of the City Superintendent
OF Schools, 1913, p. 166; Report of the Committee on the
School Inquiry, p. 64.

26
     Fourteenth Annual Report of the City Superinten-
dent of Schools, 1912, p. 131.

27
     Fifteenth Annual Report of the City Superintendent
of Schools, 1913, p. 495.

The Association of District Superintendents responded to
the idea of a decentralized curriculum by stating that
the frequent shifting of population in the metropolis
made it essential to have a uniform course of study.
Families moved so often, said the spokesman for this
body, a child transferred to a new school would be lost,
if each principal could determine his own course of study.[28]

A meeting of the High School Teachers Association
held at the High School of Commerce on Saturday, May 3, 1913,
also attacked a portion of the Hanus Survey. The teachers
denounced the proposal for large, cosmopolitan high schools,
fearing that classical subjects would be neglected in a
course of study that included manual training, and commercial subjects. The majority advocated smaller, specialized
schools, but there was a minority group who thought the
Hanus experts were correct.[29]

The Board of Superintendents had a special stake in
the Inquiry since the Hanus Report had recommended their
abolition. They therefore spent five sessions on framing
a lengthy defense. First, said the Superintendents, the
Hanus experts were biased against the New York City Department of Education and their report was based on inaccurate
and incomplete information. Professor Elliott (who suggested that the Board of Superintendents be abolished) had been

---

[28]
New York City, Department of Education, Reply of
the Association of District Superintendents of New York to
certain findings and recommendations of Professor Frank
McMurry and Professor Edward C. Elliott, (New York: 1913),
p.13.

[29]New York Times, May 4, 1913, II, p.10.

present at only one of their meetings. If it were true,
as the Committee said, that the Superintendents were too
much enmeshed in red tape, it was the fault of the
Charter, which placed such great responsibilities on them,
and not any of their own doing. They did not encourage inbreeding, continued the Superintendents, but it just happen-
ed that the men who were the best qualified to serve at
the highest echelons of administration were veterans of the
school system, while many of the problems of education in
New York City were new to the world and required experienced and delicate handling. The defense rested with a list
of their achievements, prominent among which were the
"amalgamation of thousands of foreign children of all ages,
of all degrees of education and training, immigrating into
the city..."[30]

The school system did have outside defenders. The
School Journal, a publication which normally confined itself to news of educational developments in New York City,
waxed angry in an editorial shortly after the publication
of the Hanus Report. That document lacked coherence, and
needed editing, said the Journal, and gleefully pointed
out how some of the experts disagreed with the others! The
schools of New York were too big to be surveyed by a part-

30- New York (City) Department of Education, Minutes
of the Board of Superintendents, March, 1913, (New York:1913),
pp. 178-192; New York (City) Department of Education, The
Hanus-Elliott Report: A Review and Reply by the Board of
Superintendents, pp. 3,5,7,23,25,11.

time committee, especially one on which the so-called experts
had never been administrators themselves.[31] The recommendations of Hanus and his specialists showed how inadequate
their survey was, continued the Journal. Inbreeding among
the Superintendents was not a valid criticism, because
Maxwell could get experienced assistants only from the rank
and file of the schools. The Board of Superintendents was
essential and should certainly not be abolished. Furthermore,
the plan for an advisory teachers council was "too experimental" and might disrupt the schools, while the idea of
corporal punishment was horrible! About the only finding
of the Committee with which the Journal was in agreement
was the one which recommended an elected, independent, Board
of Education. The editorial concluded by saying that the
New York City schools were very fine, considering the size
of the system, and that Maxwell had "made a new educational
New York, full of instruction for every other city in the
land..."[32]

The New York press, in general, gave the Hanus
Inquiry adequate, although not intensive coverage. The

---

[31]Actually, the Journal was wrong about the lack of
administrative experience of the Hanus experts; above p.4.

[32]The School Journal, March 13, 1913, pp. 166-167,
169,170.

World, Globe, and Times objectively reported the conflict
between the Board of Estimate and the Department of Education which led to the establishment of the Committee.[33]
When the Report was made public in January, 1913, the
Times gave it a full column and followed up with an
editorial two days later which praised the work of the
Committee, especially the recommendations for increased
flexibility in the course of study and for more vocational
education.[34]

The Herald did not have an editorial on the
subject, but did print a long review of Hanus' summary,
including interviews with members of the Board of Education, whose reactions were summarized as follows:

> Members of the Board of Education were affected
> with varying emotions respecting some of the
> recommendations, but all said there was merit
> in most of the conclusions reached by the
> commission.

The Herald indicated that Maxwell had refused to
comment and implied that the Superintendent saw little
of value in the proposals.[35]

---

[33]The New York World, October 27, 1910, p.20;
The New York Globe and Commercial Advertiser, October 26,
1910, p. 8; The New York Times, October 27, 1910, p. 10.

[34]The New York Times, January 25, 1913, p.19;
Ibid., January 27, 1913, p.8.

[35]The New York Herald, January 25, 1913, p.15.

The World covered the report in a straight seven paragraph story headed "School System of City is Defective, Professor Hanus Finds," but said nothing editorially until five days later. Then it printed a brief comment which approved McMurry's recommendation regarding the institution of corporal punishment.[36] The Globe, which was noted for its school coverage, had the longest editorial on the Hanus Report, which was to be expected. The tone of the article was favorable to the Inquiry. "The Hanus report represents the first serious attempt to grapple in a large way with the problems of urban education". The editorial went on to explain that, up to this point, city schools were just extensions of rural ones, although this should not be so. The Hanus survey, if acted upon, was a chance for New York City to show the rest of the United States what good urban education could be like. Therfore, the Globe urged the public to support the Hanus recommendations because without public pressure, the schoolmen would not implement the proposals of the Committee.[37]

---

[36]
    The New York World, January 25, 1913, p.11; Ibid., January 30, p.8.

[37]
    The New York Globe, January 25, 1913, p.8.

It would appear that press reaction was generally favorable to most of the Report, although no detailed analysis was made by any of the papers, and only the _Globe_ seemed at all excited by the conclusions. Three years later, during the controversy over the Gary Plan, the _New Republic_ hearkened back to the Hanus Report and repeated some of the charges made about the Board of Education, adding a few embellishments of its own. "The Board of Education is amateurish, feeble, too large, utterly hide-bound, insular, and a total failure." Furthermore, "...the school system works on an emergency basis only--always motivated by a desire to protect those in the system, and not the children." [38]

Professor Hanus' own estimate of the work of his group was cautiously optimistic. He saw a number of good results coming from the Inquiry, particularly greater cooperation between the Board of Estimate and the Department of Education, which he thought had been brought about by a number of factors. Superintendent Maxwell now had a statistician in his office so the previous misunderstandings about school figures would not occur again. The Board of Education, spurred by the Report, was playing a more active role, and had agreed to give more accurate

---

[38]
The New Republic, February 5, 1916, p.7.

information to the Estimate Board and the Comptroller.
The Schools were now making economies in supplies and
staff, which was in the public good. And finally, the
professional educators had been shown that the public
schools were not their private preserve and that only
when laymen and outside people took an interest in them,
could their efforts succeed.[39]

In spite of Professor Hanus' optimism, the changes
in the schools which resulted from the Inquiry were neither
very numerous nor very significant. John Purroy Mitchel
had made plans to follow up the recommendations by establishing a committee to make "more effective the results of Dr.
Hanus' investigation."

He asked Lillian Wald, as well as representatives
of other "volunteer agencies interested in the public schools"
to serve on such a body. Miss Wald declined although she
thought "Dr. Hanus' study was too important not to get
the very best thought and consideration of people who care
about the public schools" and suggested that Miss Pauline
Goldmark of the Child Labor Committee be asked in her place.[40]

---

[39] Report of the Committee on the School Inquiry,
pp. 13-18.

[40] Letter from Lillian Wald to John Purroy Mitchel,
August 25, 1912. In the Lillian Wald Collection at the
New York Public Library.

It would seem that this group had no great impact
on the school system, because even after the Report had
been publicized, the Board of Superintendents remained,
as did the large Board of Education, although unsuccessful
attempts were made by Mayor Gaynor to cut its size.[41]
Corporal punishment was not legalized, and the principals
had neither more nor less power over curriculum than
before. Most disappointing, in view of the original reason
for the Inquiry, school expenditures did not decrease, but
rather grew larger. A Teachers Council was organized in
1914, but never made any large contribution to the schools,
and only the establishment of the Division of Research and
Reference and the reorganization of the Attendance Bureau
can be considered really important changes in the structure
of the schools, attributable to the Hanus Inquiry.[42]

Superintendent Maxwell, however, evidently did not
expect so little change to result and took the precaution
of defending his administration vigorously. He had given
a statement on "Improvements in the Public Schools of the
City of New York, 1898-1911" to Professor Hanus, in

41
This is a reference to the aforementioned McKee
Bills which Gaynor supported, Above, note 8.

42
Harold McCormick, "The First Fifty Years", Fiftieth
Annual Report of the New York City Superintendent of Schools,
(New York: 1948), pp. 59,67.

September of 1911 and it was printed in volume I of the final report. Maxwell considered the unification of the schools in all the boroughs to be his greatest achievement. A close second was the professionalization of the staff and the extension of the merit system. Not far behind in importance was the organization of high schools in Manhattan and the Bronx, and their improvement in all the boroughs. Uniform salary schedules and uniform curricula had helped to modernize the schools, as had the abolition of the huge classes which were a feature of the system prior to 1902. Improvements like the "C,D. and E" classes, vacation schools, health care for the handicapped and defective, as well as the introduction of permanent record cards, fire drills, athletics, vocational education, and probationary schools were contributions of vast importance to the schools of New York, all of which had been accomplished since 1898. [43]

This thirty-eight page summary of improvements in the schools was most impressive, and strikingly similar to many of the recommendations of Professors McMurry, Courtis, et al. Actually, Maxwell and the Hanus experts had identical goals in education; both were aware of the enormous new challenges presented to the schools by the immigrant influx

---

[43] Report of the Committee on the School Inquiry, pp. 69-97.

and both wanted the schools to play an active role in the life of the city. Therefore, as has been shown in this paper, many of the projects recommended by the Hanus Committee had already been launched in New York City and were in operation.

Why then did the Committee find it necessary to criticize the schools so severely? Vocational education, junior high schools, and extension programs had been part of the educational structure of the city for some years before Professor Hanus appeared on the scene, and the very Board of Superintendents which the experts called hidebound and useless had put into operation schemes of homogeneous grouping and flexible promotion which were considerably in advance of their time. Indeed, the Hanus Committee did mention the existence of all of these programs, but indicated that they were few and largely ineffective, as they were. With the possible exception of the vacation play schools, health examinations, and evening lecture programs, most of the projects begun by the Board of Education in this period reached a very small number of pupils, and on this score, the educational authorities were vulner-able to criticism.

Maxwell was aware of the limited reach of the new projects, and of the gap between planning and implementation which existed. He attributed this to shortages of money and, to a lesser degree, to failings in his staff. Regarding

the inadequate funds, he was absolutely right. There
could be no question that the new classes, subjects and
methods would have affected many more children if sufficient
financing had been forthcoming. Without doubt, larger
appropriations would have resulted in more vocational
education, junior high schools, and special classes, to say
nothing of increased lunch programs and health services.

But contrary to the Superintendent's estimate,
money was never the entire reason for the failings of the
schools. While additional funds would have made it easier
to establish three track programs and probationary schools
like P.S. 120, it was also necessary to have creative
personnel and the drive to carry through the new projects,
once begun. In the public school system of New York City,
this vital element of creativity was in even shorter supply
than dollars, and that was the real reason why the Hanus
experts could level such telling blows on the Board of
Education.

For every Julia Richman, who carried through plans
and ideas entirely new to the schools, there were a dozen
principals who clung to traditional methods and who were
not budged very far by directives from headquarters. For
every Elizabeth Farrell, who was concerned with slow
learners, there were teachers who felt the dullards should
not be in school at all and simply ignored them until
they dropped out. For every Gustave Straubenmuller who

believed so strongly in vocational education, there were
pedagogues who continued to teach only the subjects they
had been taught, and were totally unmoved by the challenges
of industrialization. The minority of educators who were
aware of the problems and tried to be innovators were
unable to carry the entire system with them, although the
projects they began have remained and grown stronger over
the years.

Since Maxwell was demonstrably aware and desirous
of change, why could he not force implementation on his
staff? His personality was strong, his pen active, his
voice rarely still. In spite of these strengths, he was
unable to close the gap between planning and execution
because he was the prisoner of the very same bureaucracy
he had himself created; a network of superintendents and
bureaus whose pre-occupation with red-tape came between
him and the lower echelons of the staff.

This was the real divergence between the Superintendent and the Hanus Committee. Maxwell was proud of his
creation--having built a unified school system out of the
chaos which confronted him in 1898, he naturally had an
investment in its organization and therefore resented
criticism of the Board of Superintendents and the educational
bureaucracy as a whole. To an outside observer however,
it was clear that in attempting to provide much needed
unity, the Superintendent had consolidated his administration

too much, with resulting problems of overdependence on headquarters, as well as delay and inertia. In a sense, there was too much freedom for individual teachers and principals. Because the system grew too fast and soon became too large to be carefully supervised, those people who had the primary responsibility for carrying out educational plans, were able to resist change and to continue, in large part, the methods of the nineteenth century.

Overall, then, the Hanus Committee was probably correct in its criticism of the structure of the schools, and unduly harsh in its comments on programs. Most especially, the Committee did not give Maxwell and his assistants enough credit for the truly creative and innovative qualities they had exhibited, the value of which has been demonstrated by the continued existence of so many of the programs begun between 1898 and 1914, but whose implementation was somewhat restricted at the time.

This lasting quality of the changes in the schools made during this period is what most strikes the student of today. The 1965-1966 edition of the Board of Education publication, Facts and Figures, describes 50 present day departments and programs, 33 of which originated 60 to 75 years ago.[44] These programs fall into two categories:

[44] New York (City), Board of Education, New York City Public Schools, Facts and Figures, 1965-1966, (New York: 1966), passim.

administrative and substantive. In regard to the first
group, establishment of a lay, unpaid, non-partisan Board
of Education to work with a professional staff, as well as
the extension of the merit system to the teachers of all
the boroughs, and the relegation of the local school boards
to an advisory role, the establishment of the office of
superintendent of Buildings, the organization of the
Bureau of Attendance as well as the Bureau of Reference
and Research, and the erection of the entire structure of
assistant and associate superintendents are all administrative changes which originated in the early 20th century and
have remained a part of the schools today.

Similarly, the roster of substantive innovations
begun during the first decade of the century and still
prominent in the educational life of the city is very
large. The list includes the teaching of subjects such
as Health Education, Domestic Science, Manual Training,
Music, and Art, as well as the continuation of classes for
the mentally retarded, the physically handicapped, the socially maladjusted, those with speech defects, the visually
handicapped, the deaf, the gifted, and the non-English
speaking.

Furthermore, many of the special bureaus now
operating out of the Board of Education began their work
in the period under discussion. The Bureau of Attendance,
of Child Guidance, of Vocational Guidance, and of School

Lunches are all the fruit of the labors performed by
Paul Klapper, Elizabeth Farrell, Mabel H. Kittredge and
Julia Richman during the Progressive Era.

The extension activities of the schools in 1966
cover many fields, but in every case, the programs originated between 1898 and 1914. The "600" schools for the
emotionally disturbed are the direct descendents of Julia
Richman's probationary school, P.S. 120, as is the flexible
promotion policy a continuation of her experiments at P.S.
77. The after school study and play centers of today would
have gladdened Evangeline Whitney's heart, and present day
vocational, continuation, and cooperative work study
programs would have much pleased Gustave Straubenmuller.
Even the Junior high schools now being reconverted into
intermediate schools began with Maxwell's attempts to keep
the children in school past the sixth grade. Many of the
summer and evening schools for advanced, remedial, or
trade education now conducted by the Department of Education
owe their origin to the law of 1898, which allowed the
Board of Education to open school buildings after three P.M.

A number of these present day developments whose
origin has been traced to the turn of the century are
different in nomenclature, extent, and cost from their
predecessors. Most represent the flowering of what were
tiny ideas planted in the earlier period. In general,
these programs are now totally accepted as an important

part of school life, in contrast to the criticism they had
to undergo when they began. The essential similarity
between the earlier developments and those of today lies
in their purpose. Although the ethnic groups may be
different, the problems these programs are trying to solve
are comparable. To keep more children in school longer,
and give them knowledge more suited to their needs, to
provide them with training for employment, to minister to
their health, both physical and mental, are the purposes
of the public schools in New York in 1966, as they began
to be the "raison d'etre" for education sixty years earlier.

Why were the changes described in this study
undertaken? Who were the agents of reform? Was the pressure
direct or indirect, of the immigrant parents, responsible?
Or did the middle class progressives, active in so many
areas of reform during the period, stimulate the innovations?
The question is pivotal to this essay and deserves close
examination.

It is clear that many of the immigrants whose
children were the beneficiaries of the new programs were
aware that the public schools could be a vehicle for social
and economic mobility. Because they recognized this, they
encouraged their youngsters to be diligent and to take advantage of all the opportunities offered by the schools.
They could see that overcrowding and part-time schedules
made the attainment of educational success more difficult,

and they voted for Seth Low in 1901, at least in part, because he promised to see that more schools were built in the congested areas in which they lived.[45]

There also can be no doubt that politicians were aware of the popularity of good schools in all sections of the city, including those in which the immigrants predominated. When Mayor Low was campaigning for re-election in October, 1903, he made a speech on the Lower East Side in which he emphasized that his administration had spent more money for education than any other in the city's history. He also pointed with pride to his efforts to develop the use of schools as play centers, and concluded by saying, in effect, that these activities showed how cognizant he was of the needs of the East Side.[46]

In an attempt to mobilize progressive support for the Mayor, and at the same time, provide material for speeches like this one, Low's campaign managers asked Lillian Wald to summarize the ways in which she felt the Low administration had improved the city. Miss Wald's answer included a number of advances which had been made in the fields of health and welfare, but she saw one particular gain for the schools as especially important:

---

[45]
    Milo T. Bogard (ed.), The Redemption of New York (New York: 1902), p. 157.

[46]
    The New York Times, October 20, 1903, p.5.

Under our Administration, there is a very great
increase over previous school attendance, meaning
that truants and children out of school have
been gathered in, but the most important change
for the welfare of the teachers and the proper
teaching of the children is that whereas before
an exhausted teacher taught the second session
of half-time pupils, now there are two teachers
and each class has a teacher fresh for her arduous
task.   47

At least one progressive, it would appear, appreci-

ated the contribution of Seth Low to the public schools.

A few days after Low's East Side speech, however,

his opponent, George B. McClellan, also spoke on the subject

of education and attacked the incumbent's record, pointing

out how overcrowding was still a problem, and promising to

see that many more seats were made available, if he were

elected.   48   McClellan did win the contest, although Low's

school record, which really was most creditable, was hardly

the crucial factor in his victory. Indeed, this particular

campaign illustrates a pattern apparent in each of the

electoral contests of the period. All candidates, reformers

and Tammany men alike, found it necessary to speak of the

schools, and promise to remedy their deficiencies.

47
    Letter from Lillian Wald to Dr. Abbott E. Kittredge,
October 29, 1903. In the Lillian Wald Collection at the New
York Public Library.

48
    The New York Times, October 25, 1903, p.2.

In 1913, for example, the Tammany convention which
nominated Edward E. McCall, approved a platform containing
planks that any reformer could have supported. After
commending the vigor and intelligence of the Board of Education, the statement recommended more simplicity in school
administration and a flexible course of study which would be
in accord with the varied needs of the city. These regular
Democrats also favored more vocational education in both
day and evening schools and the wider use of school buildings
for recreational programs. Their campaign statement ended
with a strong attack on political interference in the administration of school affairs, which certainly was an attempt
to steal the reformer's ammunition, and indicated the extent
to which differing political groups took similar positions
on the public schools.[49]

The defeat of Mayor Mitchel in 1917, partly on the
issue of the Gary Plan which he so strongly supported, is
one of the few cases in which a difference of opinion on
school changes was a decisive factor in a municipal election.
Because many of the immigrant parents considered academic
training more important than vocational, because the
longer school day interfered with part-time jobs or religious
training, the Gary Plan was unpopular on the Lower East Side

---

[49] The New York Times, August 24, 1913, II, p.2

and in Brownsville, and John F. Hylan's victory can be attributed, partially, at least, to this issue.[50]

It would therefore appear, that since all but the newest arrivals voted, the immigrants held a powerful weapon in their hands, and no city administration could be unaware of the potential electoral power of the newcomers. The increase in school building in the congested districts, noted through the administrations of all the Mayors from Strong to Mitchel, makes it clear that no occupant of City Hall could ignore the possibility of losing votes because he neglected the schools. Similarly, the vacation schools and kindergartens were items protected from budget cutting precisely because their popularity with working class families made them a great asset to any politician who could show that he had supported them.

On the other hand, those city officials who did attempt to reduce school budgets, and thus slow down reform, suffered no backlash from indignant voters. The Coler and Grout investigations seemed to have added to the stature of the Comptrollers who initiated them, and both men were reelected after their attempts to eliminate many new programs became widely known.[51]   Members of the Board of Estimate

---

[50]
Sol Cohen, Progressives and Urban School Reform, (New York: 1964), p.98

[51]
The Literary Digest, November 16, 1901, p.593; New York Times, December 26, 1904, p.6.

generally viewed educational expansion with a jaundiced eye, but their votes on school budgets did not appear to be the primary cause of their political rise or fall.

To sum up, it would appear that all the political parties and candidates prominent in New York City's political life in the first decades of the century had to be cognizant of the potential voting strength of the immigrants and therefore, had to take a position on school matters. Implementation of their pledges might or might not follow, but the very taking of a stand indicated that attention was being paid to the electorate, as must always be the case in a democracy.

But after all these political aspects are considered, and credit given to the voice of the people as expressed at the ballot box, it is also necessary to recognize that most immigrant parents, handicapped by poverty and the need to adjust to a new life in America, could not lead the drive for better public schools, although they could and did express their views on election day.

The absence of any city-wide parent organization until 1924 meant that one avenue of citizen pressure was closed to the parents of the period. Today, the United Parents Organization of New York is a leading spokesman on school matters, drawing its strength from a membership of thousands of concerned mothers and fathers who actively

ressure the Loard of Lducation on educational affairs.
o such voice was available to parents in 1900-1914.
ndeed, principals such as Angelo Patri, who thought
arental concern would achieve many gains for education,
eplored the lack of interest on the part of the adults,
nd recorded the difficulties he experienced when he tried
                                                    52
o establish a parent teacher organization at his school.

Actually, Patri had more success than most princi-
als who tried to reach the parents of the community served
y their school. The New York Globe school page of October
6, 1910 recorded that only two parent meetings had been
eld during the previous week and said that "various schools
were) encouraging parents to cooperate with (the) teachers..."
ut the tone of the article indicated that parental interest
                            53
as not easy to arouse.

52
        Margaret Lighty and LeRoy Bowman, Parenthood in a
emocracy (New York: 1939), p.1; Angelo Patri, A Schoolmaster
n a Great City (New York: 1917), p.104; Letter from Lillian
ald to Angelo Patri, April 2, 1913. In the Lillian Wald
ollection at the New York Public Library.

53
        The New York Globe, October 26, 1916, p.15.
he two meetings described here were at P.S. 50 in the Gramercy
ark district, and at a school in the Flatbush area of
rooklyn, neither of which had high immigrant populations.

The need to earn a living and run a household
prevented working class parents from taking an active role
in school affairs. Except in a few instances, mostly related to the teaching of foreign languages, the Minutes of the
Board of Superintendents do not record evidence of parental
pressure, either from individuals or groups. The thousands
of pages of the Minutes record correspondence from teachers
and municipal officials but very little from community
groups, even when a new course of study was introduced, as
in 1902, or when a dramatic innovation such as pre-vocational education was begun in 1909. There were a few requests
for after school activities in certain areas such as
Brownsville, but in general, it would not appear that the
newcomers carried on much of a dialogue with the most powerful agency in the school system, the Board of Superintendents. [54]

Immigrant parents were not entirely mute, of course,
especially when the safety of their children was involved,
but even when an issue was of great importance to them, they
required the leadership of an outside agency; a settlement
house, or a reform organization such as the Public Education

---

[54]
Minutes of the Board of Superintendents, 1902-1914,
passim. In 1908, an increase in the number of requests for
teaching of Italian was noted. In all cases, the request
was relayed via the local school board. April 30, 1908,
p. 463. September 15, 1908, pp. 893,989.

Association. An incident which occurred in 1904 will
illustrate this point.

A meeting of parents was held at the Educational
Alliance on Sunday night, October 23, 1904 "to protest
against the recent resolution adopted by the Board of
Education which provides for the transportation of 1500
children from that part of the city (east side) to schools
on the west side as a remedy against the overcrowding of
east side schools". About 2,000 persons attended, which
indicated considerable interest. The audience was hostile
to the plan for reasons which appeared in the remarks of
the speakers. Gregory Weinstein, president of the East Side
Civic Club, under whose auspices the meeting was being held,
said the area below 14th Street had stood for "dirty streets,
grafting politicians, and overbearing policemen" but would
not stand for this school transfer plan.

David Blaustein, Superintendent of the Educational
Alliance, explained that the major objection to the scheme
came from Jewish parents who feared that the long distance
of the schools from their homes would make it impossible for
the orthodox children to say their morning prayers or attend
Hebrew school in the evenings. Other speakers placed the
emphasis on the dangers involved. Although the Board of
Education was to pay the carfare of the children, the long
trip on the "cars" would injure the health of the youngsters
and the pupils already at the West Side School were reputed

to be very tough and hostile to Jews. It would be catas-
trophic for the East Side children to have to attend these
schools of Hell's Kitchen, said one of the speakers. "We
would have a race riot every day."

The meeting closed with the passage of several resolu-
tions. One of these appointed a committee of five to appear
before Mayor McClellan and the Board of Estimate and protest
the plan. Another suggested that churches and synagogues
be used as temporary schools, until, as was much to be
desired, the Board of Education could catch up with the need
for seats. Finally, it was proposed that a temporary one-
story school be erected under and along the approaches to
the Williamsburg Bridge on land that belonged to the Parks
Department, and it was this last solution that actually
came to pass.[55]

Here is a case in which immigrant parents were
directly affected, very much aroused and successful in
changing a school decision. It was, however, an administrative arrangement, not a matter of educational policy they
were opposing, and the protest required organization by
a middle class reform group, the East Side Civic Club, and
the Educational Alliance, both of which had members with
good connections "uptown". The incident illustrates the
fact that the newcomers did take part in school affairs when
the safety of their children was concerned, and when

---

[55]
     The New York Times, October 24, 1904, p.9. Also
see above, Chapter 3, p.20.

leadership was provided.

Immigrant parents were less active when a purely educational matter created considerably controversy in the spring of 1905, although the school life of their children was directly affected. The Grout investigation of 1904, although it had not produced any changes of importance in the school system, had alerted the Board of Education to the extensive opposition that existed on the part of the city's fiscal authorities to the increasingly high school budgets. As a result, a committee of the school board was appointed in October of 1904, to investigate the possibility of revising the course of study in grades one and two. The group was also asked to look into the matter of shortening the school day in the primary grades to three and one half hours if everything but reading, writing, and arithmetic were eliminated.[56]

The committee reported in March, 1905, and stated that the majority favored leaving the school day and the course of study as it was. The chairman, however, Abraham Stern, disagreed with most of the committee and strongly advocated shortening the school day. He said that a three and one half hour day in the lower grades would mean seats for 50,000 children because classrooms could thus be utilized morning and afternoon. With so many desks available, it would not be necessary to build the fifteen new schools the Superintendent had requested and five million dollars

---

[56] The New York Times, March 19, 1905, p.5.

worth of bonds would not have to be sold.

Actually, Mr. Stern was merely recommending that a widespread policy of the Board of Education be made formal and permanent. As was pointed out in chapter three of this study, part-time devices of various kinds had been a fixture of the New York City schools for two decades. The educational authorities, however, had considered such schemes temporary evils. Now Mr. Stern was suggesting that a half-day plan was a positive good, saying, among other things, that East Side parents took proper care of their children, so there was really no harm in having them in school for only part of the day.[57]

In spite of the fact that most of the committee had not agreed with the chairman, Stern was able to convince the Board of Education to acquiesce in his plan. On March 30, the School board voted 22 to 12 to instruct the Superintendents to institute the three and one half hour day for grades one and two. Up to this point, Superintendent Maxwell had been silent, but on April 1st, he issued a statement opposing the short-time plan, and urged parents to protest.[58]

57
  Ibid., March 23, 1905, p.18.

58
  Ibid., March 30, 1905, p. 11; April 1, 1905, p.2.

Instead of parents, however, the Board of Education
was deluged with protests from reformers and settlement house
personnel. Lillian Wald, tireless worker for the immigrant,
led off the attack with a letter to the president of the
Board of Education in which she said:

> The school career of many immigrant children is
> sadly short. Many pupils are older children than
> the first year classes call for but are in them
> by reason of being newcomers...They are not only
> capable of working during the five hour session,
> but are in great need of all the instruction they
> can get.   59

Mrs. Florence Kelley of the National Consumers'
League opposed the Stern plan because every hour the children
of the poor were not in school, they would be made to work
in tenement sweatshops.   60   The New York City Child Labor
Committee pointed out "Reduce the school hours and you
surely and effectively add to the hours to be spent by little
tots of six, seven, eight, and nine...sewing at garments in
the foul air."   61   Mrs. Schuyler Van Rensalaer, president of
the Public Education Association, wrote a 480-word letter
which the *Times* printed in full, in which she gave physical
and moral reasons for the five hour school day. Her statement
also strongly defended the curriculum set up by Maxwell in

59
  Ibid., April 8, 1905, p.7.

60
  Ibid., p.8

61
  Ibid., April 13, 1905, p.6.

1902, which included the so-called "fads and frills",; sew-
[62]
ing, cooking, art, music and health education.

The barrage of protest resulted in a special hearing
at the Hall of the Board of Education at eight p.m. on
May 2, arranged to discuss the Stern plan. The following
organizations were represented and spoke against the proposal: The Association for Improving the Condition of the
Poor, the Neighborhood Workers Association, The East Side
Civic Club, the Normal College Alumnae, and the Public
Education Association. The Board decided to rescind its
order of March 30, keep the five hour day and allow the
new course of study to remain intact. [63]   It was only a
temporary and partial success, since in 1914, the four hour
day for the first grade was established, but the course of
study was not changed, and in general, the reformers could
claim a victory. [64]

Incidents such as the two just described indicate
that it was the reform elements who lead the fight for the

---

[62]
Ibid., April 22, 1905, p.10

[63]
Ibid.,May 3, 1905, p.2

[64]
Ibid.,June 15, 1905, p.2.

educational changes described in this paper, and who
watched school developments carefully in order not to
lose any hard won gains. Although their accomplishments
were many and significant, it may well be that the reformers could have achieved more extensive changes in the
schools, had they mobilized the parents and attempted
mass pressure on the Board of Estimate. In general, they
did not use this method, but relied instead on individual
influence and publicity in order to effect the policies
they favored.

A closer look at these "social progressives", a
term coined by Irwin Yellowitz in his book, Labor and the
Progressive Movement in New York State, 1897-1916, will
clarify the methods used by the groups who were the spear-
head of the movement to change the schools. These organizations shared certain common characteristics. In general,
they depended on a small inner circle of wealthy patricians,
professional men, and social workers for their financial
support and leadership.[65]   These cliques often consisted of
the same people, so that Florence Kelley,for example, could
be active in the work of the Henry Street Settlement, the
Child Labor Committee and the National Consumers' League,
at the same time.

---

[65]
   Irwin Yellowitz, Labor and the Progressive
Movement in New York State, 1897-1916 (Ithaca: 1965), p.71.

Although their major interests might differ, the
social progressives had similar goals, all of which involved the enactment of legislation which would improve
the living and working conditions of the poor, especially
the immigrant poor. Because they knew each other, often
socially as well as professionally, they worked together
easily and could quickly mobilize their forces for any
given campaign.[66]

The public schools were crucial to the goals of the
reformers because it was through the children that they
hoped to find the solutions to the social problems which
plagued New York City. For this reason, the Public
Education Association naturally exercised the most influence on the schools, but its power was multiplied many
fold because of the close ties it maintained with other
leading urban progressives, through duplication of membership and connections of friendship and family.[67]

[66]
Josephine Goldmark, Impatient Crusader: Florence
Kelley's life Story (Urbana, Ill.: 1953), pp.68-69. The
headquarters of the reform groups was at Fourth Ave. and
22nd Street in the United Charities Building.

[67]
The motivations of urban progressives, such as
those who worked for changes in the schools of New York,
have been much examined in recent years. George Mowry found
that the reformers were influenced by their Protestant
morality, strong sense of social responsibility, and belief
in the possibility of progress. Arthur Mann concluded that
the settlement house contingent among the urban reformers
were motivated by a sense of "noblesse oblige". Richard
Hofstadter saw the social progressives as victims of a
status revolution; middle and upper class people, previously accustomed to leadership, now lost in a complex America
they neither liked nor understood. To retrieve their
previous position, they embarked on a moral crusade against
the political boss and the evils generated by the new indus-
trialism. It appears that all these elements were present in
the motivations of the social progressives whose efforts
"transformed" the schools of New York.

Besides the Public Education Association, and the organizations with which it was associated, such as the Child Labor Committee and the National Consumer's League, it is possible to distinguish at least five other major elements in the coalition that transformed the schools. The settlement house residents, especially the workers of the University Settlement, Educational Alliance and Henry Street Settlement, shared equal importance with the Public Education Association. Also, the older philanthropic organizations, such as the Association for Improving the Condition of the Poor and the Childrens Aid Society participated in many of the advances recorded during this period. Newer charitable groups such as the School Lunch Committee were important in specific areas. The researches of the Russell Sage Foundation often provided the ammunition needed in order to pressure the Board of Education into a change of policy.[68]

The most important agent of all, however, was not outside of the school system, but rather at the head of it.

---

[68] Cohen, p.13.

William Henry Maxwell was a social progressive himself,
and needed only the support provided by the reform elements
to carry out the innovations in which he himself believed.[69]
Other than Julia Richman, Maxwell did not have many colleagues
who shared his point of view, but Miss Richman, connected
as she was to the Educational Alliance and associate of
many of the most influential members of the German-Jewish
community, was a lieutenant of the greatest worth. For
example, she was a close friend of Felix M. Warburg who
was part of the inner circle of the Public Education
Association in 1905, and a backer of Lillian Wald.[70]

    A close examination of ties like those which linked
Julia Richman to other reformers will help explain the power
they exercised. Mrs. Schuyler Van Rensselaer, president
of the Public Education Association from 1895 to 1905, was
at the same time a volunteer at the University Settlement
and president of its Women's Auxiliary, while James B.
Reynolds, headworker at this settlement, was a charter
member of the Public Education Association's advisory
Council.[71]

---

[69]
    Fred S. Hall, Forty Years, 1902-1942, The Work
of the New York Child Labor Committee (New York: 1942)
p. 25. This book documents Maxwell's contributions to
the Child Labor Committee.

[70]
    Interview with I. Edwin Goldwasser, February 7,
1966.
[71]
    Cohen, pp. 46,49.

The Association also cooperated with other groups, as in 1900, when a flower exhibition which became an annual event, was organized at P.S. 1 on Henry Street in cooperation with Julia Richman in her role as a director of the Educational Alliance and the Association of Normal College Alumnae.[72]

Florence Kelley of the National Consumers League and Lillian Wald of Henry Street were the closest of friends as well as co-workers.[73] The husband of Miriam Sutro Price who succeeded Mariana Van Rensselaer as president of the Public Education Association in 1905, was active in the East Side Civic Club and the Outdoor Recreation League. The wife of Board of Education president Egerton L. Winthrop was a generous donor to the Public Education Association.[74] A list of the members of the School Lunch Committee read like a "Who's Who" of reformers. The group included Lillian Wald, Mary Simkovitch, Ira Wile and Charles P. Howland of the Public Education Association and John Martin of the Ethical Culture Society.[75]

---

[72]
Ibid., p. 56

[73]
Letters from Florence Kelley to Lillian Wald, July 23, 1912, July 6, 1912, in the Lillian Wald Collection at the New York Public Library.

[74]
Cohen, p. 65, footnote 13, p.67.

[75]
The New York Times, January 12, 1913, V, p.6.

Even John Dewey, then a professor at Teachers College, was a social acquaintance of Miss Wald's.[76]

The social progressives not only knew one another well, but worked together successfully, too. The child labor campaign of 1903 is the best example of this. Robert Hunter of the University Settlement, Florence Kelley of the National Consumers League, Lillian Wald of Henry Street and William H. Maxwell of the Department of Education, share the credit for the passage of the improved law of that year.[77] Honor for introducing the school nursing program certainly goes to Miss Wald, and her lieutenant, Lina L. Rogers.[78] Mabel Hyde Kittredge began her Model Housekeeping Center from which grew the School Lunch Committee, at Henry Street.[79]

---

[76] Letter of Lillian Wald to John Dewey, October 26, 1914. In the Lillian Wald Collection of the New York Public Library.

[77] Above, Chapter 6, p.5.

[78] Above, chapter 4, p.16.

[79] Above, chapter 4, p.21.

The campaign to open the schools for recreational work owes its success to the University Settlement, the Public Education Association, and Jacob Riis, while the older Association for Improving the Condition of the Poor was decisive in the battle to establish vacation schools.[80] Pioneering efforts of the Educational Alliance lead to the formation of the "C,D, and E" classes, and the sociological investigations conducted by the Russell Sage Foundation were used in all the efforts of the social progressives.[81] Even the Junior League, not usually thought of as a reform organization, supported the work of the visiting teachers through its connection with the Public Education Association. The Committee on Special Children of the Association worked with Elizabeth Irwin of Henry Street, as well as with representatives of the Children's Aid Society, Association for Improving the Condition of the Poor, New York Child Labor Committee, and the Association of Neighborhood Workers in their efforts to bring education to the retarded children of the city.[83]

80
   Above, chapter 4, pp. 3,4.

81
   Above, chapter 5, p.3.

82
   Above, chapter 4,p.25.

83
   Cohen; p.68.

The influence of this close knit group of reformers was very great, as the extent of the changes in the schools indicate. Sometimes their pressure was direct, as in 1905, when Lillian Wald, at the request of Felix Warburg, wrote to Egerton Winthrop, president of the Board of Education, saying:

> Could not the Board of Education serve the children of the primary schools, by means of a simple and attractive lunch counter in some one school? In working out the details we should be glad to co-operate if our services could be turned to account. [84]

The educational power structure of the city was aware of the influence of the reformers. When Lillian Wald heard that Angelo Patri, a principal who had attempted to make his school "progressive" was in danger of transfer, she hastened to write to Maxwell about it. The Superintendent responded on the very next day and explained that if Patri was transferred it was because he had alienated two of the Bronx members of the Board of Education, and not because the Superintendent disapproved of his activities. On the contrary, Maxwell, as did Miss Wald, thought Patri had done a wonderful job with his school and the surrounding community. [85]

---

[84]
Letter from Lillian Wald to Egerton L. Winthrop, February 13, 1905. In the Lillian Wald Collection of the New York Public Library.

[85]
Letter from Lillian Wald to William H. Maxwell, January 23, 1911. Letter from William H. Maxwell to Lillian Wald, January 24, 1911. Both letters in the Lillian Wald Collection of the New York Public Library.

This prompt and agreeable answer is some evidence of the influence the reformers exercised on the schools.

The social progressives not only pressured Maxwell; they also hastened to defend the Superintendent whenever it was necessary. Such a situation developed in 1913. In September of that year, the Public Education Association had invited Maxwell to attend a meeting on the school budget at its office, two days before the Board of Education saw the estimate of school expenses. The Superintendent accepted the invitation, but the president of the Board, Thomas Churchill, objected and forbade him to be present. Maxwell wrote a long letter to Churchill, insisting on his right to attend, but the full Board of Education disagreed, and voted 28 to 8 to rebuke him. [86]

The Public Education Association strongly defended the Superintendent as did a _Times_ editorial. Churchill, now thoroughly angry, wrote a long letter to the _Times_, insisting on the impropriety of the meeting, which was to be held at the United Charities Building, and at which representatives of other private groups were to be present. The school board president felt the planned meeting was symptomatic of the cavalier attitude Maxwell and his reformer friends held toward the Board of Education, and thought

---

[86] _The New York Times_, September 25, 1913, p.10, October 3, p.10.

it was time the body legally charged with responsibility
for the schools, asserted itself. Eventually, a compromise
was reached. Maxwell attended the meeting, but it was held
at the Hall of the Board of Education, not the headquarters
of the United Charities.[87]

In its concluding remarks on this incident, the
Times, speaking in the voice of the same good government
forces who had won the school war of 1895, said that although
Churchill's aims were laudable, he was a politician appointed by a Tammany Mayor (McClellan) and therefore could not
be trusted as could the Superintendent, who was a professional educator, untainted by politics.[88]

This confidence in Maxwell, held in many places and
by many New Yorkers, was based on his honesty, courage,
and innovative efforts. All of the changes recorded in
this paper had the backing of the Superintendent and they
were implemented to the extent that school finances and
the opposition of the Board of Estimate permitted him to do
so. Even the Hanus Report said:

> The city of New York owes to him (Maxwell) more
> than to any other person or group of persons,
> the educational progress its schools have made
> since consolidation, and this progress, in
> spite of the defects we have pointed out, is
> very great. Without him, it is difficult to
> see how such progress could have been made.

---

[87] Ibid., September 27, 1913, p.13, September 28, IV,
p.6, October 4, 1913, p. 7.

[88] Ibid., December 4, 1913, p.8.

Great praise indeed, from a group that found so much to criticize in the schools under Maxwell's administration.[89]

The point of the matter is, that the Superintendent, stimulated and supported by a tight network of reformers, was able to make changes in the schools of the city, for the benefit of the children of the poor and the foreign born. When, as in the controversy over the Gary Plan, Maxwell split with his strongest ally, the Public Education Association, it proved impossible to implement the new system, even though the Mayor, Board of Estimate, and a large number of reformers were in favor of it. Only when Maxwell <u>and</u> the social progressives worked together, did change occur.[90]

The fact that the efforts to "transform" the schools of the 1900's were so successful may not bode well for public education in New York today. The programs of Straubenmuller, Gulick, Richman, <u>et.al.</u>, were, after all, aimed at non-English speaking, largely rural orient- ed boys and girls who had to be helped to prepare them- selves for life in an American city which was far less

---

89
     <u>Report of the Committee on the School Inquiry</u>, p. 181.
90
     Cohen, p.98, As described in chapter three, p.29, Maxwell believed the Gary Plan could achieve little without vast expenditures and if large sums <u>were</u> spent on education any plan would improve the New York <u>City</u> schools.

complex than the New York of today. While manual training
was of value to the child from Sicily, when United States
factories were expanding, it may not be the answer to the
boy from the Harlem ghetto who needs to make his way in
the highly automated society of today.

The medical and nursing programs so essential to
the tuberculosis prone Jewish child may no longer be so
important, in view of the development of Medicaid and
union welfare programs. Miss Fichman's device of homogeneous grouping, so useful to the brighter youngsters of
her day may only extend the "defacto segregation" prominent
in our schools for so long. In other words, the schools
of 1966 may be trying to win the present battle with the
weapons appropriate to another era, and may be repeating
the errors of the pre-1898 schools, that is, keeping
programs which were effective at a different time and with
different children, but which are not suited to today.

It may well be that public school education of
our time must be "transformed" anew--perhaps by parent-
school administration or by the introduction of new subjects
into the curriculum. Possibly the developmental lesson,
so long the standard in pedagogy, needs to give way to
a group participation kind of learning. Whatever the
devices chosen, the intent must be, as it was 60 years
ago, to change the schools in accordance with the changing
need of the pupils, because only this kind of responsive

ducation can be effective.

The fact that the innovations of the Progressive Era may not be the best answer to the school difficulties of today does not detract from the achievements of Superintendent Maxwell, his deputies and his allies. The improvements he listed in his answer to the Hanus Report were truly revolutionary. The very concern of the schools with the "whole child" was extraordinary, as was the attempt to continue education past regular school hours through various extension devices. The introduction of "new" subjects and abandonment of the hidebound curriculum, took considerable courage, especially in view of the manifest disapproval of the municipal fiscal authorities.

The experiments with vocational education as well as other attempts to keep the children in school longer were real achievements, worthy of respect. It is the contention of this paper, that much of this experimentation and innovation would not have taken place without the challenge posed by the vast number of immigrant children who came to the city between 1898 and 1914, because without the immigrant impact, the schools might well have continued the pattern of formalistic, limited education for some years longer. If nothing else, the shock felt by the schools from the sheer bulk of the newcomers reverberated through the Hall of the Board of Education, and required immediate attention.

There were so many, many, more children going to

school that expansion of physical facilities and staff
became absolutely essential. Because the school population became so much larger, it included the dull, and
the maladjusted in numbers too large to simply ignore.
Instead, the educational program had to be changed to cope
with all kinds of children, and vocational education, as
well as the less formal curriculum emerged. In such a
large group, there would be many more sick children and
so health care became a function of the schools. The
newcomers were poor and the bad housing and malnutrition
associated with their poverty would create still greater
difficulties for the schools if remedial measures were not
adopted. Thus recreation and lunch programs became essential. The increase in numbers meant there would be a
larger group of children of all ages and objectives and
therefore education had to be broadened to include high
schools for the adolescent and kindergartens for the very
young. The new children posed different problems from
those of native-born Americans and so required special
classes in order to resolve their difficulties. The elders
among them needed help, too, and so the evening schools
expanded and developed their work.

In sum, the public schools of New York, led by
an able, alert, Superintendent, and influenced by the
emerging social work profession,rose to the challenge

presented by a great historical upheaval, responded with new educational devices, and, in the process, became greatly changed in form and function, thus making the transition from a relatively small, hidebound, occasionally corrupt, and inefficient institution to the huge, modern system of today. The action was uneven, and not always effective, but a start was made, and the foundation for the schools of today, with all their faults and virtues, was laid.

FIGURE 4. THE ORGANIZATION OF THE DEPARTMENT OF EDUCATION IN 1914.*

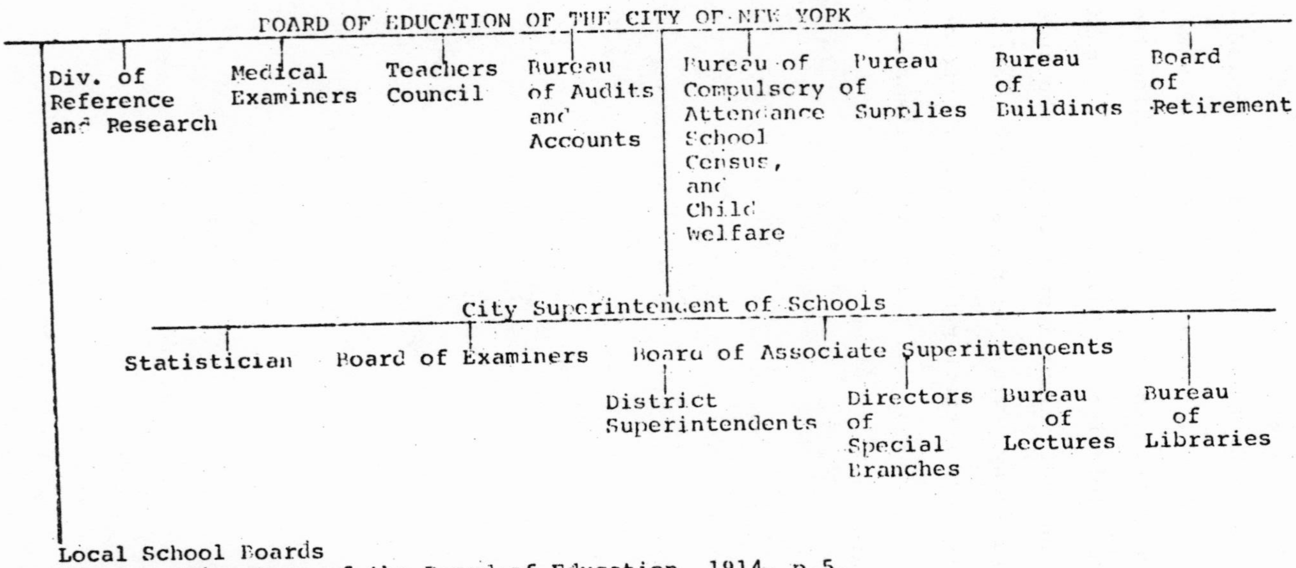

BOARD OF EDUCATION OF THE CITY OF NEW YORK

Div. of Reference and Research — Medical Examiners — Teachers Council — Bureau of Audits and Accounts — Bureau of Compulsory Attendance — Bureau of Supplies — Bureau of Buildings — Board of Retirement

School Census and Child Welfare

City Superintendent of Schools

Statistician — Board of Examiners — Board of Associate Superintendents

District Superintendents — Directors of Special Branches — Bureau of Lectures — Bureau of Libraries

Local School Boards

*Source: Directory of the Board of Education, 1914, p.5.

374.

BIBLIOGRAPHY

This bibliography is arranged in two sections:
an essay on the sources which attempts to describe and
evaluate the most important sources of information used
in the study, and a list of _all_ the materials examined,
grouped under topical headings.

ESSAY ON THE SOURCES

PART I. PRIMARY SOURCES OF INFORMATION

A. DOCUMENTS OF THE NEW YORK CITY DEPARTMENT OF EDUCATION

More than any other material, the sixteen Annual
Reports of the City Superintendent of Schools (New York,
1899-1914) were basic to this study. These volumes
contain much more than what their title implies. As
the school system grew more complex, so did the reports,
and, especially after 1902, the various appendixes are
of as much interest as the body of the reports themselves.
In addition to Superintendent Maxwell's clear, often
caustic, and always direct summaries and recommendations,
many of the directors of special programs wrote statements
about their work which were of the utmost value. For a
period of six years, from 1904 to 1910, the Associate
Superintendents presented the developments occuring in
their divisions as part of these reports, and especially
in the case of Division I, (the Lower East Side), these
additions were very important. The statistics tabulated
for these annual surveys show the astonishing growth of
the system and were essential to the study. Of course,
care had to be used in reading the Superintendent's
reports. They do, after all, present the picture as it
was seen at headquarters, and although Maxwell was far
more candid than many administrators, and the subject of
education had not yet developed its present "jargon",
the reports do tend to give a one sided view.

In an attempt to cross-check the Superintendent,
a careful study of other Board of Education documents
was made. Perhaps not surprisingly, in view of some of
the criticisms made of this body, the Journals of the
Board of Education (New York, 1899-1914) and the Annual
Reports of the Department of Education (New York, 1899-
1914) are not at all revealing. The former recite the
pettiest of administrative details only, and the latter
merely repeat the Superintendent's summaries. Except
in a very few instances, (C. B. Snyder's reports on
building plans, for instance), the thousands of pages

which make up these documents are not of much value.
If the minutes of the committee meetings of the Board,
especially the powerful executive committee, had been
kept, it might have been possible to gain new insight
into the matters considered. This, however, was not
done; no trace of them exists at the Board of Education headquarters, nor was it possible to locate them
anywhere else in the city.

On the other hand, the Minutes of the Board of
Superintendents (New York, 1902-1914) are of more value,
although here too, one feels that the real discussion
took place at committee meetings, no record of which is
available. But the Minutes do give a picture of school
developments, mostly through the communications received
by the Superintendents, and the decisions made by this
powerful group. Fortunately, there are indexes to the
Minutes, which makes the student's task somewhat easier.

Of great interest are the Directories of the Board
of Education (New York, 1910-1914) which give the names
and addresses of every teacher, supervisor, and adminis-
trator in the system and are easily available, as are all
the Board of Education documents, at the New York Public
Library and at Board of Education Headquarters.

While of less overall value, the many special
reports of the Department of Education are essential.
The Report of the Special Committee of Five (New York,
February 24, 1904) to answer the Grout Inquiry; the
pamphlet of The School Lunch Service in New York City
(Bulletin #3 of the Division of Reference and Research
New York, 1914); the announcement of the Murray Hill Pre-
Vocational School for Boys (New York, n.d.); the Syllabus
for the teaching of English to Grade "C" Classes in the
Elementary Day Schools (New York, 1900); the report on
The Teachers Council: Its history, purpose, organization,
work (New York, 1916); The Report of the Committee on
Truancy of the Teachers Council (New York, 1914); William
Wirt's Report on a plan of Organization for Co-operative and
Continuation Classes (New York, 1914); as well as the Reply
of the Board of Superintendents to the Hanus-Elliott Report
(New York, 1913); and the Reply of the Association of
District Superintendents to the Findings of Professor
Edward C. Elliott-(New York, 1914) are absolutely essential
to an understanding of the progress and problems of the
Department of Education in this period. Similarly, the Maps

of the Local School Boards (New York, 1910) show the
districts and divisions of the city and help make the
educational structure somewhat clearer.

While not an official document of the Department
of Education, William H. Maxwell's A Quarter Century of
Public School Development (New York, 1912) is a very
important summary of the changes which took place in the
school from the point of view of the head of the system.
Another basic, although semi-official source was A.E.
Palmer's History of the New York City Public Schools
(New York, 1905). Mr. Palmer was the Secretary to the
Board of Education from 1898 to 1905 and was an eye-
witness to many of the developments he described; he
had as well access to a number of documents, since lost.
In spite of his position, Palmer wrote an objective,
very dull, but very valuable history of the schools and
was not especially an apologist for his employers. For
background on public education in New York City in an
earlier period, prior to the establishment of the Board
of Education, William O. Bourne's History of the Public
School Society (New York, 1873) is invaluable, while
Public Education in the City of New York (New York, 1869)
by Thomas Boese tells the story of the Board of Education
from its establishment in 1842 to 1869.

Harold McCormick was active in the research division of the Board of Education for many years and wrote
The First Fifty Years (New York, 1948) as part of the
Annual Superintendent's Report for that year. Although
he was a contemporary of many of the changes he describes,
the work is based on Board of Education records, many of
which are no longer available. Mr. McCormick indicated
that the Board had little sense of history, since much
of the material he used was later stored in the basement
and later yet, disposed of. His study, therefore, became
the only history of the New York City schools from 1898
to 1948, and is, as a result, more valuable than it might
otherwise be. It is objective and factual, dispassionate,
discreet and useful. In sum, the work of Bourne, Boese,
Palmer, and McCormick, tell the story of public education
in New York City from the point of view of insiders.

Two recent publications of the Board of Education
are important for an understanding of the continuity of
the programs. Frederick Shaw's Fifty Years of Research
in the New York City Board of Education (New York, 1964)
is valuable for the background of the Hanus Inquiry and

for the history of the Bureau of Research. Facts and Figures, 1965-66, (New York, 1966), a small guidebook to the school system of today, was also useful.

In room 732 of the Livingston Street headquarters of the Board is a filing cabinet, labeled V.F. 902 which contains a number of mimeographed and manuscript documents relating to this study. The Invitation to and Program of the tribute to Maxwell held at Carnegie Hall in October, 1912, was located there, as was a fine photograph of the Superintendent, a press release on his Election as Superintendent Emeritus in 1918, and summaries of the work of Elizabeth Farrell, Gustave Straubenmuller, and Albert Shiels. Of special interest was a copy of the Appreciation of a Great Educator, Julia Richman;(New York 1916), written by her sisters, Bertha R. Proskauer and Addie R. Altman, which gave some much needed background on this exceptional teacher.

Additional information which was of some use were the Addresses Delivered Upon the Opening of the New Hall of the Board of Education, 1900; the Minutes of the Organization of the School Board of Manhattan and the Bronx, 1901; and a reprint of a speech entitled The Board of Education by Thomas Churchill, President of that Body in 1914.

D. OTHER GOVERNMENTAL DOCUMENTS

The documents published by municipal governmental units other than the Department of Education, which bore on this study, came mostly from the Board of Estimate. The two Reports of an Investigation Concerning the Cost of Maintaining the Public Schools for 1904 and 1905 (the Grout Inquiry) and the Report of the Committee on the School Inquiry of 1911-1913, (the Hanus Committee) as well as, to a lesser extent, the Minutes of a Hearing of the Sub-Committee of the Committee on the Board of Education on Vocational Guidance, 1914, all of which were very critical of the Department of Education, were extremely important, in order to balance the picture received in the Superintendent's reports.

Although the interest and influence of New York State in the city's educational progress was quite limited, certain documents emanating from Albany were important. Basic, of course, were the New York City Charters of 1897

and 1901, chapter 378 of the Laws of 1897 and chapter
466 of the Laws of 1901, especially the educational
provisions. In addition, it was necessary to consult
the Compulsory Education Laws of 1896 and 1897, 1903 and
1913, chapter 606, section 3; chapter 415, sections 70-76;
chapter 184, sections 70-73; chapter 151, sections 174-179a;
chapter 748, section 622.

The Report of the New York State Immigration Commission of 1909 was of some use, as was the Annual Report of
the New York State Department of Education for 1917 which
dealt with immigrant education.

Much more significant were the reports of various
Federal agencies, The Abstracts of the 11th (1890), 12th
(1900), 13th (1910), and 14th (1920) Census were essential,
as was the Abstract of the Statistical Review of Immigration to the United States, 1820-1910, (Washington, 1911)
The massive Report of the United States Immigration Commission of 1911, (often known as the Dillingham Report)was
of the greatest importance, especially volume 66, Immigrants
in Cities and the Abstract of the Report on Children of
Immigrants in the Schools. The Seventh Special Report
of the United States Commissioner of Labor, entitled The
Slums of Great Cities (Washington, 1894) although published a little too early for this study, was consulted for
background purposes. Similarly just a bit too previous
but still important was the Report of the United States
Industrial Commission on Immigration (Washington, 1901)
especially Vol. 15, which contains Kate Claghorn's informa-
tive summary on "The Foreign Immigrant in New York City".
Not surprisingly, the United States Bureau of Education
Bulletins were very useful, especially #51, Report of a
Conference on Education and Immigrants, 1913; , and #5,
American Schoolhouses, 1910 as well as theReports of the
Education Commissioner for 1913, 1916 and 1918 which
deal with the nation-wide efforts to Americanize the
immigrant.'

C. REPORTS OF PRIVATE ORGANIZATIONS

As the study makes clear, private organizations
played a very important role in the story of the immigrants
and the schools. As a result, the reports of the various
organizations concerned with the problem are almost equal
in importance to the documents published by governmental

units. The Childrens Aid Society's Crusade for Children
(New York, n.d.) tells of the many activities of this
organization during the period under examination. Of
greater value are the fifteen years of Reports of the
Educational Alliance, 1897-1912, because of the pioneering work of this unique settlement house. The surveys
of the schools made by Charles C. Wehrum, Description of
Grammar and Primary Schools in the City of New York, 1894
and by Good Government Club E, Public School Buildings
in New York, 1895, were of interest as was the Citizens
Union's More and Better Schools, 1897. The Report of
the Committee on the Congestion of Population, entitled
The True Story of the Worst Congestion in Any Civilized
City, (New York, 1911) was useful and revealing. In a
category by itself was the Public Education Association.
The Bulletins of this pressure group, especially numbers
16 to 20 on the Hanus Report (1913) and #23 (1914) on
the Gary Plan controversy, #10, "Shall the Schools Serve
Lunch?", 1913 and #2 on the Permanent Census Board(1912)
were very useful, as were the Official Wirt Reports to
the Board of Education, (1916), with an introduction
by Howard W. Nudd, the executive secretary of the organization, and the Primer of Public School Progress (1914).
The New York Association for Improving the Condition of
the Poor was active in a number of projects, and the
Report of the Department of Schools on Vacation Schools
(1905) of the AICP was particularly valuable. The
Reports of the University Settlement for 1897, and 1903
were useful as background for the school extension and
child labor campaigns.

D. INTERVIEWS

Originally, a number of interviews with retired
school personnel or individuals who were students during
the period under examination, were planned; the object
being to get first hand information on the execution of
the programs so much discussed in the official reports
of the Department of Education. This plan proved hard to
implement. The retired teachers, when located, were often
not able to give an interview, mostly for reasons of
health and advanced age; and when they were available,
proved to have faulty memories, or were totally uninformed.
Part of this lack of knowledge was significant, because
it was further proof of the uneven nature of the various

changes. It was evidently quite possible to have been a student or a teacher in New York between 1898 and 1914 and not have participated in any of the new programs. But as a result of this, the interviews became less important to the study, and were used more for color and detail, than for basic information.

Dr. Jacob Ross, however, was rather an exception to this general statement. He came to the United States in 1892, from Russia, and was enrolled at P.S. 75 on Norfolk Street immediately after his arrival. After graduation from the College of the City of New York preparatory school, and the college itself, he became a teacher at P.S. 189 on Catharine Street in 1904, and thus began a career which saw him rise through all the levels of the school system until he retired as Principal of Midwood High School in Brooklyn in 1954. Because of this background, his reminiscences were very valuable. Dr. Ross referred me to Mr. Milton B. Perlman, whose years on the Lower East Side and in the school system were roughly the same, and whose memories were colorful. Dr. Harold McCormick, at the Board of Education, was a young teacher in 1910, but knew many of the individuals mentioned in the study. He referred me to one of the survivors, Dr. Morris E. Siegel, whose information on the evening school division was very important.

Closer to home, the manuscript autobiography of my father, Hyman Cantor, was of value because it gave so much of the background of the "new" immigration, in his own words. Similarly, the school experiences of my brother-in-law, Joseph Winick, who came to New York in 1907, at the age of 12, and went through "D" classes and the advanced summer schools, helped make these programs real to me.

D. MEMOIRS

These latter sources were really in the nature of memoirs, of which the literature abounds. Mary Antin's The Promised Land (Boston, 1912) is well known, as is Michael Gold's Jews Without Money (New York, 1930), Marcus Ravage's An American in the Making (New York, 1917), Mary Simkovitch's Neighborhood, My Story of Greenwich House, (New York, 1938), Lillian Wald's House on Henry Street (New York, 1915), Leonard Covello's The Heart is the Teacher (New York, 1958), Angelo Patri's A Schoolmaster in a Great City (New York, 1917), Constantine Panunzic's The Soul of the Immigrant (New York, 1922) and Anzia Yezierska's Children of Loneliness (New York, 1923).

Most memoirs of the children of immigrants are interesting because the consciousness of being between

two cultures influenced the way in which these marginal
men and women viewed the world around them as Oscar
Handlin explains in his introduction to Children of the
Uprooted (New York, 1966).

F. CONTEMPORARY SURVEYS

Many other works, contemporary in nature, but
not memoirs, were of the greatest value. The Redemption
of New York (New York, 1901) edited by Milo Pogard, sheds
light on the election of Seth Low as Mayor in that year,
while a private individual, Wirt Howe, lawyer and Republican activist, provided a view of New York at the Turn
of the Century (Toronto, 1940) which, if read with care,
is revealing. Howe was a typical "WASP" and his opinions
about Tammany and Mayor Van Wyck, are a bit one sided,
but interesting none the less. The Gentleman and the
Tiger (New York, 1956) edited by Harold Syrett, gives a
picture of George McClellan as Mayor, in his own words.

Fred S. Hall, member of the New York Child Labor
Committee for many years, wrote a brief history of its
activities entitled Forty Years (New York, 1942) which
describes the campaigns to enact the Child Labor Laws of
1903 and 1913.

The Russian Jew in the United States (Philadelphia,
1905) edited by Charles E. Bernheimer, was useful in
general, but the essay by J. K. Paulding on the Russian
Jewish immigrant and his school adjustment in New York
City was a mine of information. Abraham Cahan's novel,
The Rise of David Levinsky (New York, 1913) was based so
completely on the real life of the ghetto, it was almost
a survey of social conditions there. Robert Hunter's
Poverty (New York, 1904) was one of the earliest analyses
of that social problem and very moving, as was John
Spargo's The Bitter Cry of the Children (New York, 1909).
Both of these works are in the same "genre" as Jacob
Riis' two powerful books, The Children of the Poor (New York,
1892) and the Battle with the Slum (New York, 1902), as is
Joseph Lee's Constructive and Preventive Philanthropy
(New York, 1902). These "muckraking" type books are
joined by Charles Zueblin's Decade of Civic Development
(Chicago, 1905) and his American Municipal Progress (New
York, 1916) both of which give a more optimistic view
of urban life, as does Hutchins Hapgood's Spirit of the
Ghetto (New York, 1902). A Columbia University graduate

student, Thomas Jones, studied the Sociology of a New York City Block, (New York, 1904) and discovered much of interest regarding the patterns of life among the Italians of East Harlem. At the same time, in Boston, Robert A. Woods and his associates at South End House published Americans in Process (Cambridge, 1902) and The City Wilderness (Cambridge, 1892) both of which contain much information regarding the immigrant impact in Boston.

An investigation conducted under the auspices of the Special Committee of the Eighth New York State Conference of Charities and Corrections resulted in a report by the Secretary of its Committee on the Standard of Living, Robert C. Chapin, entitled The Standard of Living Among Workingman's Families in New York (New York, 1909), which helped explain the economic reasons for child labor.

Bertha Boody did a pioneering Psychological Study of Immigrant Children at Ellis Island (Baltimore, 1926) a little after the period but dealt with Jewish and Italian children, and her results were therefore valuable. The well-known books of Myra Kelly, Little Aliens (New York, 1910), Little Citizens (New York, 1904), and Wards of Liberty (New York, 1907) are amusing and instructive because they tell the story of a young Irish middle class teacher assigned to a ghetto school, and her troubles and triumphs. The stories are largely autobiographical, since Miss Kelly taught on the Lower East Side for years before she became an author.

Less interesting, but more valuable, are Leonard Ayres' Laggards in our Schools (New York, 1915), and Harriet Johnson's The Visiting Teacher in New York City (New York, 1916), all of which are surveys of special aspects of the schools of the period done under the auspices of private groups. A different sort of investigation, done earlier, was the one by Dr. Joseph Mayer Rice, The Public School System (New York, 1893) which graphically portrayed the inadequacies of the New York City schools in that year. An even better survey was the one done by Adele Marie Shaw for World's Work magazine during 1903 and 1904. In a series of nine articles, she reported on the deficiencies and strengths of public school systems in rural and urban communities. The first and eighth installments were about New York City, and described both the regular day schools and certain extension programs such as the vacation schools, under the title, "The True Character of the New York Public Schools" (Volume VII, pp. 4204-21, 1903 and volume VIII, pp. 505-514, 1904).

The National Education Association, powerful
organization of the profession, had much of importance
in the Proceedings of its 54th meeting in 1916, especially an article on truancy, and one on health education
in the New York City schools. A subsidiary of the National
Education Association, the National Society for the Study
of Education, in its 10th (1911) and 14th (1915) yearbook
dealt with evening schools and community centers in an in-
formative manner.

F . MANUSCRIPTS

A word about the absence of manuscript materials
in this study is necessary. An extensive campaign to uncover
the papers of William H. Maxwell has so far ended in frustration. The Lillian Wald Collection at the New York Public
Library yielded documentary evidence of the links which bound
the "social progressives".

About Julia Richman, little success can be recorded. Her nephew, Mr. Richman Proskauer, and her close
friend, Mr. I. Edwin Goldwasser believe her papers may be
in existence, but up to the time of writing, they were
not uncovered. Fortunately, all these leading figures
wrote extensively in periodicals and for reports, and
the study has made use of this kind of material in lieu
of the manuscripts which would have been so valuable, if
only they had been available.

G. CONTEMPORARY PERIODICALS

A very important source for this study was found
in the periodicals of the day. So voluminous was this
literature, it would be difficult to list every article of
value. The footnotes can be consulted for those essays
most used, but in addition, some of the others should be
mentioned, because they added considerably to the information needed.

I. IMMIGRATION

Kate Claghorn's "Immigration and Dependence"

Charities, XII, (1904), 501-504 cleared up some of the
stereotypes concerning the pauperism of the "new" immigrants,
as did her "Immigration in Relation to Pauperism" Annals
of the American Academy of Political and Social Science,
XXIV, (1904), 187-205. Jacob Riis'"Special Needs of the
Poor in New York" Forum, XIV, (1892), 492-502 is an
abbreviated version of the main themes of his books.
John Carr spoke favorably of the "Coming of the Italian"
Outlook, LXXXII (1906),419-431,while the Jewish Immigrants
received the attention of Albert Friedenberg in "The
Problem of Jewish Immigration" Jewish Comment, XVI (1903)
1-3 and from Edward Steiner in "The Russian and Polish
Jew in New York" Outlook LXXII (1902) 528-539. The East
Side was discussed by William F. Walling in "What the
People of the East Side Do" University Settlement Studies
I, (1903) 79-85 and by Zalman Yoffeh in "The Passing of
the East Side", Menorah Journal, XVII (1929), 265-275.

2. AMERICANIZATION

F. T. Hill's articles, "From Americanization to
Adult Education" Survey, LXII (1929) 366-367) and
"Contributions of Americanization to Education" School
and Society, XXXIII(1931), 160-164 explain how the
adult education program grew out of the Americanization
movement of the World War I period. The major force behind
this campaign in New York was Frances Kellor, secretary
of the New York State Commission on Immigration of 1909,
founder of the New York Committee of the North American
Civic League for Immigrants and chief investigator of
the New York State Bureau of Industries and Immigration.
Her articles, "Education of the Immigrant", Educational
Review, XLVIII, (1914), 21-36), and "A Domestic Policy"
Immigrants in America Review, I, (1915) 9-22 reveal the
prevailing attitudes of the "WASP" regarding the need to
educate the alien. Frank Lenz "Education of the Immigrant"
Educational Review, LI, (1916), 469-477, reinforces Miss
Kellor's position. S. J. Schuster's "What the Evening
School is Doing for the Alien." Journal of Education,
LXXIX (194) 201-202 is too laudatory, as is L. H.
Wheaton's "United States Bureau of Education and the
Immigrant" Annals of the American Academy of Political
and Social Science, LXVII, (1916), 273-283.

3. SCHOOLS

The subject of the schools was a fertile source of magazine articles during this period. Some that were particularly interesting were "The Gap Between the Secondary and the Elementary School" School Review, X (1902), 701-707; Physical Disability of New York City School Teachers" by L.I. Dublin School and Society, IV, (1916), 564-569, 602-607; "Problems of the Backward Child" by Andrew Edson, School Journal, (1906), 60-62; and "How a Great Free Lecture System Works" by George Iles, World's Work, V, (1903), 3328-3334. Somewhat critical was "What Ails the Schools?" by Tristram Metcalfe, Globe School Bulletin, (March, 1912), as was the article on "Our Medieval High Schools" by William H. Mearns in the Saturday Evening Post, CLXXXIV, (1912), 18-19. William McAndrew, principal of Washington Irving High School, described "A Day's Work in a New York Public School", World's Work, IV, (1902), 2634-2643. James K. Paulding of the University Settlement gave his views on "The Public School as a Center of Community Life" in Educational Review, XIII (1898) 147-154.

When Seth Low unsuccessfully ran for re-election in 1903, Outlook magazine tried to help his campaign with an article called "What Reform has done for Children" LXXV, (1903), 201-202. Lina Rogers discussed her pioneer work in "School Nursing in New York City" University Settlement Studies Quarterly, III, (1905), 141-147, while Talbot Winthrop overpraised the work of P.S. 4 on Rivington Street in "A Public School in the Slums that Does Its Work" World's Work, XVIII, (1909), 11567-72. Florence Woolston made an investigation of the children applying for working papers in October 1909 which was entitled "Our Untrained Future Citizens", Survey, XXIII, (1909) 21-35 and very critically discussed the failure of the schools to prepare the dropout for citizenship and employment.

4. PERIODICALS EXAMINED IN DEPTH

In addition to particular articles, certain periodicals proved consistently valuable. The School Journal which had been established in 1870, claimed to be the first nationwide weekly educational newspaper in the United States, and was published in both New York City and Chicago. Its columns contained professional news of interest to the classroom teacher. In 1913, it changed ownership and became the

"National representative organ of progressive education",
published monthly from New York. Post-1913, the Journal
was more theoretical and sophisticated, and less oriented
to the grade school teacher. It consistently spoke for the
professional educator, and against the layman, especially
if he was a politician. The Educational Review and Education, were also very useful. Survey, World's Work, Outlook,
and the Forum were all worth close examination, as was the
Literary Digest which summarized press opinion on a variety
of issues connected with this study. The New York Times
was outstanding in its coverage of school developments,
although the lack of a good index for the years 1900 and 1912
made it somewhat difficult to use. The World, Globe, and
Herald were useful for the Grout and Hanus investigations.

PART II - SECONDARY SOURCES OF INFORMATION

There was no shortage of information on the city,
the immigrants, or the schools in books written after the
events which they describe had occurred.

A. DISSERTATIONS

Three dissertations, among a number examined,
were particularly valuable. Morris I. Berger's, The Settlement,
The Immigrant and the Public School (Columbia, 1956) explains
the influence of the Educational Alliance on the public school
changes of the period; Sister Mary Fabian Matthews' The Role
of the Public School in the Assimilation of the Italian Immigrant
Child in New York City, 1900-1914 (Fordham, 1966) provided
information on the children of this ethnic group, who were
generally not as well documented as was the Jewish child.
Leonard Covello's three volume study on The Social Background
of the Italo-American School Child (New York University, 1944)
was enormously revealing of parental school attitudes among
South Italians and the reasons for this posture.

B. THE CITY

In regard to events in New York City in general in
the first decade of the 20th century, Allan Nevins and John
Krout's (editors) collection of essays, The Greater City
(New York, 1948) provided a very useful place to start,
while David Ellis; et al., Short History of New York State

(Ithaca, 1957) is a basic text important to consult. Harold
Syrett's City of Brooklyn (New York, 1944) is essential for
the history of that Borough prior to consolidation. Wallace
Sayre's and Herbert Kaufman's Governing New York City (New
York, 1960) was important to consult as was David Truman's
The Governmental Process (New York, 1951). Of even greater
value because he has a long introductory chapter on the
Progressive Era in New York was Charles Garrett's The La
Guardia Years (New Brunswick, 1961). For statistics, Walter
Laidlaw's Population of the City of New York, 1890-1930
(New York, 1932) was useful, although much of the data
that concerned me was readily available elsewhere. Grace
Mayer's Once Upon a City (New York, 1958) shows the history
of New York City in pictures which were interesting, although
for my purposes, the great photographs in the Jacob Riis
Collection of the Museum of the City of New York were better.
Cleveland Rodgers and Rebecca Rankin wrote a survey of
New York City History entitled New York: The World's Capital
City (New York: 1948) which is somewhat useful but a bit too
much in the nature of a guidebook. A scholarly and important
work is Frederick Shaw's History of the New York City Legislature (N.Y., 1954) which provided essential information about
the municipal agency whose attitudes affected school events
so much. Irwin Yellovitz has written of the relationship
between Labor and the Progressive Movement in New York State,
1897-1916 (Ithaca,1965) and detailed the wide ranging activities
of the "social progressives".

C. IMMIGRATION

     The literature on the immigrant can only be des-
cribed as gigantic. The best general history of immigration
to the United States is Maldwyn Jones' American Immigration
(Chicago, 1960), which tells the full story, using the best
of modern historical technique and clarity of language. Marcus
Hansen's The Immigrant In American History (New York, 1940)
although limited to the 19th century was suggestive in many
ways. A convenient survey and collection of readings is
Michael Kraus' Immigration: The American Mosaic (Princeton,
1966) whose title is particularly apropos. Outdated, but
useful for some basic facts is George Stephenson's History
of American Immigration (Boston, 1926) while Carl Wittke's
We Who Built America (New York, 1939) is staunchly for the
immigrant and his contributions. Perhaps the most stimulating
work in this field is Oscar Handlin's The Uprooted (New York,
1951), which tells the compelling story of the great human

migration to the United States from the point of view of the immigrants
themselves. More precise is his Immigration as a Factor in
American History (Englewood Cliffs, 1959) and especially
relevant to the modern New York City situation is his work on
The Newcomers (Cambridge, 1959). Handlin's most recent contribution to the field of immigration studies is his Children of
the Uprooted (New York, 1966) in which he edits the memoirs of
a number of 2nd generation Americans.

D. THE IMMIGRANTS

A fairly recent work by two sociologists, Nathan
Glazer and Daniel Moynihan, Beyond the Melting Pot (Cambridge,
1963) was stimulating and instructive because it deals with
the adjustment of the major ethnic groups who have peopled
New York City in the 20th century. Also of recent vintage
and considerable value were two books on social problems in
which the impact of immigration is discussed. Robert Bremner's
From the Depths (New York, 1956) discusses the "discovery"
of poverty as a social problem in the United States at the
turn of the century, while Roy Lubove's The Progressives and
the Slums (Pittsburg, 1962) is an extremely worthwhile study
of tenement house reform in New York City.

In the field of nativism, John Higham's Strangers
in the Land (New Brunswick, 1955) has no peer, while the
legal aspects of the movement to restrict immigration is
adequately covered by R. L. Garis in Immigration Restriction
(New York, 1927).

Most of the material on the two immigrant groups
of concern to this study had to be used with care because
the authors were frequently members of the ethnic group they
were describing and were consequently extremely defensive.
Such a criticism could be made of Harry Linfield's The Jews
in the United States (New York, 1927) and Peter Wiernik's
Jews in America (New York, 1912) which were semi-contempor-
aneous studies. More objective and very valuable was Samuel
Joseph's Jewish Immigration to the United States, (New York,
1914) and History of the Baron de Hirsch Fund (New York,
1935) both of which were quite basic to at least a part of
this investigation. Of the greatest value, was Moses Rischin's
The Promised City (New York, 1964) which covers in loving
detail the life and labor of the Eastern European Jews who
came to New York between 1870 and 1914. For statistical
information, especially regarding organizations formed by
the Jewish immigrants C. M. Horowitz' and L. Kaplan's The
Jewish Population of the New York Area, 1900-1975 (New York,

1959), was useful while Alexander Dushkin's Jewish Education in New York City (New York, 1918) gave a very complete picture of the non-public schooling of the Jewish youngsters of New York City and makes the point that most Jewish parents preferred their children to attend secular schools and receive their religious education after three p.m.

The definitive work on the Italian immigration to the United States is Robert Foerster's Italian Emigration of our Times (Cambridge, 1924) which, in completeness and detail, is unmatched by any other book in this field. Other works on the Italians which were consulted were Elliott Lord's The Italians in America (New York, 1906); John Mariano's The Italian Contribution to American Democracy (Boston, 1921); Lawrence Pisani's The Italian in America (New York, 1957); Philip Rose's The Italians in America (New York, 1922) and Antonio Stella's Some Aspects of Italian Immigration to the United States (New York, 1924), but Foerster's work was much the best. Of considerable value, because it is more scholarly and does not suffer from the need to defend is Phyllis Williams' South Italian Folkways in Europe and America (New Haven, 1938). The Federal Writers Project produced a work on the Italians of New York (New York, 1938) which is somewhat useful, although not entirely accurate. The same group's New York Panorama (New York, 1938) is too general to be of much value.

F. AMERICANIZATION

The subject of how best to assimilate the immigrant has produced many books, as often sociological in orientation as historical. I.B. Berkson's Theories of Americanization (New York, 1920) is a general study of the Americanization of the Jews, introducing the well-known themes of the "melting-pot" and cultural pluralism. Immigration and Race Attitudes (Boston, 1928) by Emory Bogardus is an early attempt to explore race relations in a pluralistic society, while his Essentials of Americanization (Los Angeles, 1919) tries to clarify the aims of that movement. David Bowers Foreign Influences in American Life (Princeton, 1944) is a collection of suggestive essays and bibliographies designed to lead to further investigation of the topic. Francis J. Brown and Joseph S. Roucek edited a collection of essays on the various immigrant groups who have peopled the United States under the heading Our Racial and National Minorities (New York, 1937) while Lawrence Brown's Immigration: Cultural Conflicts and Social Adjustments (New York, 1933) is a digest of a number

of sociological studies in the field. John P. Commons,
best known as a labor historian, is the author of Races
and Immigrants in America (New York, 1930) a generally
concerned survey of the "new" immigration to which he was
a contemporary. Maurice Davie's World Immigration (New
York, 1936) has valuable information on the Americanization
movement of the World War I era, as well as many other
details on immigration in the 20th century. Even more
useful is Immigration and Americanization (Boston, 1920)
edited by Philip Davis, which is a collection of articles
by experts in various aspects of Americanization and
immigration, of which the essay by E. A. Goldenweiser, who
was a staff member for the Dillingham Commission in 1911
is particularly significant. A publication of the United
Nations Educational, Social and Cultural Commission, edited
by W. D. Borrie, entitled The Cultural Integration of
Immigrants (Paris, 1959) was interesting as a survey of
how immigrants have fared culturally in countries other
than the United States.

Grace Abbott, who was the director of the
Immigrant's Protective League of Chicago between 1911 and
1918 wrote The Immigrant and the Community (New York, 1917)
which discusses the problems of the alien from the point
of view of a social worker and is very critical of the
lack of adequate facilities for the integration of the
immigrant in the United States as a whole. Horace Kallen's
Culture and Democracy in the U.S. (New York, 1924) is an
interesting series of philosophical essays on the value
of cultural pluralism. On the same subject, but much more
concrete is Julius Drachsler's Democracy and Assimilation
(New York, 1920) which pleads for multi-faceted society
in the United States rather than forced Americanization,
and advocates the use of the public school as the medium
with which to accomplish this. The definitive work in the
field of Americanization history is The Movement to
Americanize the Immigrant (New York, 1948) by Edward
Hartmann which is extremely detailed, complete and has an
enormous and valuable bibliography which I used with profit.
The sources listed in William Smith's Americans in the
Making (New York, 1939) were likewise useful. Although
dealing with Cleveland, Ohio, not New York City, Herbert
Miller's The School and the Immigrant (Cleveland, 1916)
which was part of the Cleveland Foundation's Survey
of education in that city was very useful because, by detail-
ing the deficiencies of the Cleveland schools in regard to
to the immigrant, it made the New York efforts more significant.

Three books, among many in the Americanization
Series published between 1920 and 1921, were outstanding.
Foremost was Frank Thompson's Schooling the Immigrant
(New York, 1920) which was a detailed study of the public
schools and the immigrant, nation wide, and which praised
the innovations of the New York City schools in this field
very highly. Robert Park and Herbert Miller's Old World
Traits Transplanted was useful for the immigrant background, and Sophinista Breckenridge's New Homes for Old
(New York, 1921), which dealt especially with immigrant
mothers, was also necessary for information relating to
the newcomer's families.

F. THE SCHOOLS

For the purposes of this study the single most
important book in the field of educational history was
Lawrence Cremin's The Transformation of the School
(New York, 1961) which is an excellent history of the
origins of progressive education in the late 19th and
early 20th centuries, and convincingly develops the
author's thesis that progressive education was another
aspect of the progressive movement in politics and
economics. In a more philosophical vein is Professor
Cremin's The Genius of American Education (Pittsburgh,
1965) a reprint of a Horace Mann lecture he delivered.
The History of Education in American Culture (New York,
1953) co-authored by Dr. Cremin and Freeman Butts is
an excellent survey of the field. Older, less objective,
but very interesting because they illustrate the
pedagogical opinion of his era are the works of Ellwood
Cubberly; Public Education in the United States (Cambridge,
1919) and Changing Conceptions of Education (Boston, 1909.
I. L. Kandel's American Education in the 20th Century
(Cambridge, 1957) discusses pedagogical changes from a
more conservative point of view than Cremin, while
Twenty-Five Years of American Education (New York, 1929)
edited by Kandel, is a collection of essays by former
students of Paul Monroe on different aspects of 20th
century American education. The Cyclopedia of Education,
New York, 1918) edited by Paul Monroe himself, contained
much that was useful, especially an article by Ellwood
Cubberly on education in New York City in volume IV.
Deservedly famous and important for background was

Merle Curti's Social Ideas of American Educators (Paterson, 1959), while Philip Curoe's Educational Attitudes and Policies of Organized Labor in the United States (New York, 1926) helped explain the union viewpoint on vocational education. The small volume by John and Evelyn Dewey, The Schools of Tomorrow (New York, 1915) gave an idea of the many different forms progressive education took, especially in its early years.

Nicholas Murray Butler edited a collection of essays under the heading Education in the United States (New York, 1910) three of which were quite valuable. One described a New York City school building in detail, another was a general survey of education in the United States in 1909 by famed educator William Torrey Harris, and the last was a report on high schools by United States Education Commissioner, E. E. Brown. At approximately the same time, Andrew S. Draper, New York State Education Commissioner, published American Education (Cambridge, 1909) which contained the arguments for keeping the traditional liberal arts subjects of the schools intact.

Two recent studies were most provocative. Rush Welter's Popular Education and Democratic Thought in America (New York, 1962) draws a number of parallels between educational developments and the progress of social and political ideas in the United States, which was illuminating. Similarly, Raymond Callahan's Education and the Cult of Efficiency (Chicago, 1962) maintains that most of the educational changes since 1900 arose in response to demands that the schools become more efficient and cost less, and offers the Gary Plan controversy as an example of this.

A number of works on specialized types of educational problems were of value. Edith Abbott and Sophinisba Breckenridge did a study of Truancy and Non-Attendance in the Chicago Schools (Chicago, 1917) which demonstrated that most of the causes of this problem were not unique to New York City. Charles Bennett's History of Manual and Industrial Education (Peoria, 1937) was a necessary source of information on this type of education. M.L. Greene's Among School Gardens (New York, 1910) was a fervent plea for the inclusion of nature study in the urban schools while Educational Extension (Cleveland, 1916) by Clarence Perry similarly urged the development of recreational programs. William Sharlip and others cooperated on a text on Adult Immigrant Education (New York, 1925) which was illustrative of the recommended methodology for teaching the foreign

born. John F. Carr edited Bridging the Gulf in Library
Work with the Foreign Born (New York, 1917) which contains
a most valuable essay by Ernestine Rose, who was a librarian
at the Seward Park Branch of the New York Public Library.

In the roster of books relating specifically to
educational developments in New York City, Rose Cohen's
The Financial Control of Education in the Consolidated
City of New York (New York, 1948) ranks very high. Miss
Cohen did a painstaking analysis of the fiscal relations
between the Departments of Education and Finance and her
work is essential to an understanding of the Grout
Inquiry, as well as the entire financial struggle of the
schools. Lewis Mayer's Columbia dissertation, The Organiza-
tion and Procedure of the Board of Education of the City of
New York (1913) gives the structure and operation of the
Department of Education in great detail at the time that
the Dept. was under severe attack by the Hanus Committee.
Luther Gulick and Leonard Ayres explained how Medical
Inspection in the Public Schools (New York, 1913) was
carried out, while Abbie T. Graham's biography of Grace H.
Dodge (New York, 1926) gave some interesting facts on the
background of this advocate of industrial education. The
one existing biography of Dr. William H. Maxwell (New York,
1934) by Samuel Abelow is too adulatory to be entirely
trusted, but is of some interest, although John S. Brubacher's
article on Maxwell in the Dictionary of American Biography
(New York, 1933) vol. 12, pp. 445-446 gives the basic facts
in a more objective manner.

Although the United Parents Association of New
York City was organized after 1914, Parenthood in a
Democracy (New York, 1939) by Margaret Lighty and Lee
Bowman, which is a history of that organization, does
give some information on the weakness of parent groups in
the earlier period. S. Willis Rudy's The College of the
City of New York (New York, 1949) is a detailed, all-in-
clusive history of New York's first municipal college
and was important because of the large number of Jewish
immigrant youngsters who attended the preparatory school,
as well as the college itself. In 1927, Josephine Chase
wrote New York at School (New York, 1927) which described
the various programs and practices of the public schools
at that time and was useful for tracing the continuity
of programs begun in the earlier period, and reported in
William H. Allen's High Spots in the New York Schools
(New York, 1916).

A dissertation by Richard Whittemore entitled
Nicholas Murray Butler and Public Education (Columbia,
1962) provided information regarding the "great school
war" of 1895, but even more valuable in this regard was
Sol Cohen's excellent Progressives and Urban School Reform
(New York, 1964) which, although primarily a history of
the Public Education Association, also gives a description
of the various currents and movements among the reform
groups of the city in the Progressive Era in so far as
they related to the schools. Dr. Cohen's pages on the
"Gary Fight", its origins and implications is very well
done and was of great value to this study.

Two articles by present day researchers were read
with profit: Alan M. Thomas Jr. wrote on "American Education
and the Immigrant" in the Teachers College Record LV,
(1953) 253-267 and demonstrates his belief that American
education, as a whole, was thoroughly changed by the need
to respond to the immigrant's problems. Timothy Smith's
"Progressivism in American Education" in the Harvard
Educational Review XXXI (Spring, 1961) 168-193 makes the
same connection between reform in education and in other
spheres in the years between 1880 and 1900, as do Sol
Cohen and Lawrence Cremin for a slightly later period.

LIST OF MATERIALS CONSULTED

THE CITY

PRIMARY AND RELATED MATERIALS.

Bogard, Mile (ed.) The Redemption of New York,
New York: 1902.

Howe, Wirt. New York At the Turn of the Century.
Toronto: 1946. (reissued after private printing
earlier)

New York City Committee on the Congestion of
Population. The True Story of the Worst Congestion in any Civilized City. New York: 1911.

New York (State) Laws of 1897. Chapter 378.
Charter of the City of New York. Albany: 1897.

New York (State) Laws of 1901. Chapter 466. Charter
of the City of New York. Albany: 1901.

Syrett, Harold C. (ed.) The Gentleman and the
Tiger: The Autobiography of George B. McClellan,
Jr. New York: 1956.

Veiller, Lawrence and DeForest, Robert. The
Tenement House Problem. New York: 1903.

Zueblin, Charles. American Municipal Progress.
New York: 1916.

_____. A Decade of Civic Development.
Chicago: 1905.

SECONDARY WORKS.

Ellis, David, et.al. A Short History of New York
State. Ithaca: 1957.

Flick, Alexander C. (ed.). The History of the
State of New York. 10 vols. New York: 1937.

Garrett, Charles, The LaGuardia Years: Machine and
Reform Politics in New York City. New Brunswick,
New Jersey: 1961.

Goldmark, Josephine. Impatient Crusader:
Florence Kelley's Life Story. Urbana, Ill.,
1953.

Laidlaw, Walter (ed.) The Population of the
City of New York 1890-1930. New York: 1932.

Lubove, Roy. The Progressives and the Slums:
Tenement House Reform in New York City,
1890-1917. Pittsburgh: 1962.

McKelvey, Blake. The Urbanization of America
New Brunswick, N.J.: 1963.

Mayer, Grace. Once Upon a City, New York,
New York, 1890-1910. New York: 1958.

Nevins, Allan and Krout, John (eds.) The Greater
City. New York: 1948.

Rankin, Rebecca and Rodgers, Cleveland. New York:
The World's Capital City. New York: 1948.

Sayre, Wallace and Kaufman, Herbert. Governing
New York City: Politics in the Metropolis.
New York: 1960.

Shaw, Frederick. The History of the New York City
Legislature: New York: 1954.

Syrett, Harold C. The City of Brooklyn, 1865-1898.
New York: 1944.

Truman, David. The Governmental Process: Political
Interests and Public Opinion. New York: 1951.

Yellowitz, Irwin. Labor and the Progressive Movement
in New York State, 1897-1916, Ithaca: 1965.

THE IMMIGRANTS

PRIMARY AND RELATED MATERIAL

Abbott, Edith (ed.) Immigration: Select Documents
and Case Records. Chicago: 1924.

American Jewish Committee. American Jewish Yearbook. Philadelphia: 1914.

Antin, Mary. The Promised Land. Boston, 1912.

Bernheimer, Charles S. (ed.) The Russian Jew in the United States. Philadelphia: 1905.

Blaustein, Miriam (ed.) Memoirs of David Blaustein. New York: 1913.

Cahan, Abraham. The Rise of David Levinsky, New York: 1913.

Chapin, Robert, Standard of Living of Workingman's Families. New York: 1909.

Cohen, Elliott (ed.) Commentary on the American Scene: Portraits of Jewish Life in America. New York: 1953.

Covello, Leonard. The Heart is the Teacher. New York: 1958.

Gold, Michael. Jews Without Money. Garden City, N.Y.: 1946.

Handlin, Oscar. (ed.) Children of the Uprooted. New York: 1966.

Hunter, Robert. Poverty. New York: 1904.

Hapgood, Hutchins. The Spirit of the Ghetto. New York: 1902.

James, E.J. (ed.) The Immigrant Jew in America. New York: 1907.

Jencks, J.W. and Lauck, W.J. The Immigration Problem: A Study of American Immigrant Conditions and Needs. New York: 1912.

Jewish Communal Register of New York City. New York: 1918.

National Civic Federation. Conference of the Immigration Department. New York: 1906.

New York (State). Commission on Immigration. <u>Report</u>.
Albany: 1909.

Panunzio, Constantine. <u>The Soul of the Immigrant</u>.
New York: 1923.

Patri, Angelo. <u>A Schoolmaster in a Great City</u>.
New York: 1917.

Ravage, Marcus. <u>An American in the Making</u>. New
York: 1917.

United States. Census Office. <u>Abstract of the
Eleventh Census, 1890</u>. Washington: 1896.

_____.Census Office. <u>Abstract of the Twelfth
Census, 1900</u>.Washington: 1904.

_____.Census Office. <u>Abstract of the
Thirteenth Census, 1910</u>. Washington: 1913.

_____.Census Office. <u>Abstract of the
Fourteenth Census, 1920</u>. Washington: 1923.

_____.Immigration Commission. <u>Abstract of
the Statistical Review of Immigration to the
United States</u>, 1820-1910. Washington: 1911.

_____ Immigration Commission. <u>Immigrants
in Cities</u>. Washington: 1911.

_____. Industrial Commission. <u>Reports on
Immigration</u>. Vol. 15. Washington: 1901.

_____.Commissioner of Labor. <u>The Slums of
Great Cities</u>. Washington: 1894.

Wiernik, Peter, <u>Jews in America</u>. New York: 1912.

Yezierska, Anzia, <u>Children of Loneliness</u>. New
York: 1923.

SECONDARY WORKS

Baskerville, Beatrice. <u>The Polish Jew</u>, New York:
1906.

Berkson, Isaac. <u>Theories of Americanization</u>.
New York: 1920.

Bogardus, Emory. Immigration and Race Attitudes. Boston, 1928.

Boody, Bertha M. A Psychological Study of Immigrant Children at Ellis Island. Baltimore: 1926.

Bowers, David F. Foreign Influences in American Life. Princeton: 1944.

Breckenridge, Sophinisba P. New Homes for Old. New York: 1921.

Bremner, Robert. From the Depths: The Discovery of Poverty in the United States. New York: 1956.

Brown, Francis J. and Roucek, Joseph S. (eds.) Our Racial and National Minorities. New York: 1937.

Brown, Lawrence G. Immigration: Cultural Conflicts and Social Adjustments. New York: 1933.

Commons, John F. Races and Immigrants in America. New York: 1930

Davie, Maurice R. World Immigration. New York: 1936

Davis, Philip. (ed.) Immigration and Americanization. Boston: 1920

Dushkin, Alexander. Jewish Education in New York City New York: 1918.

Fairchild, Henry. Immigration: a World Movement and its American Significance. New York: 1913.

Federal Writers Project. The Italians of New York. New York: 1938

———————————————————— New York Panorama. New York: 1938.

Foerster, Robert F. Italian Emigration of Our Times. Cambridge: 1924.

Garis, R.L. Immigration Restriction. New York: 1927.

Glazer, Nathan. American Judaism. Chicago, 1957.

_____ and Moynihan, Daniel Beyond the Melting Pot. Cambridge: 1963.

Hall, Prescott F. Immigration and its Effect Upon the United States. New York: 1920.

Handlin, Oscar, The Uprooted. New York: 1951.

_____. Immigration as a Factor in American History. Englewood Cliffs, New Jersey; 1959.

_____, The Newcomers. Cambridge: 1959

Hansen, Marcus. Immigrant in American History. New York: 1940.

Haskin, Frederic J. The Immigrant: An Asset and A Liability. New York: 1913.

Higham, John. Strangers in the Land. New Brunswick, N.J.: 1955

Hirschfeld, Charles, Baltimore, 1870-1900. Baltimore: 1941

Horowitz, C. Morris and Kaplan, Lawrence. Jewish Population of the New York Area.1900-1975. New York: 1959.

Jewish Encyclopedia, Vol. IX. New York: 1909.

Jones, Maldwyn A. American Immigration. Chicago: 1960.

Jones, Thomas J. The Sociology of a New York City Block. (Columbia University Studies in History, Economics & Public Law, Vol. XXI). New York: 1904.

Joseph, Samuel A History of the Baron de Hirsch Fund: The Americanization of the Jewish Immigrant. Philadelphia: 1935.

_____. Jewish Immigration to the United States, 1881-1910 (Columbia University Studies In History, Economics and Public Law (Vol. LIX) New York: 1914.

Kraus, Michael. Immigration, The American Mosaic
Princeton: 1966

Linfield, Larry. The Jews in the United States.
New York: 1929

_____. Statistics of Jews and Jewish
Organizations. New York: 1939.

Lord, Elliott. The Italian in American. New
York: 1906.

Mariano, John. The Italian Contribution to
American Democracy. Boston: 1921.

Lasserman, L. and Laker, G. The Jews Come to
America. New York: 1932

Panunzio, Constantine. Immigration Crossroads.
New York: 1927.

Park, Robert E. and Miller, Herbert A. Old World
Traits Transplanted. New York: 1921.

Pisani, Lawrence. The Italian in America. New
York: 1957.

Richin, Moses. The Promised City: New York"s
Jews, 1870-1914 New York: 1964.

Roberts, Peter. The New Immigration. New York:
1912.

Rose, Philip. The Italians in America. New York
1922.

Stella, Antonio, Some Aspects of Italian Immigration to the United States. New York: 1924.

Stephenson, George M. History of American Immigration Boston: 1926.

Warne, Frank J. Immigrant Invasion. New York:
1913.

Williams, Phyllis. South Italian Folkways in
Europe and America.New Haven: 1938.

Wittke, Carl. We Who Built America. New York: 1939.

Woofter, T. J. Jr. Races and Ethnic Groups in American Life. New York: 1933.

ARTICLES:

Brandt, Lillian. "A Transplanted Birthright," Charities, XII (January, 1904), 494-499.

Brudno, Ezra S. "The Russian Jew Americanized", World's Work., VIII (March, 1904), 4555-4567.

Carr, John F. "The Coming of the Italian", Outlook, LXXXI (February, 1906), 419-431.

Claghorn, Kate H. "Immigration and Dependence", Charities, XI (January, 1904), 501-504.

Davis, Philip. "Making Americans of Russian Jews", Outlook, LXXX (July, 1905), 631-637.

Durland, Kellog and Sessa, Louis. "The Italian Invasion of the Ghetto", University Settlement Studies I, (January, 1906) 106-117.

"Foreign Born of the United States", National Geographic, XXVI (September, 1914) 265-271.

Friedenberg, Albert. "The Problem of Jewish Immigration", Jewish Comment, XVI, (February, 1903), 1-3.

Goldenweiser, E.A. "Immigrants in Cities", The Survey, XXV (January, 1911) 596-602.

Hendrick, Burton J. "The Jewish Invasion of America", McClure's Magazine, XL (March, 1913), 125-165.

Riis, Jacob A. "Special Needs of the Poor in New York", Forum, XIV, (December, 1892), 492-502.

Steiner, Edward A. "The Russian and Polish Jew in New York", Outlook, LXXVII (November, 1902) 529-539.

Walling, William L. "What the People of the East Side Do", University Settlement Studies Quarterly, 1, July, 1903, 79-85.

Yoffeh, Zalmen. "The Passing of the East Side", Menorah Journal, XVII, (December, 1929), 265-275.

Young, Pauline. "The Reorganization of Jewish Family Life in America", Social Forces VII (December, 1928), 238-244.

IMMIGRANTS AND SCHOOLS

PRIMARY AND RELATED MATERIALS

Carr, John F. (ed.) Bridging of the Gulf in Library Work with the Foreign Born. New York: 1917.

Childrens Aid Society. The Crusade for Children: A Review of Child Life in New York during Seventy Five Years, 1853-1928. New York: 1928.

Educational Alliance. Reports. 1897-1912.

Kelly, Myra. Little Aliens. New York: 1910.

_____. Little Citizens. New York: 1904.

_____. Wards of Liberty. New York: 1907.

Lee, Joseph. Constructive and Preventive Philanthropy. New York: 1902.

New York (City). Department of Education. Division of Research and Reference. The School and the Immigrant. New York: 1915.

New York (State). Department of Education. Annual Report. Vol. II. Albany: 1917.

Riis, Jacob A. The Children of the Poor. New York: 1892.

_____. The Battle with the Slum. New York: 1902

Sinkhovitch, Mary K. Neighborhood, My Story of
Greenwich House.   New York: 1938.

Spargo, John. The Bitter Cry of the Children.
New York: 1909.

University Settlement Reports,1897-1903.

United States. Immigration Commission. Abstract
of the Report on the Children of Immigrants
in the Schools. Washington; 1911.

Wald, Lillian. The House on Henry Street.
New York: 1915.

Woods, Robert A. (ed.). Americans in Process.
Cambridge, 1902.

_____ (ed.). TheCity Wilderness.
Cambridge: 1898.

SECONDARY WORKS

Abbott, Edith and Breckenridge, Sophinisba.
Truancy and Non-Attendance in Chicago Schools.
Chicago: 1917.

Abbott, Grace. The Immigrant and the Community.
New York: 1917.

Bierstadt, Edward H. Aspects of Americanization
Cincinnati: 1922.

Bogardus, Emory S. Essentials of Americanization.
Los Angeles, 1919

Borrie, W.D. et.al. The Cultural Integration of
Immigrants. Paris: 1959.

Drachsler, Julius. Democracy and Assimilation:
The Blending of Immigrant Heritages in America.
New York: 1920.

Hartmann, Richard. The Movement to Americanize
the Immigrant. New York: 1948.

Kallen, Horace. Culture and Democracy in the
United States. New York: 1924.

Miller, Herbert A. The School and the Immigrant.
Cleveland: 1916.

Sharlip, W. et.al. Adult Immigrant Education:
Its Scope, Content, and Methods. New York 1925.

Smith, William C. Americans in the Making. New
York: 1939.

Thompson, Frank V. Schooling the Immigrant.
New York: 1920.

ARTICLES

Abbott, Clarence. "On the Education of the
Immigrant", American Leader, III (June, 1913),
698-701.

Abbott, Grace. "Education of Foreigners in
American Citizenship," Proceedings of the
Buffalo Conference for Good City Government,
Sixteenth Annual Meeting of the National
Municipal League. New York: 1910, 375-384.

Abelson, Paul. "The Education of the Immigrant",
Journal of Social Science, XLIV (September, 1906)
163-172.

Addams, Jane. "The Public School and the
Immigrant Child". Proceedings of the National
Association, 1908, 99-102.

Betts, Lillian. "The Child Out of School Hours",
Outlook, LXXV (September, 1903), 209-216.

Claghorn, Kate H. "Immigration in Relation to
Pauperism", Annals of the American Academy of
Political and Social Science, XXIV, (September
1904), 187-205.

Cody, F. "Americanization Courses in the Public
Schools", English Journal, VII (December, 1918)
615-622.

Dine, H. B. "The School Center and the Immigrant",
Playground, X (February, 1917) 456-461.

Dugmore, A.R. "New Citizens for the Republic",
World's Work, V (January, 1903), 3323-3326.

"Education of the Immigrant", Elementary School
Teacher, XIV, (February, 1914) 261-263,

Fisher, Winifred, "Cities Provide Educational
Opportunities for Foreign Born Women",
School Life, XV, (September, 1929), 8-9.

Gaus, John M. "A Municipal Program for Educating
Immigrants in Citizenship", National Municipal
Review, VII (May, 1918) 237-244.

Hill, R. T. "From Americanization to Adult
Education", Survey, LXII (June, 1929), 366-367.

_____."Contributions of Americanization to
Education in the United States", School and
Society, XXXIII, (January, 1931).

_____. " Letting Johnny do It: Educating
Parents Through Their Children", Survey, LXI
(January, 1929) 504.

Kellor, Frances A. "Education of the Immigrant",
Educational Review, XLVIII (June, 1914), 21-36.

_____. "A Domestic Policy", Immigrants
in America Review, I (March, 1915) 9-22

Lenz, Frank. "Education of the Immigrant", Educational Review, LI (May, 1916), 469-477.

Murdoch, Katherine. "A Study of Race Differences
in New York City", School and Society, XI
(January, 1920), 147-150.

Peters, A. "The Duty of America to the Adult
Immigrant", Education. LII (September, 1931)
19-23.

Robbins, Jane E. "The Settlement and the Public
Schools", Outlook, XCV (August, 1910), 785-787.

Schuster, S.J. "What the Evening School is Doing
for the Alien", Journal of Education, LXXIX
(March, 1914), 261-262.

Straubenmuller, Gustave. "The Work of the
New York Schools for the Immigrant Class", Journal
of Social Science, XLIV (September, 1906,) 175-
182.

Strook, Samuel "The Night School and the Immigrant", Jewish Immigration Bulletin, VI (August, 1916) p. 6-16

"Teaching Immigrants and Illiterates", Elementary School Journal XVIII (June, 1918) pp. 729-732.

Thomas, Alan. "American Education and the Immigrant", Teachers College Record, LV (November, 1953), pp. 253-267.

Wheaton, H.H. "Survey of Adult Immigrant Education", Immigrants in America Review, I (June, 1915), pp. 42-71.

_____. "United States Bureau of Education and the Immigrant", Annals of the American Academy of Political and Social Science, LXVII (September, 1916) pp. 273-283.

THE SCHOOLS

PRIMARY AND RELATED MATERIALS

Ayres, Leonard P. Laggards in our Schools. New York: 1909.

Boese, Thomas, Public Education in the City of N.Y. New York: 1869.

Bourne, William O. History of the Public School Society. New York: 1873

Childs, Clinton. A Years Experiment in Social Center Organization. New York: 1918.

Churchill, Thomas. The Board of Education. New York: 1915.

Citizens Union. More and Better Schools. New York: 1897.

Flexner, Abraham, I Remember, New York: 1940

Good Government Club E. Public School Buildings in New York City. New York: 1895.

Hall, Fred S. Forty Years, 1902-1942; The Work of the New York Child Labor Committee, New York 1942.

Irwin, Elizabeth. Truancy, A Study of Mental,
Physical, and Social Factors in the Problem
of Non-Attendance at School. New York: 1915.

Johnson, Harriet. The Visiting Teacher in New
York City. New York: 1916.

Maxwell, William Henry. A Quarter Century of
Public School Development.(New York: 1912)

National Education Association. Addresses and
Proceedings of the 54th Meeting. New York:
1916.

National Society for the Study of Education.
Tenth Yearbook. Chicago: 1911.

_____. Fourteenth Yearbook. Bloomington,
Ill.: 1919.

New York Association for Improving the Condition
of the Poor. Report of the Department of
Schools and Institutions on Vacation Schools.
New York: 1895.

New York (City) Board of Education. Report of
the Special Committee of Five, February 24, 1904.
New York: 1904.

New York (City), Department of Education. Addresses
delivered upon the opening of the New Hall of
the Board of Education, February 22, 1900. New York:
1900.

_____. Annual Reports of the Department
of Education of the City of New York. 1898-1914.

_____. Division of Reference and Research.
The School Lunch Service in New York City.
New York: 1914.

_____, Directory of the Board of
Education of the City of New York, 1910-1914.

_____. Journals of the Board of Education
of the City of New York. 1898-1914.

_____. Journals of the Board of Superintendents of the City of New York, 1902-1914.

_____. Maps of the local School Boards. New York: 1910.

_____. Murray Hill Pre-Vocational School for Boys. New York: 1913.

_____. Board of Superintendents. The Hanus-Elliott Report: A Review and Reply. April 23, 1913.

_____. Association of District Super-intendents. Reply of the Association of District Superintendents of New York to Certain Findings and Recommendations of Professor Frank McMurray and Professor Edward C. Elliott. New York: 1914.

_____. New York City Public Schools, Facts and Figures, 1965-66. New York: 1966.

_____. Department of Education. Board of Superintendents. A Syllabus for the Teaching of English to "Grade C" classes in the Elementary Day Schools. September 27, 1906.

_____. The Teachers Council, Its History, purpose, organization, work. Mimeographed. 1916.

_____. The Teachers Council. Report of the Committee on Truancy and Delinquency of the Teachers Council. March, 17, 1914.

_____. Wirt, William. A Report on a Plan of Organization for Cooperative and Continuation Courses. July 30, 1914.

_____. Organization of the School Board for the Boroughs of Manhattan and the Bronx. February 13, 1901.

_____. Annual Reports of the City Superintendents of Schools of New York City. 1899-1914.

New York (City). Board of Estimate and Apportionment. Reports of an Investigation concerning the cost of maintaining the Public School System in the City of New York. June, 1904.

_____ .Reports of an Investigation Concerning the cost of maintaining the Public School System of the City of New York. October 31, 1905.

_____ Report of the Committee on the School Inquiry. 3 vols. 1911-1913.

_____ . Minutes of a hearing on a Report of the Sub-Committee, Committee on High Schools and Training Schools, Board of Education, on Vocational Guidance. June 16, 1914.

New York (State) Dept. of Education. Finegan, Thomas. The Organization of the City School System: An Address Delivered before the Council of School Superintendents. Albany: 1912.

_____ . Laws of the State of New York, 1897, Charter 415, Section 73 (Child Labor)

_____ . Laws of the State of New York 1896. Chapter 606. Section 3. (Compulsory Education)

_____ .Laws of the State of New York, 1903, Chapter 151. Section 174-179a. Chapter 184 Sections 70-73. (Child Labor Law) (Compulsory Education Law)

_____ . Laws of the State of New York, 1913. Chapter 748. Section 622. (Compulsory Education Law)

Palmer, A.E. History of the New York Public Schools, New York: 1905

Public Education Association. A Primer of Public School Progress. New York: 1914.

_____ . Bulletins 16-20, 1913.

_____ . Bulletin #10 Shall the Schools Serve Lunches? Feb. 25, 1913.

Public Education Association. Official Wirt Reports to the Board of Education of New York City. New York: 1916.

_____. Bulletin #2. The Permanent Census Board. March 15, 1912.

_____. Bulletin #23. The Schools of Gary. June 5, 1914.

Rice, Joseph Mayer. The Public School System. New York: 1893.

United States, Bureau of Education. Bulletin #51 1913.

_____. Bulletin #5, 1910. Washington: 1911.

_____. Report of the Commissioner of Education, 1914, 1916, 1918.

Behrum, Charles C. Description of Grammar and Primary Schools in the City of New York and their Requirements. New York: 1894.

SECONDARY WORKS

Abelow, Samuel. Dr. William H. Maxwell. Brooklyn: 1934.

Allen, William H. High Spots in the New York Schools. New York: 1916.

Bennett, Charles A. History of Manual and Industrial Education, 1870-1917. Peoria, Ill. 1937.

Butler, Nicholas M. (ed.) Education in the United States. New York: 1910.

Callahan, Raymond. Education and the Cult of Efficiency. Chicago: 1962.

Cattell, J. McKeen (ed.) Leaders in Education. New York: 1932.

Chase, Josephine, New York at School. New York: 1927.

Cohen, Rose N. The Financial Control of Education in the Consolidated City of New York. (Teachers College, Columbia University Contributions to Education, #943) New York: 1948.

Cohen, Sol. Progressives and Urban School Reform:
The Public Education Association of New York
City, 1895-1954. New York: 1964.

Cremin, Lawrence A. and Butts, Freeman. History
of Education in American Culture. New York: 1953.

Cremin, Lawrence A. The Genius of American
Education. Pittsburgh: 1965.

_____. The Transformation of the Schools.
New York: 1961.

Cubberly, Ellwood. Public Education in the United
States. Cambridge: 1919.

Cubberly, Ellwood. Changing Conceptions in Educa-
tions. Boston: 1909

Curoe, Philip R. V. Educational Attitudes and
Policies of Organized Labor in the United States.
(Teachers College, Columbia University Contribu-
tions to Education, # 201). New York: 1926.

Curti, Merle. Social Ideas of American Educators.
Paterson, N.J.: 1959.

Draper, Andrew S. American Education. Cambridge:
1909

Farnsworth, Philo T. Adaptation Processes in
Public School Systems. (Teachers College,
Columbia University Contributions to Education,
801.) New York: 1940

Goldmark, Josephine, Impatient Crusader: Florence
Kelley's Life Story. Urbana, Ill.: 1953.

Graham, Abbie. Grace H. Dodge, Merchant of Dreams.
New York: 1926.

Greene, M. Louise. Among School Gardens. New York:
1910.

Gulock, Luther and Ayres, Leonard. Medical Inspection in the Schools. New York: 1913.

Jessup, Walter A. The Social Factors Affecting
Special Supervision in the Public Schools of the
United States. (Teachers College, Columbia University Contributions to Education, #43(New York:
1911.

Kandel, I. L. (ed.) Twenty-Five Years of American
Education, New York: 1929.

_____. American Education in the Twentieth
Century. (Cambridge: 1957).

Lighty, Margaret and Bowman, LeRoy. Parenthood
in a Democracy. New York: 1939.

McCormick, Harold. "The First Fifty Years". Fiftieth Annual Report of the Superintendent of
Schools. New York: 1948.

Dewey, John and Dewey, Evelyn. The Schools of
Tomorrow. New York: 1915.

Brubacher, John S. "William Henry Maxwell",
Vol. XII, Dictionary of American Biography. Edited
by Dumas Malone. New York: 1933.

Monroe, Paul (ed.), Cyclopedia of Education.
Vols. III, IV. New York, 1918.

Perry, Clarence. Educational Extension. Cleveland:
1916.

Proskauer, Bertha and Altman, Addie. Appreciation
of a Great Educator, Julia Richman, New York:
1916.

Rudy, S. Willis. The College of the City of New
York: A History. New York: 1949.

Shaw, Frederick. "Fifty Years of Research in the
New York City Board of Education". Educational
Program Research and Statistics.Publication #226.
New York: 1964.

Welter, Rush. Popular Education and Democratic
Thought in America. New York: 1962.

ARTICLES

"Administration of New York's Public Schools," Harper's Weekly, L, (February 1906) p.257

Ballard, Walter. "Adult Education in New York City", Journal of Education, LXVIII (November, 1908), 540-541.

Brody, Catherine, "A New York Childhood", American Mercury, XIV (May, 1928), 57-66.

Duck,Winifred, "Work and Play in the Public Schools", Outlook, LXXX (July, 1905), 725-732.

"City Superintendent Maxwell of New York", Educational Review, XXVII (Jan. 1904), 1-18.

Cremin, Lawrence A. "The Revolution in American Secondary Education, Teachers College Record, LVI (November, 1954), 295-308.

Donahue, J. L. "The Gap Between the Secondary and the Elementary School", School Review, X (November, 1902), 701-707.

Dublin, L. I. "The Physical Disability of New York City School-teachers", School and Society, IV (October, 1916) 564-569, 602-607.

Edson, Andrew W. "Instruction of Exceptional Children in the New York City Public Schools", Education, XXXI (September, 1910), 1-10.

_____. "Problem of the Backward Child", School Journal, (July 21, 1906) 60-62.

Flexner, Mary. "The Visiting Teacher in Action", Survey, XXX (May, 1913), 179-182.

"Hanus Experts", Education XXXIII (May, 1913), 573.

Hendrick, Burton. "Six Thousand Girls at School", McClure's Magazine, XLI (May, 1913), 46-57.

Hendrick, Burton and Kennaday, Paul. "Three Cent Lunches for School Children", McClure's Magazine, XLII (October, 1913), 120-28.

Hill, Marion. "The Star-Spangled Banner", McClure's Magazine, XV (September, 1900) 262-267.

Iles, George. "How a Great Free Lecture System Works", World's Work, V (February, 1903), 3328-3334.

Johnson, Eleanor H. "Social Service and Public Schools", Survey, XXX, (May, 1913), 173-178.

Kittredge, Mabel H. "The Needs of the Immigrants", Survey, XXX (April, 1913) 188-192.

Klapper, Paul. "Bureau of Attendance and Child Welfare", Educational Review, L. (November, 1915), 369-391.

Low, Seth. "The New York Schools", Educational Review, XXIV (November, 1902), 427-430.

Lynch, Ella F. "Is the Public School a Failure?", Ladies Home Journal, XXIX (August, 1912), 3-5.

Maxwell, William Henry, "My Ideals as Superintendent", Educational Review, XLII (November, 1911), 451-459.

_____. "The Present Needs of the Public Schools", Nation, LXXXIV (April, 1907), 379-381.

_____. "School Achievements in New York", Educational Review, XLIV (October, 1912)., 275-309.

_____. "On a Certain Arrogance in Educational Theorists", Educational Review, XLVII (February, 1914), 165-182.

_____. "The City and the Child". Publications of the National Recreational Association of America. XXVI, (no date) 7-8.

_____. "The Schools of New York", Municipal Affairs IV (December, 1900), 742-750.

_____. "Stories from the Lives of Real Teachers, World's Work, XVIII, (August, 1909), 11877-11880.

McAndrews, William. "The High School Itself", Proceedings, National Education Association, 1910, pp. 450-457.

_____. "A Day's Work in a New York Public School", World's Work, IV, (October, 1902), pp. 2634-2643.

Mearns, William H. "Our Medieval High Schools", Saturday Evening Post, CLXXXIV (March, 1912) pp 18-19.

Metcalfe, Tristram W. "What Ails the Schools?" Globe School Bulletin, (March, 1912), pp. 1-13.

Morse, D. LC. "From Grammar to High School", School Review, X (October, 1902), pp. 620-625.

"New York Campaign: What Reform has Done for Children", Outlook LXXV (September, 1903), pp. 201-202.

"The New York City Board of Education", Educational Review, XLII, (November, 1911), pp. 429-430.
"The New York City Schools", Educational Review, XII (September, 1896), pp. 206-208.

Nudd, Howard, "The Gary Plan and Its Social Bearing", Proceedings, National Conference of Charities and Corrections, 1916, pp. 559-566.

Paulding, James K. "The Public School as a Center of Community Life", Educational Review, XIII (February, 1898) pp. 147-154.

Phillips, Helen C. "Elizabeth Farrell", Review of International Council for Exceptional Children I., (Feb. 1935), pp. 73-76.

"Politics Against the Schools" New Republic, VI (February, 1916) pp. 32-33.

Richman, Julia, "A Successful Experiment in Promoting Pupils", Educational Review, XVIII (June, 1899), pp. 23-29.

_____. "What Can Be Done in a Graded School for the Backward Child?", Survey, XIII (October, 1904), pp. 129-131.

419.

_____ "The Incorrigible Child", Educational Review, (May, 1906), pp. 484-506.

_____ "A Social Need of the Public Schools", Forum, XLIII, (February, 1910), pp. 161-169.

Rogers, Lina L. "School Nursing in New York City", University Settlement Studies Quarterly, III (October, 1905), pp. 141-147.

Rosenfeld, Jessie, "Special Classes in the Public Schools of New York", Education, XXVII (October, 1906) pp. 92-100.

Russell, Isaac. "Is Our Public School System Behind the Times?", Craftsman XX (May, 1911), pp. 140-145.

"School Situation in New York", New Republic, VI (February, 1916), pp. 6-8.

Scott, Colin A. "The Manual Arts in the City of New York", Educational Review, XXXI (April, 1906), pp. 411-419.

Shaw, Adele Marie. "The True Character of the New York Public Schools", World's Work, VII (November, 1903), pp. 4204-4221; VIII (October, 1904), pp. 5405-5414; IX (November, 1904) pp. 5480-5485.

Simkhovitch, Mary K. "The Enlarged Function of the Public Schools", Proceedings, National Conference of Charities and Correction, 1904, pp. 471-486.

Smith, M.G. "Foreign Child and Teacher", Education, XXXVIII, (March, 1918), pp. 504-507.

Smith, Timothy, "Progressivism in American Education, 1880-1900", Harvard Educational Review, XXXI (Spring, 1961), pp. 168-193.

Snedden, D.S. "The Public School and Juvenile Delinquency", Educational Review, XXXIII (April, 1907), pp. 374-385.

Spargo, John. "The Regeneration of Ikey", Craftsman, XII, (September, 1907), pp. 642-646.

Straubenmuller, Gustave. "Industrial Education", Education, XXX (April, 1910), pp. 519-521.

Talbot, Winthrop, "A Public School in the Slums that does its Job", World's Work, XVIII (June, 1909), pp. 11567-11572.

Van Rensselaer, Mariana. "Our Public Schools: A Reply", North American Review, CLXIX (July, 1899), pp. 77-89.

Woolman, Mary, "The Manhattan Trade School for Girls", Educational Review, XXX (September, 1905), pp. 178-188.

Woolston, Florence. "Our Untrained Citizens", Survey, XXIII, (October 2, 1909), pp. 21-35.

Woolston, Howard. "Socialized Education in Public Schools", Charities, XVI, (September, 1906), pp. 570-578.

DISSERTATIONS

Berger, Morris I. "The Settlement, the Immigrant, and the Public School". Unpublished Ph.D. dissertation, Columbia University, 1956.

Covello, Leonard, "The Social Background of the Italo-American School Child". 3 vols. Unpublished Ph.D. Dissertation, New York University, 1944.

Matthews, Sister Mary Fabian, "The Role of the Public School in the Assimilation of the Italian Immigrant Child in New York City, 1900-1914." Unpublished Ph.D. dissertation, Fordham University, 1966.

Mayers, Lewis. "The Organization and Procedure of the Board of Education of the City of New York". Unpublished Ph.D. dissertation, Columbia University, 1913.

Whittemore, Richard. "Nicholas Murray Butler and Public Education". Unpublished Ph.D. Dissertation, Columbia University, 1962.

MANUSCRIPTS AND OTHER SOURCES

FILED PAPERS

In vertical file #902, in room 732 at the Board of Education, 110 Livingston Street, Brooklyn, N.Y.

Election of William H. Maxwell as Superintendent Emeritus, Press Release, 1913.

Invitation to a Tribute to Superintendent Maxwell on the 25th Anniversary of his service to the schools. October, 1912.

Program of the Tribute to Superintendent Maxwell on the 25th Anniversary of his service to the schools. October, 1912.

Photograph of William Henry Maxwell.

Mimeographed summaries of the work of:
    Elizabeth Farrell
    Albert Shiels
    Gustave Straubenmuller

INTERVIEWS

I. Edwin Goldwasser	February, 1967
Harold McCormick	October, 1966
Milton B. Perlman	October, 1966
Jacob Ross	October, 1966
Morris E. Siegel	November, 1966
Joseph Winick	November, 1966

MANUSCRIPTS

Autobiography of Hyman Cantor, 1935. In the Author's possession. Lillian Wald Collection, 1897-1914. At the New York Public Library.

NEWSPAPERS AND PERIODICALS

New York Globe, 1903-1904, 1911, 1913.

New York Herald. 1903-1904, 1911, 1913.

New York Times. 1898-1914

New York World. 1903-1904, 1911, 1913.

Literary Digest. 1898-1914

School Journal.　1898-1914.

AUTOBIOGRAPHICAL STATEMENT

Selma Cantor Berrol was born in Brooklyn, New York on June 7, 1924, and was educated in the public schools. After receiving a B.A. degree from Hunter College in 1945, she went on to earn an M.A. at Columbia University, where she wrote a Master's thesis on "The First State Governments in New York and South Carolina: A Comparison", under the direction of Professor John A. Krout.

Mrs. Berrol then served as an instructor in the Department of History at Hunter College for three years, after which she was appointed as a permanent teacher of Social Studies in the New York City high schools.

She was married to Edward Berrol in 1948, and is the mother of a son and a daughter. Since September, 1964, she has been a doctoral student in the Department of History at the City University of New York. Her article "The Schools of New York in Transition" was published in the Urban Review, in December, 1966. Mrs. Berrol plans to teach American History at the college level.

BILINGUAL-BICULTURAL EDUCATION IN THE UNITED STATES

An Arno Press Collection

Allen, Harold B. **A Survey of the Teaching of English to Non-English Speakers in the United States.** 1966

Allen, Virginia F. and Sidney Forman. **English As A Second Language.** [1967]

Aucamp, A.J. **Bilingual Education and Nationalism With Special Reference to South Africa.** 1926

Axelrod, Herman C. **Bilingual Background And Its Relation to Certain Aspects of Character and Personality of Elementary School Children** (Doctoral Dissertation, Yeshiva University, 1951). 1978

Bengelsdorf, Winnie. **Cthnic Studies in Higher Education.** 1972

Berrol, Selma Cantor. **Immigrants at School: New York City** (Doctoral Dissertation, City University of New York, 1967). 1978

Cordasco, Francesco, ed. **Bilingualism and the Bilingual Child.** 1978

Cordasco, Francesco, ed. **The Bilingual-Bicultural Child and the Question of   Intelligence.** 1978

Cordasco, Francesco, ed. **Bilingual Education in New York City.** 1978

Dissemination Center for Bilingual Bicultural Education. **Guide to Title VII ESEA Bilingual Bicultural Projects, 1973-1974.** 1974

Dissemination Center for Bilingual Bicultural Education. **Proceedings, National Conference on Bilingual Education.** 1975

Fishman, Joshua A. **Language Loyalty in the United States.** 1966

Flores, Solomon Hernández. **The Nature and Effectiveness of Bilingual Education Programs for the Spanish-Speaking Child in the United States** (Doctoral Dissertation, Ohio State University, 1969). 1978

Galvan, Robert Rogers. **Bilingualism As It Relates to Intelligence Test Scores and School Achievement Among Culturally Deprived Spanish-American Children** (Doctoral Dissertation, East Texas State University, 1967). 1978

Illinois State Advisory Committee. **Bilingual/Bicultural Education.** 1974

Levy, Rosemary Salomone. **An Analysis of the Effects of Language Acquisition Context Upon the Dual Language Development of Non-English Dominant Students** (Doctoral Dissertation, Columbia University, 1976). 1978

Malherbe, Ernst G. **The Bilingual School.** 1946

Mandera, Franklin Richard. **An Inquiry into the Effects of Bilingualism on Native and Non-Native Americans** (Doctoral Dissertation, University of Illinois, 1971). 1978

Materials and Human Resources for Teaching Ethnic Studies. 1975

Medina, Amelia Cirilo. **A Comparative Analysis of Evaluative Theory and Practice for the Instructional Component of Bilingual Programs** Doctoral Dissertation, Texas A&M University, 1975). 1978

National Advisory Council on Bilingual Education. **Bilingual Education.** 1975

Peebles, Robert Whitney. **Leonard Covello: A Study of an Immigrant's Contribution to New York City** (Doctoral Dissertation, New York University, 1967). 1978

Reyes, Vinicio H. **Bicultural-Bilingual Education for Latino Students** (Doctoral Dissertation, University of Massachusetts, 1975). 1978

Rodriguez M[unguia], Juan C. **Supervision of Bilingual Programs** (Doctoral Dissertation, Loyola University of Chicago, 1974). 1978

Royal Commission on Bilingualism and Biculturalism. **Preliminary Report and Books I & II.** 3 vols. in 1. 1965/1967/1968

Streiff, Paul Robert. **Development of Guidelines for Conducting Research in Bilingual Education** (Doctoral Dissertation, University of California, Los Angeles, 1974). 1978

Streiff, Virginia. **Reading Comprehension and Language Proficiency Among Eskimo Children** (Doctoral Dissertation, Ohio University, 1977). 1978

Ulibarri, Horatio. **Interpretative Studies on Bilingual Education.** 1969

United Kingdom, Department of Education and Science, National Commission for Unesco. **Bilingualism in Education.** 1965

United Nations Educational Scientific and Cultural Organization. **The Use of Vernacular Languages in Education.** 1953

United States Bureau of Indian Affairs. **Bilingual Education for American Indians.** 1971

United States Commission on Civil Rights. **Mexican American Education Study.** 5 vols. in 1. 1971-1973

United States House of Representatives. **Bilingual Education Programs.** 1967

United States House of Representatives. **United States Ethnic Heritage Studies Centers.** 1970

United States Senate. **Bilingual Education, Health, and Manpower Programs.** 1973

United States. Senate. **Bilingual Education, Hearings.** 1967

Viereck, Louis. **German Instruction in American Schools.** 1902